The middle years of the twentieth century marked a particularly intense time of crisis and change in European society. During this period (1930-1950), a broad intellectual and spiritual movement arose within the European Catholic community, largely in response to the secularism that lay at the core of the crisis. The movement drew inspiration from earlier theologians and philosophers such as Möhler, Newman, Gardeil, Rousselot, and Blondel, as well as from men of letters like Charles Péguy and Paul Claudel.

The group of academic theologians included in the movement extended into Belgium and Germany, in the work of men like Emile Mersch, Dom Odo Casel, Romano Guardini, and Karl Adam. But above all the theological activity during this period centered in France. Led principally by the Jesuits at Fourvière and the Dominicans at Le Saulchoir, the French revival included many of the greatest names in twentieth-century Catholic thought: Henri de Lubac, Jean Daniélou, Yves Congar, Marie-Dominique Chenu, Louis Bouyer, and, in association, Hans Urs von Balthasar.

It is not true — as subsequent folklore has it — that those theologians represented any sort of self-conscious "school": indeed, the differences among them, for example, between Fourvière and Saulchoir, were important. At the same time, most of them were united in the double conviction that theology had to speak to the present situation, and that the condition for doing so faithfully lay in a recovery of the Church's past. In other words, they saw clearly that the first step in what later came to be known as *aggiornamento* had to be *ressourcement* — a rediscovery of the riches of the whole of the Church's two-thousand-year tradition. According to de Lubac, for example, all of his own works as well as the entire *Sources chrétiennes* collection are based on the presupposition that "the renewal of Christian vitality is linked at least partially to a renewed exploration of the periods and of the works where the Christian tradition is expressed with particular intensity."

In sum, for the *ressourcement* theologians theology involved a "return to the sources" of Christian faith, for the purpose of drawing out the meaning and significance of these sources for the critical questions of our time. What these theologians sought was a spiritual and intellectual communion with Christianity in its most vital moments as transmitted to us in its classic texts, a communion that would nourish, invigorate, and rejuvenate twentieth-century Catholicism.

The *ressourcement* movement bore great fruit in the documents of the Second Vatican Council and has deeply influenced the work of Pope John Paul II.

The present series is rooted in this renewal of theology. The series thus understands *ressourcement* as revitalization: a return to the sources, for the purpose of developing a theology that will truly meet the challenges of our time. Some of the features of the series, then, are a return to classical (patristic-medieval) sources and a dialogue with contemporary Western culture, particularly in terms of problems associated with the Enlightenment, modernity, and liberalism.

The series publishes out-of-print or as yet untranslated studies by earlier authors associated with the *ressourcement* movement. The series also publishes works by contemporary authors sharing in the aim and spirit of this earlier movement. This will include any works in theology, philosophy, history, literature, and the arts that give renewed expression to Catholic sensibility.

The editor of the Ressourcement series, David L. Schindler, is Gagnon Professor of Fundamental Theology and dean at the John Paul II Institute in Washington, D.C., and editor of the North American edition of *Communio: International Catholic Review,* a federation of journals in thirteen countries founded in Europe in 1972 by Hans Urs von Balthasar, Jean Daniélou, Henri de Lubac, Joseph Ratzinger, and others.

Divine Likeness: Toward a Trinitarian Anthropology of the Family
Marc Cardinal Ouellet

The Portal of the Mystery of Hope
Charles Péguy

In the Beginning:
A Catholic Understanding of the Story of Creation and the Fall
Joseph Cardinal Ratzinger

In the Fire of the Burning Bush:
An Initiation to the Spiritual Life
Marko Ivan Rupnik

Hans Urs von Balthasar: A Theological Style
Angelo Scola

The Nuptial Mystery
Angelo Scola

DIVINE LIKENESS

Toward a Trinitarian Anthropology
of the Family

MARC CARDINAL OUELLET

Translated by

Philip Milligan
and
Linda M. Cicone

WILLIAM B. EERDMANS PUBLISHING COMPANY
GRAND RAPIDS, MICHIGAN / CAMBRIDGE, U.K.

Published 2006 by
Wm. B. Eerdmans Publishing Co.
255 Jefferson Ave. S.E., Grand Rapids, Michigan 49503 /
P.O. Box 163, Cambridge CB3 9PU U.K.

Printed in the United States of America

11 10 09 08 07 06   7 6 5 4 3 2 1

Library of Congress Cataloging-in-Publication Data

Ouellet, Marc, 1944-
[Divine ressemblance. English]
Divine likeness: toward a Trinitarian anthropology of the family /
Marc Cardinal Ouellet; translated by Philip Milligan and Linda M. Cicone.
p.   cm.   — (Ressourcement)
ISBN-10: 0-8028-2833-7 / ISBN-13: 978-0-8028-2833-0 (pbk.: alk. paper)
1. Family — Religious aspects — Catholic Church.   2. Trinity.
I. Title.   II. Series: Ressourcement (Grand Rapids, Mich.)

BX2351.O94   2006
261.8'3585 — dc22

2005035466

www.eerdmans.com

CONTENTS

vii

CONTENTS

Pope John Paul II bequeathed a priceless legacy of teaching concerning the place of marriage and family in the Church's mission at the beginning of the Third Millennium. His courageous and untiring defense of the family was part not only of an organic vision of human rights, but also of an ecclesiology that gives weight to the family's mission and evangelizing potential. Indeed, his teaching went well beyond the realm of moral exhortation to lay the base for an anthropology and ecclesiology of the family that responds to the drift of contemporary culture. His eminently prophetic message deserves the special attention of theologians and pastors, who should draw from it inspiration to pursue a broader and deeper scholarship aimed at elucidating and supporting the ecclesial mission of the family in today's world.

The theology of marriage has experienced a remarkable development in the last thirty years thanks to the renewal inaugurated by the Second Vatican Council. The same cannot be said of the theology of the family, which is still a huge quarry waiting to be mined — even though the apostolic exhortation *Familiaris Consortio* is rightly regarded as a *magna charta* of the family. On the theological level, much work remains to be done in the way of developing a consistent and comprehensive vision that responds both to the requirements of theological science and the needs of pastoral action today. The crisis of man, which has exploded into evidence in the wake of the secularization of society, also makes necessary a theological deepening of anthropology in the light of Jesus Christ and, so, of the Trinity.

The study that I present here is part of this theological investigation into the relationship between theology and anthropology and, more precisely, between the Trinity and the family. It is the fruit of a series of lectures organized by the bureau for family ministry of the Italian Episcopal Conference (CEI) and by the Pontifical John Paul II Institute for Studies on Marriage and Family. I recall with gratitude the organizers of these initiatives, especially Msgr. Renzo Bonetti and His Excellency Msgr. Angelo Scola, who also took pains to ensure the scholarly quality and interdisciplinary character of the resulting investigations. The first part, entitled "Toward a Trinitarian Anthropology," reproduces the McGivney Lectures, which I gave at the invitation of the John Paul II Institute in Washington, D.C., in 1996. My sincere thanks to Carl Anderson for his encouragement to publish these lectures. The interest that they created was a stimulus to develop the reflection further, and to develop a conjugal and familial spirituality having its theological basis in the Trinity. Hence the second part of this study, "Perspectives of Trinitarian Spirituality for Marriage and Family," which I gave in Rome between 1998 and 2000 at the invitation of the CEI, as a contribution to the Conference's study weeks on marriage and family. I am also and especially grateful to the numerous families whose active and joyful involvement made them not only an enriching forum for discussion, but also a veritable laboratory for spiritual and missionary research.

The context in which this study was born explains its particular character, marking it as a type of reflection that, while not fulfilling all of the critical requirements of academic theology, opens up new horizons for investigation, which can be developed without loss of, or modification to, the fundamental orientation staked out already in Chapter One. My hope is that this modest contribution will help theologians, pastors, and believers to develop fruitfully the legacy of Pope John Paul II and to carry forward the theological and existential quest to bring the Trinity and the family into reciprocal illumination for the good of the contemporary world.

MARC CARDINAL OUELLET
Primate of Canada

PART 1

Toward a Trinitarian Anthropology

CHAPTER I

Theology of the Family:
An Ongoing Project

At the dawn of the third Christian millennium the evangelization of the world is more and more centered on the family. "In the future, evangelization will depend largely on the domestic Church," John Paul II affirmed already at the very beginning of his pontificate, at the inauguration of the Bishops Assembly for Latin America (CELAM) in Mexico.[1] He was encouraging even then the development of a vigorous ministry to the family that would orient and sustain the liberating dynamism of Latin American Christianity. With the Synod on the Family, followed by the apostolic exhortation *Familiaris Consortio* (1981), he began to multiply his efforts to situate the family at the heart of the project for a new evangelization. The many Wednesday catechetical sessions around these themes, the Exhortation *Mulieris Dignitatem* and the *Letter to Families,* illustrated John Paul II's concern with highlighting the future of evangelization by means of an appropriate theology which would make explicit God's plan for marriage and the family.[2] Among these many initiatives, the founding of the

1. Cf. Discourse at the Third General Assembly of the Latin American Bishops, January 28, 1979, IV, in *Acta Apostolicae Sedis* 71 (1979), p. 204.

2. John Paul II, *Familiaris Consortio* (Rome: Libreria Editrice Vaticana, 1981), apostolic exhortation on the duties of the Christian family in today's world; *Mulieris Dignitatem* (Rome: Libreria Editrice Vaticana, 1988), apostolic letter on the occasion of the Marian year; *Letter to Families* (Rome: Libreria Editrice Vaticana, 1994), on the occasion of the international year of the family; cf. various authors, *La famiglia cristiana nell'insegnamento di Giovanni Paolo II* (Milan, 1988).

John Paul II Institute for Studies on Marriage and Family and the development of the Pontifical Council for the Family certainly marked an important step in the development of the Holy Father's pastoral priorities. In a certain way they crystallized and concretized the project of developing a theology of the family following the intuitions of the Second Vatican Council.

The significance of these initiatives should be measured in the long term by the impact of new experiences and research not only concerning the evangelization of the family, but above all concerning evangelization *by the family*. This is so because theological reflection on the family increasingly reveals the evangelizing potential of this fundamental institution. Until recently the family was considered a terminal point, a field for applying, in a certain sense, the Church's pastoral decisions. This time has gone. The post–Vatican II appreciation of the family as "domestic Church," "theological locus," and "sacramental reality," now opens to it undreamed-of perspectives of participation in the salvific mission of the Church.

The very concept of evangelization could well be modified and enriched, particularly in light of the ecclesiology of communion promoted by the Second Vatican Council. In fact, the accent on communion, with a corresponding positive appreciation of personhood and of community, invites us to go beyond an evangelization conceived predominantly as the transmission of doctrinal contents or even as a process of inculturation of the faith. The new evangelization by the family reveals and inspires a new sense of God's presence in the faith community; it invites the flowering of a new theological awareness that shapes from within the sacramental relationships of love, faithfulness, and fecundity in the service of the Gospel. Hence the recurring theme of a "civilization of love" in the texts of John Paul II, a theme which Christians are called upon to promote in a world increasingly disillusioned and hungry for fundamental values, both human and spiritual. It could well be that the evangelization of the world will henceforth come by way of family life understood, in its simplicity and despite its fragility, as a sacrament of Trinitarian communion.

The theology of the family is still in its infancy, in spite of the vigorous impulse given to this noble cause by John Paul II and by institutes aimed at meeting the challenge of the new evangelization. There were, no doubt, significant developments in the theology of marriage in Germany between the two wars,[3] and conjugal spirituality did make some progress in France after the Second World War;[4] however, there remain a deficiency and in some ways a delay in developing the theology of the family. No comprehensive overview of a systematic theology of the family exists as yet.[5] The 1980 Synod on the Family drew attention to both the void and the need. While the apostolic exhortation *Familiaris Consortio* remedied this in part, it was hoped that theologians would pursue in depth the nature and mission of the family within the global framework of theological anthropology. Our purpose here is not so much to provide a complete presentation as to indicate a direction wherein a synthesis might eventually be developed. Hence the "programmatic" title given to these reflections: *Toward a Trinitarian Anthropology of the Family*. This perspective invites us to study the relationship between Trinity and family from a theological point of view. Contrary to what is generally believed, the question is not new. It is rooted, as we will see, in a tradition as yet scarcely known, but which nonetheless finds renewed relevance today in light of an exegesis of the *imago Dei* and of contemporary trends in thought, notably personalism.

This reflection is not intended as a purely speculative endeavor. It will consider theology before all else, but it aims to bring out the basis for a spirituality of marriage and the family in response to the deep orientations of the Second Vatican Council. Almost half a century has elapsed since Karl Rahner and Hans Urs von Balthasar deplored the fact that Trinitarian theology had little impact on the spiritual and ecclesial life of believers. Balthasar voiced this criticism in 1953, in a prophetic little book that anticipated the renewal that would come with Vatican II:

3. Cf. D. von Hildebrand, *Die Ehe* (Munich, 1928). English translations: *Marriage* (1942); *Marriage: The Mystery of Faithful Love* (Manchester, N.H.: Sophia Institute Press, 1984). Also H. Doms, *Vom Sinn und Zweck der Ehe, eine systematische Studie* (Breslau, 1935). English translation: *The Meaning of Marriage* (New York: Sheed and Ward, 1939). Also B. Krempel, *Die Zweckfrage der Ehe in neuer Beleuchtung* (Zurich, 1941); N. Rocholl, *Die Ehe, als geweihtes Leben* (Dumel-in-Westfalen, 1937).

4. Cf. C. Massabki, *Le sacrement de l'amour* (Paris, 1946); J. Leclercq, *Le mariage chrétien* (Tournai-Paris, 1947); "Mystère et mystique du mariage," *L'Anneau d'Or*, n. 50 (1957), pp. 70-87; H. Rondet, *Introduction à l'étude de la théologie du mariage* (Paris, 1960).

5. Some pioneering essays exist, written by the likes of G. Ceriani. *Teologia della famiglia* (1950); E. Rollan, *Signification totale de la famille: Pour une théologie de la famille* (Paris, 1950); more recently one finds attempts in: José Silvio Botero, *Per una teologia della famiglia* (Rome: Borla, 1992); Maurice Emynian, *Theology of the Family* (Malta: Jesuit Publications, 1994).

What place does the doctrine about the triune God have in Christian existence? And what place has it had in theology, in which this doctrine seems to have stood still, half-congealed and dried up after Augustine's psychological speculation? There would be so many other paths besides that of Augustine, perhaps ever better paths. . . . Why does no one seek these paths and follow them out? Christian proclamation in the school, from the pulpit, and in the lecture halls of the universities could be so much more alive, if *all* the theological tractates were given a completely trinitarian form![6]

The essay presented here aims to echo this wish, because theology of the family should follow the Christocentric and Trinitarian perspective that Vatican II opened up for contemporary theological reflection. This is why we will next consider the contemporary issues arising from the family, issues whose seriousness was already perceived during the Council. Our introduction will state the presuppositions of a Trinitarian anthropology of the family, while the subsequent chapters will develop its implications and its scope.

Issues Arising from the Family in Today's World

The contemporary family has been categorized as "nuclear," meaning perhaps its lowest common denominator. In this atomic age, however, it could also mean that family, like the atom, can be just as easily split with the accompanying cataclysmic devastation.

These words were pronounced by Dr. Eric McLuhan, son of Canadian philosopher Marshall McLuhan, introducing his talk on "The Family in the Electronic Age" at an International Congress on the Family held in Milan in 1981.[7] They express a widely held conviction among philosophers, psychologists, theologians, writers and pastors: the situation of the family has become precarious in today's world, and the consequences of a breakdown of the family can be measured by the large number of problems and the in-

---

6. Hans Urs von Balthasar, *Razing the Bastions* (San Francisco: Ignatius Press, 1993), p. 29.

7. Eric McLuhan, "The Family in the Electronic Age," in *Mass Media and the Family,* Proceedings of the International Congress on the Family (Milan: CISF, 1981), p. 38.

tense suffering with which we are, alas, too familiar.[8] Since *Gaudium et Spes* alluded to the anxieties of contemporary man, the shadow cast over the family (an image from *Familiaris Consortio*) grows ever longer, in what appears to the Western world to be the slow sunset of the family.

The tragic situation of the family is reflected in the profound and accelerated changes so evident at the end of the third millennium. The twentieth century will always be identified with major upheavals within the family, the end and seriousness of which are still unknown.[9] It has become commonplace to say that the evolution of the family in this modern age is characterized by the progressive movement from family seen as extended, molecular, patriarchal, to family seen as restricted, nuclear, and conjugal, comprising only the husband and wife and their children, even when other persons (uncles, in-laws, etc.) live with them. This evolution, according to sociologists of the family, has been caused by industrialization and urbanization. As a result profound changes have occurred in the very functioning of the family. It has ceased to be, as in the agrarian society of the past, a unit and a center of production. It has also lost its traditional functions of protection and prevention, which have been largely taken over by the State. "Thus the family today is reduced to a function that is conjugal, parental, and fraternal. It has only one role left: the formation, development, and human promotion of persons."[10]

One of the most salient traits of the contemporary family is the fact that it has ceased to base itself upon a marriage of convenience, reason, or interest; its foundation now rests on the personal love of the couple. While this evolution is more respectful of the equality of the sexes and of the freedom of individuals, it does give rise to a high coefficient of instability. This signals a major crisis in the institution of marriage and the family. In a climate of secularization love becomes increasingly removed from traditional religious values and mores, and asserts itself in an autonomy that

---

8. See Jack Dominian, *Marital Breakdown* (Chicago: Herald Press, 1968); Stanley L. Saxton, Patricia Voydanoff, and Angela Ann Zukowski, eds., *The Changing Family* (Chicago: Loyola University Press, 1984); Tony Anatrella, "Faiblesses et défis de la famille," *La famille chrétienne dans le monde d'aujourd'hui,* (Montreal: Bellarmin, 1995), pp. 15-46.

9. H. Wattiaux, "La famille a-t-elle encore un avenir?" in *Esprit et vie* 40 (1992), pp. 265-69, 529-44; Michel Berger, "La famille aujourd'hui: État des lieux," *La Pensée Catholique* 275 (1995), pp. 10-27.

10. P. Adnès, "Mariage et vie chrétienne" in *Dictionnaire de Spiritualité*, vol. 10 (Paris, 1995), p. 357.

leads to a diversity of breaking points: (1) domestic relations become disconnected from marriage; (2) sexuality is disconnected from love and procreation; (3) the family is relegated to the sphere of private life.[11] Add to this the almost complete absence of family policies in most of the secularized western societies. Family law becomes increasingly permissive, due to the influence of pressure groups who impose their views on lawmakers, who themselves are less and less informed by basic principles.[12] There results a growing gap between civil laws and Christian morality. This clouds the conscience of the faithful on such fundamental values as fidelity, indissolubility, and openness to life (FC 7). The most striking signs are a marked increase in divorces, the plague of abortion, the increasingly frequent use of sterilization, the dominance of a contraceptive mentality, and, finally, abandonment of marriage as a sacrament.

In such a context the Church can no longer count on the State to defend the rights of the family as society's original and primary cell. It has to fight ceaselessly this unequal fight against the dangers which threaten family life at the level of demographic policies of both state and international organizations.[13] This dramatic situation, however, awakens both the prophetic conscience of the Church and its pastoral responsibility for proclaiming God's plan for marriage and the family (FC 3). This proclamation is neither wholly positive nor wholly negative; it calls for discernment of the "shadows and lights" of today's family (FC 4-10). The "shadows" which have just been mentioned must not cancel out the "lights" of which John Paul speaks in number 6 of *Familiaris Consortio:* "A more vivid awareness of human freedom and greater attention to the quality of interpersonal relations in marriage, to the promotion of the dignity of women, to responsible procreation, to the education of children." These values show that the current socio-cultural trends, ambiguous as they are, could also open a phase of growth in the understanding of one's own being and of the meaning one ascribes to marriage and the family. The challenge facing a theol-

11. Berger, "La famille aujourd'hui," p. 11; cf. *Familiaris Consortio* no. 6; see also Carl Anderson, "Marriage and Family in Western Society," in *Anthropotes* 2 (1991), 273-85.

12. In the United States and in Canada, the evolution of jurisprudence protects the individual more than it protects marriage: "The new legal framework actually promotes tendencies which enhance individuality and separation of the marital couple rather than tendencies which support unity and mutuality," Anderson, "Marriage and Family," pp. 283-84.

13. The role of the Vatican's delegation at the 1994 Cairo Conference on population is a good example of this difficult struggle.

ogy of the family lies in the integration of these values and their development in such a way as to counterbalance the signs of "a disturbing degradation of some fundamental values" (FC 6). This requires the practice of an evangelical discernment as well as the incorporation of positive values within a theological horizon which fully guarantees the dignity of the human person and its blossoming within the family.

The Need for a New Theological Synthesis

The situation of the family has given rise to significant pastoral reflection in our century. First, the theology of marriage has been marked by the evolution from a juridical and naturalistic conception of the ends of marriage toward an increasingly personalistic conception accentuating love and the communion of persons. Hence the progressive integration of the two final ends of marriage (unitive and procreative) within conjugal love, whose very nature and sacramental dimension call for openness to life. The Pastoral Constitution *Gaudium et Spes* marked a turning point on this issue when it defined marriage as "a community of deep life and love," an institution born "of a human act based on mutual self-giving and receiving" (48). According to W. Kasper, this represents a radical break from a previous, predominantly legalistic tradition based on a static view of nature. The same author held, twenty years ago, that the doctrine of the church had not yet succeeded in "creating a new and satisfactory integration of the diverse dimensions of marriage from a personalistic viewpoint."[14]

It is in this context that one must situate the violent reaction to the encyclical *Humanae Vitae,* which seemed to take a step backward from the advances of Vatican II. Criticism of the Church's position on contraception was directed mainly toward a certain "biologism" which, in the mind of many, was not in accord with the "personalism" of *Gaudium et Spes.*[15] The persistent opposition to this official teaching signaled a serious malaise in the Church and the fragility of the Magisterium vis-à-vis the contemporary world. This pointed to the need for further theological depth in explaining why contraception is morally unacceptable in a Christian con-

14. W. Kasper, *Teologia del matrimonio cristiano* (Bologna: Queriniana, 1985), p. 18.
15. Michel Séguin, *La contraception et l'Église, Bilan et Prospective* (Montreal: Pauline & Mediaspaul, 1994), pp. 87-104.

text. Important elements for reflection were brought forth by John Paul II, re-affirming the teaching of Paul VI. Also, these elements were intended to demonstrate the fact that the "personalism" of Vatican II is not opposed to the objective moral norm inscribed in the nature of the conjugal relationship between man and woman.[16] The expansion of a contraceptive mentality has led to an erosion of family values. This only serves to show how just and wise the Church's pastoral orientation was. However, much remains to be done to remove the persistent malaise and illustrate the solid ground and theological coherence of this teaching.

From the dogmatic point of view, *Familiaris Consortio* represents an important step in the search for a theological anthropology open to contemporary personalistic aspirations. Critics have, moreover, given a positive reception to the broad orientations provided by this document. One author even saw it as an official confirmation of the most advanced theological reflection on the family, the image of the Trinity, a "meeting between Catholic and Eastern theologies on the theme of the family."[17] Others would have hoped for a still clearer affirmation on this subject. Maurice Emynian, for instance, notes that while it affirms the creation of man and woman in the image of God (FC 11), "one looks in vain in it for an explicit statement regarding the Trinitarian dimension of the family."[18] Nonetheless, John Paul II himself gave us more explicit reflections in his Wednesday catechetical sessions between 1979 and 1982. During his first major apostolic trip, he said to the inhabitants of Pueblo: "We must make this beautiful and deep consideration: our God is not a solitude, but a family, because there is within himself paternity, filiation, and the essence of the family, which is love. This love in the divine family is the Holy Spirit. The theme of the family, then, is not at all extraneous to the divine essence."[19] This family analogy was probably not yet ripe for integration in a document as official as a post-synodal exhortation.

The solemn beginning of *Familiaris Consortio* n. 11 does contain a beautiful passage about man as the image of the God of Love: "God created man in his own image and likeness: calling him to existence *through love,*

16. *Familiaris Consortio* n. 32. Cf. Michel Séguin, *La contraception et l'Église,* ch. 9: "Un personnalisme integral," pp. 143-83.

17. Botero, *Per una teologia della famiglia,* pp. 42, 65.

18. M. Emynian, *Theology of the Family,* p. 43.

19. *Insegnamenti di Giovanni Paolo II,* Vol. II, n. 1 (Rome: Libreria Editrice Vaticana), p. 182.

He called him at the same time *for love.*" John Paul II goes on to explain how the humanity of man and woman bears within itself a vocation to love and communion, and how marriage and virginity are two complementary expressions of this. In doing so he does not go much further than the affirmation of marriage as a sacramental sign of the union between Christ and the Church. There is no explicit integration in any analysis of conjugal and familial love seen from a Trinitarian perspective. Rather, we remain with the more general idea of a communion of persons which reflects the God of Love. It remains the case, however, that the emphasis on the communion of persons, as well as concern for the promotion of women and insistence on love's duties as "a vivid and real participation of the love of God for humanity" (FC 17), provide a doctrinal basis for a Trinitarian interpretation of conjugal and familial love, open to further developments which could fulfill more explicitly the aspirations of contemporary personalism. The argument based on the dignity of the human person is particularly open to this; however, Msgr. Philippe Delaye considers that within *Familiaris Consortio,* "in spite of a fundamental compatibility and the possibility of a progressive synthesis, this latter has not yet been achieved."[20] This view is akin to Kasper's, and points to the need for a theology of the family which restates the systematic advances of recent decades on a more ample and theological basis. The theological developments on the family as image of the Trinity, promoted by such theologians as Häring, Balthasar, Moltmann, and Adnès, still await an official confirmation, but important steps have been taken in this direction. This is why we can say that *Familiaris Consortio,* while representing a true charter of doctrine as well as of ministry to families, remains a transitional document in relation to what is aimed at by a Trinitarian anthropology of the family.

Presuppositions of a Trinitarian Anthropology of the Family

A Trinitarian anthropology of the family cannot develop without a hermeneutic of Vatican II, especially of the chapter on theological anthropology. The Council, in its preparatory stage, had seen heated debates in the commission on doctrine with regard to the question of the supernatural. This

20. P. Delaye, "La pastorale familiale dans l'optique de Familiaris Consortio," *Esprit et Vie* 46 (1982), p. 631.

had also been keenly debated in the 1940s and 1950s, following the publication of Henri de Lubac's historical study.[21] The Council did not directly re-
open the debate but chose a more pastoral language and opted for a
"Christocentric"[22] approach. This set the stage for the Church's more open
and dynamic orientations in its dealings with the world. Without a doubt,
the Pastoral Constitution *Gaudium et Spes* is the most explicit in this regard. One can, however, sense a certain tension between the doctrine of the
image of God as expressed in no. 12 and the Christology of no. 22. Although
complementary, these do not yet seem well-integrated. This lacuna (especially evident in the preceding version) was severely criticized by Joseph
Ratzinger in 1968 in his commentary on no. 12 on the dignity of the human
person: "the text was criticized for only apparently choosing a theological
starting point in the idea of man as the image of God, whereas in reality it
still had a theistically-colored and to a large extent nonhistorical view. In
opposition to this, it was urged that the starting point should be Christ, the
second Adam, from whom alone the Christian picture of man can be cor-
rectly developed."[23] As a result, a certain tension remains in the first exposi-
tion of man as image of God because it lacks a Christological reference.

Underlying this tension one finds the modern inheritance of a conception of the natural and the supernatural as two juxtaposed entities
without any close connection. If there is to be in the future a truly personalist conception of marriage and family, it is important to distinguish between a "theistically colored" theology of the image of God, and a
"Christocentric" theology of creation.[24] It seems right to say with Carl Anderson that "this Christocentric theology is foundational to each of the
magisterial documents of John Paul II and provides the context for the

21. Henri de Lubac, *Surnaturel* (Aubier, 1946); most recently in English, *The Mystery of
the Supernatural* (New York: Crossroad, 1998).

22. Cf. E. Michelin, *Vatican II et le "surnaturel," Enquête préliminaire 1959-1962* (Venice:
Editrice Notre Dame de Vie, 1993). The author analyzes the evolution of vocabulary in the
preparatory texts for the Council and comes to the conclusion that a basic option was
adopted concerning the relations between man and God, particularly concerning man's "divine vocation": while at the same time avoiding "supernatural" vocabulary as far as possible.
It is clear that the reality remains, but the way of expressing it changes so as to be more easily
understood by contemporary man.

23. J. Ratzinger, "The Dignity of the Human Person," *Commentary on the Documents of
Vatican II*, ed. H. Vorgrimler (New York: Herder & Herder, 1967), p. 120.

24. D. Schindler, "Christology and the *Imago Dei:* Interpreting *Gaudium et Spes,"*
Communio (Spring 1996).

new evangelization of marriage and family." John Paul expresses the main reason for his choice in his first encyclical: "Precisely because Christ has united himself with each human person, man 'is the primary and fundamental way for the Church' (RH 14) and therefore the family is 'the first and the most important' path for the Church's mission."[25]

Vatican II's Christocentric emphasis had a liberating effect for the development of an ecclesiology of communion, the nerve center and backbone of a Trinitarian anthropology of the family. The Council's way of conceiving the unity of the Church from the standpoint of the supreme model of a "Trinity of persons in the unity of the one God, Father, Son and Holy Spirit"[26] became more mystery-oriented than juridical. It is a Trinitarian model destined to influence directly the unity of the "domestic Church," and thus the natural and supernatural relationships that are the life and beauty of the Christian family within the mystery of the Church. At the center of John Paul II's reflections on the family are the *communio personarum* and the "unity of the two." These concepts presuppose a deeper theological grounding than the usual view of the human person (even when enriched by an account of grace). From this angle, it does seem that a radically Christocentric understanding of the person depends upon the possibility of a thoroughly integrated familial community and Trinitarian communion at the heart of the mystery of the Church. This will receive considerable attention in our reflection.

In this context, the question of the sacramentality of marriage and the family seems important. What is the specific nature of the sacrament of marriage, and to what extent can the family participate in this sacramentality? What can guide our understanding if we are to think not only in terms of each individual's personal relation to the Trinity, but also in terms of a real interpenetration of the familial and the Trinitarian relations? Through the grace of baptism and of the sacrament of marriage, those who love each other "in Christ" are sustained, animated, and perfected by God's love and faithfulness in Christ. In fact, *Gaudium et Spes* affirms that "authentic conjugal love is caught up into divine love, and is directed and enriched by the redemptive power of Christ and the salvific action of the Church" (GS 48). May we reach the same conclusion as Kasper: "the love

---

25. C. Anderson, "Criteria and Content of the Intellectual Formation of Future Priests with Regard to Marriage and Family," *Seminarium* A. XXXV (1995), n. 4, p. 655.

26. Decree on Ecumenism, no. 2.

and fidelity of Christian spouses is not only a sign and symbol of God's love, but an efficacious sign, a full symbol, a real actualization, an epiphany of the love of God manifested in Jesus Christ?"[27] What is the ultimate meaning of this real actualization of Trinitarian love in the world? Can we interpret the participation of the family in the Trinitarian relations in terms of sacramentality? With these queries, the question of the "domestic Church" and the basis of its ecclesiality is wholly set out.

Dealing with this fundamental issue presupposes several preliminary questions bearing upon the Trinity-family relationship. These can be approached from the point of view of a theology of creation, or from the point of view of a covenant theology. In each case the analogy between the Trinity and the family has a different impact. Is the family an image of the Trinity? On this point, can Augustine's negative verdict be challenged? On the other hand, are the positive contemporary openings convincing? Have we sufficiently integrated Christology and the doctrine of the *imago Dei* (image of God)? Has the advent of the hypostatic union made possible any existential participation of family relations in the Trinitarian relations? These are fundamental questions which must be addressed by a Trinitarian anthropology of the family, bearing in mind the unity of God's plan, and the distinction between the order of created things and the order of supernatural fulfillment in Christ. The answers to these questions should enable us to rethink not only the place of the family in the mission of the Church, but also, even more profoundly, the participation of the family in the Trinitarian missions.

All of these questions require an integration of theological anthropology in a global view that is Christocentric and Trinitarian. In view of this, a second, methodological, presupposition is required. Catholic theology has always ascribed a special place to analogy and this is more timely than ever. The analogical method proceeds from the bottom up, beginning with creatures and rising toward God. It presupposes a balance of affirmation and negation in expressing the resemblance and difference between creature and Creator. However, this method does not exhaust all of the possibilities for expressing the relations between God and his creatures. There is a complementary procedure which Hans Urs von Balthasar has described as katalogical.[28] This method reverses the perspective and starts from on high

---

27. W. Kasper, *Teologia del matrimonio cristiano,* p. 37.

28. H. U. von Balthasar, *Theologik II: Wahrheit Gottes* (Einsiedeln: Johannes, 1985), pp. 159-200.

to enlighten created realities. What this means, for example, is that instead of proceeding exclusively from the family to the Trinity (analogy), one can proceed also from the Trinity to the family (katalogy). The harmonious integration of the two methods should allow us to go beyond the limits present in the tradition of the familial analogy of the Trinity, a tradition that restricts itself to a rather essentialist approach to resemblances and differences between Trinity and family. While still relying on this tradition, and at the same time interpreting it with Christ as the starting point, the essential question will be not so much: What can the family bring to our grasp of the Trinitarian mystery? But rather: What does the Trinity wish to express through the family in a global context of covenant? This should lead us to rethink the familial analogy of the Trinity in a descending perspective, dynamic and existential, which opens naturally into the mystery of the Church as communion, concretized in the "domestic Church." Such a "katalogical" approach should allow us to deepen theological understanding of the covenant between the Trinity and the family, and the significance of this covenant as a missionary reality and as service for the glory of God.

To adopt a katalogical perspective, always from the point of view of theological method, is also to say that "it is only in the mystery of the Word made flesh" that man's deepest identity becomes clear (GS 22). This hermeneutical principle conditions any interpretation of Scripture. It implies that we agree to consider the book of Genesis in light of eschatology: the Alpha in light of the Omega, the first Adam in light of the second Adam. A scrupulous exegesis of the texts of the Old Testament should not prevent a theological approach from re-reading the first steps and the promises of the first Covenant from the starting point of the unhoped-for and unforeseen fulfillment they receive in Christ. Otherwise we condemn ourselves to see only a purely factual link between Christ and creation. This would mean that we would consider the family simply as a provisional reality, to be overcome, leading to an "extrinsic" supernatural view detached from its anthropological foundation. In this light it would be important to see how and to what extent the creation of man, as man and woman, in the image of the Trinity, implies that a person's humanness necessarily comes by way of the family.

Familiaris Consortio is no stranger to this katalogical approach since it makes explicit "God's plan for marriage and the family," beginning with the Word of God. The 1981 Synod wanted to "return to the beginning" (Mt. 19:4) out of respect for Christ's teaching (FC 10). It wanted, consequently, to adopt God's point of view on marriage and the family. This move does not preclude, of course, recourse to the human sciences; but it does point out their limits and their subordinate role. In virtue of the unity of the divine plan of creation and redemption, one must give an authentic place to all the multiple aspects which created reality involves and which require the competence of the human sciences. From this comes the necessity for dialogue between theological anthropology and the human sciences. They will not dictate to theology, however, the ultimate logic which integrates the tenets of creation within the eschatological accomplishments fulfilled in Christ. Here again, the way of conceiving the relationship between nature and grace directly affects the way in which one conceives the relationship between philosophy and theology, the human sciences and theology, human experience and the gift of grace. In a unified Christocentric vision which respects distinct orders, these relationships are founded on nature and reason's receptivity and obedience with regard to grace and the Word of God. The resulting anthropology must correct to a certain extent the excessive modern emphasis on a person's subjective autonomy and subjective dynamism. On the other hand, this anthropology underlines the openness of reason and human availability in the face of a transcendent fulfillment received as an unexpected marvel of grace and freedom.

In delineating the presuppositions of a Trinitarian vision of marriage and family, I must insist, in conclusion, on placing anthropology within the framework of a Trinitarian theocentricism. What does this mean? Simply this: the ultimate meaning of human existence is revealed against the background of Trinitarian love envisaged not only as the *Bonum diffusivum sui* of philosophers, but as an exchange of love *between* the divine Persons. In this direction, Hans Urs von Balthasar has opened up unexpected perspectives which radically transform the horizon of theological anthropology.[29] These perspectives take up again the question of the meaning of creation as service for the glory of God, but from an explicitly Trinitarian point of view. In line with St. Thomas Aquinas, Balthasar sees the divine work *ad extra* as the prolongation of the intra-Trinitarian processions. However, unlike Aquinas, who hesitates to include the distinction

---

29. H. U. von Balthasar, *Theo-Drama: Theological Dramatic Theory*, Volume II, *Dramatis Personae, Man in God;* Volume III, *Dramatis Personae, Persons in Christ;* Volume IV, *The Action;* Volume V, *The Last Act* (San Francisco: Ignatius, 1989-1995). Cf. Marc Ouellet, *L'existence comme mission: L'anthropologie théologique de Hans Urs von Balthasar* (Rome: Pontifical Gregorian University, 1983).

of the Persons in the common work *ad extra*, Balthasar states clearly, in light of the primacy of Christ, that all work *ad extra* is integrated in the exchange of love *between* the divine Persons: "it is a gift of the Father to the Son, a gift which the Son then returns to the Father and which is transfigured by the Holy Spirit as the love between the Father and the Son. It is in this sense, and only in this sense, that the cosmos becomes a *diffusio bonitatis divinae*."[30] This bold viewpoint rests on the universal mediation of the hypostatic union, which places Christ the Lord at the summit of creation as mediator of the participation of creatures in divine life. All creation, which is dependent upon Him and belongs to Him becomes, in Him, part of the Trinitarian dialogue: "The mutual gifts of the Trinity are the creature's place and home. . . ."[31]

Scrupulously safeguarding the gratuity and freedom of God's work of creation, Balthasar affirms nonetheless that "[the reason for creation] follows from the fact that the creature is drawn into the reciprocal acts of love within the Godhead, so that the collaboration of each Divine Person in the work of creation is intended to magnify the 'glory' of the Others."[32] Father and Son glorify each other in one and the same Spirit, by creating, saving and glorifying the creature. They glorify each other in and by creation itself. The Holy Spirit is the key to this self-glorification of God in his creation because it is He who is eternally the witness and the crowning of the Glory of God: "he makes the life of love well up, not in front of us nor above us, but in us, and thereby empowers us to 'glorify' through our life the glory that has been given to us as his own."[33] To the extent to which spiritual creatures allow themselves to be indwelt by the Spirit of Love, they are elevated to the incomparable dignity of being servants of God's Glory. The eminent dignity of this service consists in expressing in a created manner the exchange of uncreated love between the divine Persons. From such a perspective man finds himself already situated between God and God and solicited by the Spirit to let himself become caught up in the very reciprocity of Father and Son. The discovery of this "theological

30. H. U. von Balthasar, *The Glory of the Lord: A Theological Aesthetic*, Volume I, *Seeing the Form* (San Francisco: Ignatius, 1982), p. 506; see also Volume VII, *Theology: The New Covenant* (San Francisco: Ignatius, 1989), pp. 515-16; *Theo-Drama: Theological Dramatic Theory*, Volume V, *The Last Act* (San Francisco: Ignatius, 1998), p. 506.

31. H. U. von Balthasar, *The Glory of the Lord* VII, p. 516.

32. H. U. von Balthasar, *Theo-Drama* V, p. 507.

33. H. U. von Balthasar, *The Glory of the Lord* VII, p. 389.

locus" makes possible the integration of the anthropology of desire and the Augustinian *cor inquietum* in an anthropology of obedience of love and service. This integration opens out into an affirmation of the ultimate meaning of human existence, in which, without falling into any sort of pantheism, we see that not only does God have meaning for man but also man for God.

The nature and importance of the participation of persons and of human relations in intra-Trinitarian love will form the backdrop of our reflections and will serve as an axis for integrating all our anthropological and ecclesial developments. In my opinion, this is the key to reaching beyond the simple relation of exemplarity between the Trinity and the family. With Balthasar and John Paul II, we wish to speak of "the 'sincere gift of self' as the way and the fundamental content of the authentic realization of self."[34] A Trinitarian anthropology of the family must be placed, I think, in this "theo-logical," that is to say Trinitarian, context, which surpasses the modern anthropocentric perspective, even as it integrates it. The demands of contemporary personalism, notably the inviolable dignity of the person, the primacy of love, the intersubjectivity and the communion of persons, should derive new and decisive confirmation from such a Trinitarian theocentrism. Besides this, the most significant advances of post-conciliar theology, notably the Christocentrism of John Paul II, the theme of liberation and participation, and that theme of the "domestic Church" and Church-Communion, should also find themselves reaffirmed and better articulated in a global Trinitarian perspective. This perspective is already in gestation in post-conciliar theology but its development has yet to overcome some resistance and to avoid excessive simplification. On one hand, a certain Augustinian and Thomistic tradition easily leaves a suspicion of anthropomorphism and even of tritheism hanging in the air around any systematic approach to the Trinity-family relationship. On the other hand, there exists a certain exploitation of the Trinity, be it anthropocentric or purely symbolic, which opens the way to egalitarian and democratic ecclesiologies. These two tendencies, whose extreme expressions are integrism and progressivism, show to what extent it is difficult to discern, with the respect and seriousness owed to an *analogia entis,* what is an authentic Trinitarian logic and what is a human projection of this logic.

---

34. John Paul II, *Pastores Dabo Vobis,* no. 34; cf. *Gaudium et Spes* no. 24.

Conclusion

We are now closer to working out a Trinitarian anthropology of the family along certain lines and with certain presuppositions, both hermeneutical and methodological. The project is vast and requires convergent approaches whose fruitfulness will be illustrated in the second part of this book. I shall discuss first the theme of the family as image of the Trinity in Scripture and Tradition. I will then take up the theme of the "domestic Church," specifically its theological identity, its anthropological and pneumatological foundation, and the sacramental implications of its relations. We will see how Divine Love gives itself to man through the sacraments of Christ and the Church, notably through Baptism, Eucharist, and Marriage, elevating the family to the dignity of being a sacred sanctuary of God's presence, of the communion of persons, and of life. In this way, questions of family spirituality and ethics will appear in a new light, from the starting point of the ecclesial identity of marriage and family. Finally, in the light of the Trinitarian christocentrism mentioned previously, the contemporary mission of the family will be considered in the "theo-dramatic" context of the Church and the world at the dawn of the new millennium.

CHAPTER II

The Family, Image of the Trinity

"The original model of the family must be sought in God himself, in the Trinitarian mystery of his life."[1] In these bold words John Paul II spoke to families in 1994, during the year designated by the United Nations as the International Year of the Family. Thirteen years after the apostolic exhortation *Familiaris Consortio* he returned even more explicitly to the relationship between the Trinity and the family, against the background of the doctrine of the *imago Dei*. Yet this theme of the family, image of the Trinity, is still far from being unanimously welcomed. It has yet to rally those who follow the long tradition founded upon the authority of Augustine of Hippo and Thomas Aquinas, who preferred the "psychological" or "intra-subjective" analogy as an approach to the Trinitarian mystery. Are we on the verge of taking leave of this tradition to venture onto new paths more in line with current sensitivity? Have we taken sufficient account of the impact that such an option might have on the way of understanding Divine love and human love?

In the second part of his *De Trinitate*, while looking for a real image of the Trinitarian God, Augustine presents the opinion of theologians who purported "to discover the divine image of the Trinity in a trinity of persons which belong to the natural human order: an image which would be realized in marriage by the presence of man, woman, and child." Augustine does not hide his total opposition to this opinion, which he por-

---

1. John Paul II, *Letter to Families* (Rome: Libreria Editrice Vaticana, 1994), no. 6.

trays as "so unfounded" and "so strange and so false that it is very easy to rebuke it."[2] Has John Paul II taken the risk of rehabilitating an analogy set aside as inadequate for so long? It is true that the first quotation given above is preceded by very prudent wording: "In the light of the New Testament, it is *possible to glimpse* the original model of the family which must be sought in God himself in the trinitarian mystery of his life." It is possible to glimpse. Note the pope's extreme prudence in affirming what he knows to be in contrast with a predominant tradition. He continues: "the divine 'We' constitutes the eternal model of the human 'we' which is formed by man and woman, created in the image of God, according to his likeness" (LF 6). Has personalist philosophy, which nourished John Paul's thought and which he has contributed to developing, finally overcome the objections of the great African master whose authority has once again been confirmed by the *Catechism of the Catholic Church?*

The title of this chapter, if formulated as a question, recognizes the theological challenge that an analogy between the Trinity and the family represents. One must measure the meaning and range of the challenge that John Paul II takes up with originality and boldness. For the meaning of the relationship between the Trinity and the family depends upon whether or not the man-woman relationship is included within the *imago Dei.* If man — man and woman — is the image of the Trinity, then the communion and participation of the family "we" in the Trinitarian "We" goes far deeper. Conjugal love and family relations take on an undreamt-of theological and sacramental dimension. We must therefore answer as thoroughly as possible the following question: does a family analogy of the Trinity really exist? If so, what is its foundation, what are its limits, and what is its scope? A brief consideration of Tradition and Scripture shall allow us to answer these questions and so to grasp more fully the value and the scope of John Paul II's teaching in *Mulieris Dignitatem* and in the *Letter to Families.*

The Family Analogy of the Trinity in the Tradition

"The history of theology confirms the existence of an analogy between the creating Trinity and the created human family."[3] By these words, Lionel

2. Augustine, *De Trinitate* XII.V.5, Corpus Christianorum Series Latina 50 (1968), pp. 359-60.

3. Lionel Gendron, *Mystère de la Trinité et Symbolique familiale* (Rome, 1975). I will

Gendron, a specialist on the topic, does not hesitate to state the conclusion of his historical study on the family analogy of the Trinity. This analogy built itself around a reading of Genesis 1:26 ff ("Let us make man in our image . . ."), interpreted in both a Trinitarian and a family perspective. A first meaning, which Gendron calls the "typical" family analogy, appeared during the fourth century to illustrate the divine personality of the Holy Spirit and the consubstantial unity of the Trinity. It is found in the fifth *Theological Discourse* of Gregory of Nazianzen,[4] who is its major proponent, and in the twelfth book of *De Trinitate* of Augustine, who is its main opponent but nonetheless presents it in a remarkable way. "On the basis of engendering, different from *ekporeusis* (procession in the strict sense), and of particular modes of existence, this analogical structure has the Father and Adam corresponding to one another as 'un-engendered' and the Son and Seth (or Abel) as 'engendered,' and finally the Spirit and Eve as 'coming forth by *ekporeusis.*'"[5] This first analogy thus focuses precisely on the resemblance between the Father and Adam who are both un-engendered, as well as on the Son and Seth (or Abel) who are both engendered, and finally on the Spirit and Eve who both proceed otherwise than by generation, indicated by Gregory as *ekporeusis* (procession).

Augustine's major objection to this analogy is the impossibility of realizing a true unity, that is to say a substantial unity, within a human family; in the three human *hypostases* of man, woman, and child there exists such a disparity that any real unity is inconceivable. Note here that for the Eastern Fathers, notably the Cappadocians, this objection presents no major problem, for in their understanding human beings who partake in one human substance are one not only specifically but also numerically.[6] "For these Fathers it was relatively easy to show the consubstantial unity of the

---

draw largely from this historical study, whose author has summarized the conclusions in two articles. The first is "Le Foyer chrétien: une Église véritable?" *Communio* XI:6 (1986), pp. 65-83, from which the above quotation is taken, p. 71. The second is "La famille: reflet de la communion trinitaire," in *La famille chrétienne dans le monde d'aujourd'hui* (Montreal: Bellarmin, 1995), pp. 127-48.

4. Gregory of Nazianzen, *Oratio XXXI (Theol. V)*, Patrologia Graeca 36, p. 144.

5. L. Gendron, "Le Foyer chrétien," p. 72.

6. In his essays to illustrate this unity, Basil named Paul, Sylvan, and Timothy (Patrologia Graeca 32, 773 B) and Gregory of Nazianzen named Adam, Eve, and Seth. This last example has the advantage of showing the specific and numerical unity of the three terms in presence, not only by the communion which they realize in one human substance, but also by the fact that each term comes from another whose substance carries on through him.

Trinity thanks to the image of the human family, and particularly thanks to the first family."[7] For them, Eve and Seth originated from the same third person, Adam; and thus man, woman, and child come from the same primordial *anthropos,* to a certain extent.

For his part, Augustine cannot conceive of a valid analogy unless it be "a trinity of terms distinct from one another and yet forming a true unity."[8] The family does not seem to Augustine to offer this possibility because of his notion of person, still imprecise and even hesitating between two extremes: "Sometimes Augustine makes of the person an absolute which excludes any idea of relativity, sometimes he makes of the Father, Son, and Holy Spirit pure relatives which exclude any idea of subsistence."[9] Thomas Aquinas's flash of genius in defining the divine Persons as subsisting relations did not yet permit a reconciliation of these opposites. We must, however, note in all honesty that Aquinas will share the reservations of his master with regard to the family analogy and will prefer to deepen the intrasubjective analogy.[10] In short, Augustine's influence marks a halt in the spread of the typical family analogy carried by the Greek tradition. Nevertheless, it offers other approaches which, once they are taken up by subsequent tradition, will allow the family analogy to be revived.

A first approach stems from the analysis of love of neighbor in the light of God who is Love. "What therefore is love, so praised, so celebrated by the divine Scriptures, if not the love of Good? But love comes from one who loves, and by love something is loved. Here then are three things: one who loves, that which is loved, and love itself."[11] Would there then be a trinity in love, wonders Augustine? He sees that human love might serve as the basis for a social analogy of the Trinity. Unfortunately, overcome by a kind of remorse, he ends his development there. Where we might have ex-

---

7. L. Gendron, *La famille,* p. 133.

8. M.-R. Sciacca, "Trinité et unité de l'esprit," *Augustinus Magister,* vol. I (Paris, 1954), p. 522.

9. A. Malet, *Personne et Amour dans la théologie trinitaire de saint Thomas d'Aquin* (Paris, 1956), p. 22.

10. Thomas Aquinas, *Summa Theologiae* I, q.27, a.2; q.92, a.2; q.36, a.3.1: "[I]n truth, this example borrowed from a previous source does not seem well chosen to represent the immaterial procession of the Divine Persons"; for the discussion, cf. Bertrand de Margerie, *La Trinité chrétienne dans l'histoire* (Paris: Beauchesne, 1975), pp. 367-82, esp. 368-75. (English edition: *The Christian Trinity in History* [Still River, Mass.: St. Bede's Publications, 1982].)

11. Augustine, *De Trinitate* VIII.XIV (our translation).

pected an intersubjective explanation of love, Augustine puts all "his attention on intrasubjective love whose *mens* is both subject and object."[12] It is hard to explain why. The personalist philosopher Maurice Nédoncelle has tried to answer. He notes that neither one nor the other love, the intrasubjective and the intersubjective, succeeds in showing adequately the mystery of the Trinity; the intrasubjective love does not show the distinction of the Persons, and the intersubjective love does not show their unity in nature. He comes to this conclusion: "The second lack is worse than the first in Augustine's view. He therefore sets aside the comparison of friends in favor of the other, for he approaches the divine mystery by considering that which best explains the nature and not the Persons."[13]

We have not yet exhausted Augustine's contribution to the family analogy of the Trinity. Gendron has traced back a second starting point that effectively leads to a rediscovery, paradoxically, of the family theme. In his *Tractatus XXXIX,* while describing Church unity founded on the charity between the community members, Augustine states that therein lies an analogy of the unity which exists between the divine Persons.[14] He observes, in fact, that love possesses the capacity to create a common soul and a common heart among those who love one another. He perceives this capacity especially in God, in whom the Holy Spirit appears as the bond and the fruit of the mutual love of Father and Son. However, he also sees it in ecclesial love, which the Holy Spirit brings to life and consecrates within the community. This analogy will henceforth become the most fruitful and most adequate approach to the Trinitarian mystery. The Orthodox theologian Sergius Bulgakov considers that Augustine's approach to the Trinity as Love and the meaning of the *hypostasis* of the Spirit as bond of love constitutes his major contribution to Trinitarian theology.[15] For this social or intersubjective analogy, subsequent tradition would bring about developments that reintegrate the theme of the family as image of the Trinity.

In the twelfth century, Richard of Saint-Victor took up this tradition and developed a vision of the Trinity as communion in Love, presenting the image of three Friends gathered together as one in love: a Lover, a Be-

---

12. J. Racette, *Le livre neuvième du De Trinitate,* SE (1956), p. 50.

13. M. Nédoncelle, "L'intersubjectivité humaine est-elle pour saint Augustin une image de la Trinité?" *Augustinus Magister,* vol. I (Paris, 1954), p. 586.

14. Cf. *Tractatus XXXIX: In Joannis Evangelium,* n. 5, in Patrologia Latina 35, 1684 and CCSL 36, pp. 347-48. Quoted in Gendron, *La famille,* p. 136.

15. S. Bulgakov, *Le Paraclet* (Paris, 1946), p. 49.

loved, and a *condilectus* loved by both. In his mind there is thus a social analogy. But in pursuing further his analysis to determine the distinct processions in God, he has to call upon the auxiliary concept of kinship or even family. "It is from Adam's substance that Eve, Seth and Enoch proceed. But the first procession alone was immediate, the second was both mediate and immediate: for Seth proceeded from Adam's substance immediately, in that he was procreated by him, and also mediately, in that he is also engendered by Eve."[16] The originating processions in God follow this double immediate and mediate mode: the Son proceeds immediately from the Father, whereas the Spirit proceeds from the Father by the mediation of the Son. From this, one can conclude "that the intersubjective analogy which Augustine had initiated has become in Richard of St. Victor a social analogy, first the interpersonal one of the three friends, then the social analogy of a privileged family expression."[17]

St. Bonaventure, disciple of Augustine and Richard, would in turn carry on this doctrine and give a remarkable complement to the family analogy. To illustrate how the Holy Spirit is in truth the Love of the Father and the Son, he calls upon the family experience where love between husband and wife finds its personalized expression in the child. The child is in some way the communion of the spouses incarnated in a third person. In Bonaventure's view, even if the child is more "the loved one" than "love," he is more than Richard's *condilectus;* he is the hypostasis of the parents' love. "This new analogy thus takes up as its own the social analogy, no longer only favoring the family dimension but this time insisting on it. For this reason, we believe that it may indeed be called a typically familial-social analogy of the Trinity."[18]

It must be noted that the family analogy, which has been referred to in two different and complementary expressions, the first associating Eve with the Spirit and the second associating the child with the Spirit, did not play a major role in theological tradition. It was forgotten with the decline of scholasticism. Petau and Tommasinus took the family analogy up again in the seventeenth century, in their rediscovery of patristics, but it disappeared once again soon after to return in strength in the twentieth century

16. G. Salet, *Richard of St. Victor, La Trinité* (Paris: Cerf, 1999).

17. L. Gendron, *La famille*, p. 139.

18. L. Gendron, *La famille*, p. 140. See also the fine developments that St. Bonaventure inspires in Klaus Hemmerle: "Matrimonio e Famiglia in una antropologia trinitaria," *Nuova Umanità* 6 (1984), 3-31, esp. n. 31.

under the impulse of Scheeben. Now it is fast developing in Trinitarian theology, as in the theology of marriage,[19] at the prompting of personalist philosophers.[20] In stating prudently that "the original model of the family must be sought in God himself, in the Trinitarian mystery of his life" (LF 6), John Paul II draws upon a modest yet respectable tradition. Even though the family analogy has been limited over the centuries, it nevertheless remains that solid points of support authorize the doctrinal development which we are currently witnessing.[21] However, before coming to a conclusion about its authenticity, we must finally take a look at Scripture itself in the light of current exegesis of the *imago Dei*.

Contemporary Exegesis of the *Imago Dei*

Emil Brunner's words are often quoted: "It is the doctrine of the *imago Dei* that decides the destiny of all theology." It actually decides the fate of man's vital relationship to God, and the fundamental link between theology and anthropology. The question of the dignity of the person also hinges on it, as does the balance between body and soul, man and woman, the individual and the community. Balthasar is in agreement with Brunner and Barth in affirming that the theme of image-likeness deserves a major place in dogmatic theology. "It must be said, however, that this topic, which was central in the patristic period and still received adequate attention in Scholasticism, scarcely plays any part in works of the more modern dogmatic theologians."[22] Let us leave this paradox for the moment and see what exegesis says of the *imago Dei*. The revealed foundation of this doctrine is found in Gen. 1:26-27: "Let us make man in our image, according to our

19. M. J. Scheeben, M. Schmaus, and H. Muhlen have used it extensively in Trinitarian theology; H. Doms, B. Häring, and Th. Rey-Mermet in the theology of marriage. P. Evdokimov, K. Barth, J. Moltmann, and Hans Urs von Balthasar put it at the heart of the anthropology of the *imago Dei*.

20. Among those philosophers who give important consideration to this analogy, let us note Gabriel Marcel, Maurice Nédoncelle, Jean Guitton, Joseph de Finance, Jean Lacroix, and P. L. Eintralgo.

21. Cf. Blanca Castilla y Cortàzar, "La Trinidad como familia," *Annales theologici* 10 (1996), pp. 381-416.

22. H. U. von Balthasar, *Theo-Drama: Theological Dramatic Theory*, vol. II: *Dramatis Personae: Man in God* (San Francisco: Ignatius, 1990), p. 317. Balthasar's reference to Brunner is taken from *Zwischen den Zeiten* (1929), p. 264.

likeness. . . ." Does this narrative of the creation of man imply an analogical relationship between the Trinity and the family? Some would like to think so, but most exegetes deem it anachronistic to reread the creation narratives in the light of the New Testament. Notwithstanding these methodological scruples, it is possible to identify, on a strictly exegetical basis, a certain number of elements which authorize an interpretation of the image-likeness that includes the couple and their fruitfulness, in other words, the family. We will try to briefly evoke some of these elements.[23]

As a preliminary observation, let us first note that the theme of "man created in the image and likeness of God" is rather rare in the Old Testament. Except for the revival in Ecclesiasticus 17:1-3 and Wisdom 2:23, it is practically limited to the priestly history of the origins: Genesis 1:26-28; 5:1-3; 9:6b. At the level of interpretation we can say that current exegesis is moving beyond two extremes. On the one hand, one finds the purely spiritual interpretation — which is the commonly held opinion of Christian exegesis since Philo — that the notion of image of God concerns only the spiritual dimension of man, allowing him to have dominion over animals and things. On the other hand, there is the purely material interpretation of the image: the fact that the Hebrew term *ṣelem* (sculpture, statue) would bring us back to the bodily configuration proper to man, that is, his vertical posture. The majority of exegetes can currently be found between these two opinions, maintaining that the image-likeness in Genesis 1:26-27 refers to the fact "that Adam is the royal representative of God himself, embodying and exercising God's own authority in regard to the earth and all that lives in it."[24] Another group maintains with Claus Westermann that "the image of God is to be found in the divinely conferred capacity for relation to God."[25] Properly understood in its context, the narrative of the creation of man would express God's will to give himself a partner capable of dialogue with him. For our reflection, the most important fact is to note how

23. The most developed presentation of current exegesis is found in the meticulous and well-balanced study of Gunnlaugur A. Jonson, *The Image of God: Genesis 1:26-28 in a Century of Old Testament Research,* Conjectanea Biblica, Old Testament Series, 26 (Stockholm: Almquist & Wiksell International, 1988).

24. Francis Martin, "A Summary of the Teaching of Genesis Chapter One," *Communio: International Catholic Review* (Summer 1993), p. 247.

25. F. Martin, "A Summary of the Teaching of Genesis Chapter One," p. 258. See Claus Westermann, *Genesis I–II: A Commentary* (Minneapolis: Augsburg, 1984), pp. 147-61 and especially pp. 157-58.

exegesis of Genesis 1:27-28 according to the priestly tradition assists in integrating the relationship man-woman within image-likeness.

Indeed, if rather than separating the two narratives of creation, we allow the first to be illuminated by the second (Gen. 2:18-24) and by Genesis 5:3, it appears clear that the male-female reciprocity, in the image-likeness of God, allows man to represent him on earth and to imitate him in participating in his creative power. The insistence in the priestly tradition upon the bodily differences of the sexes serves to express the fundamentally relational characteristic of the human being, on the horizontal axis of a relationship between man and woman, as well as on the vertical axis of a relationship with God. This is why the exegesis of the priestly tradition manages to link closely the theme of image and that of the family. "Adam images God, that is, makes his power and authority present and interacts with God, in the relating of man and woman."[26] Régine Hinschberger comes to the conclusion that Genesis 1:26 suggests "a relationship of likeness between God who creates and man, male and female, who blessed by him, procreates." Thus "the expression 'God made him in his likeness' means that God made man to be fecund like him."[27] Moreover, if it is emphasized with Walter Brueggemann that God created them, man and woman, to mirror himself in *them* as in his image and likeness, then it may be concluded: "Only in community of humankind is God reflected. God is, according to this bold affirmation, not mirrored as an individual but as a community."[28] Add to that the deliberate plural "Let us make," which introduces the doctrine of image, and it can be rightfully concluded that this exegesis of the *imago Dei* according to the priestly tradition, duly completed by New Testament revelation, constitutes a solid scriptural basis upon which to found the family analogy of the Trinity.

It is clear that Genesis does not make this analogy explicit in regard to the correspondence of the members of a family to the Persons of the Trinity. The exegesis of image-likeness only puts in a dialogical relationship a fruitful couple and a still undetermined divine "We," indicating God's creative power in the procreative union. Hinschberger continues: "In other words,

---

26. F. Martin, "A Summary of the Teaching of Genesis Chapter One," p. 259.

27. L. Gendron, *La famille*, pp. 142-43. The first quotation is taken from an article of R. Hinschberger, *"Image et ressemblance dans la tradition sacerdotale,"* in *RSR* 59 (1985), 192. This article is a brief presentation of the paper *Image et ressemblance dans la tradition sacerdotale* (Strasbourg, 1983), from which is drawn the second quotation, p. 52.

28. W. Brueggemann, *Genesis: Interpretation* (Atlanta: John Knox Press, 1982), p. 34.

our priestly tradition does not seem to make a connection between the being of God and the being of man, but rather between the creative "doing" of a God who brings forth life and the procreative "doing" of a man who is able to multiply upon the face of the earth."[29] This dynamic view of the image actualizing its likeness by means of the procreative union fits well within the idea of a covenant *(berit)*, which forms the global context of the doctrine of the *imago Dei*. In fact, God creates man in his image in view of a relationship with him, in view of a Covenant, which is expressed in a privileged way in the history of Israel. The message of Genesis is that this covenant structure is already set within the complementarity between man and woman, whose fruitful reciprocity resembles and suits the Creator's gift. When Eve gives birth to her first son she cries out: "I have given birth to a man with the help of the Lord" (Gen. 4:1), underlining God's creative intervention in the gift of life. Taken in all its scope, this story of the Covenant, already begun in the creation of Adam and Eve, culminates in Christ, the new Adam of whom the first Adam is the figure. For he is in fact above all "the Image of God" (II Cor. 4:4), "the image of the invisible God" (Col. 1:15). It is therefore in him that the family analogy of the Trinity reaches its highest point and at the same moment goes beyond this towards a deeper analogy founded no longer on God's creative act alone but on the gift of Grace.

It is not possible here to elaborate, even briefly, upon the New Testament exegesis of the *imago Dei*, with its implications for the interpretation of Genesis 1:27-28. Let us content ourselves in pointing out the Christological setting offered by the doctrine of the two Adams, which Paul develops in Chapter 5 of the Letter to the Romans (5:12ff), and which highlights the Christocentric direction of all creation (Col. 1:15-17). Paul sees the relationship between man and woman as being part of the *imago Dei;* the fecundity of this relationship announces Christ who, in union with the Church, will fill the world with his fullness *(plērōma)* (cf. Eph. 1:23). The union of man and woman as one flesh is thus the prophetic prefiguring of the greater mystery: the union of Christ and the Church (Eph. 5:21-32). Let us also mention Matthew 19:4-6, where Jesus restores marriage to its original dignity: "The Creator, in the beginning, made them male and female. . . . Thus they will no longer be two, but become one flesh."[30] Jesus

---

29. R. Hinschberger, *"Image et ressemblance dans la tradition sacerdotale,"* p. 192.

30. For an interpretation of Gen. 2:24 in the light of Mt. 19:6, see M. Gilbert, "Une seule chair," *Nouvelle Revue Théologique* 100 (1978), pp. 68-89.

adds a mysterious phrase, which he declares to be beyond understanding without a gift of God (11:15; 13:9): "There are eunuchs who have made themselves so for the sake of the Kingdom of heaven" (Mt. 19:12). This word opens the eschatological horizon, and leads to new possibilities of inter-subjective analogy between the Trinity and the Church. Indeed, the ecclesial relationships founded on the grace of virginity develop new possibilities for communion and therefore of interpersonal analogy in which the limits of the family analogy are integrated and superseded. To recognize this, one need only consider the Holy Family of Nazareth and the relationships which arise between Jesus, Mary, and John at the Cross. The spiritual fecundity of virginal relationships transcends the natural fruitfulness of the conjugal union, yet without allowing the man-woman complementarity to lose all meaning. The family analogy blossoms, so to speak, in the "domestic Church," in which the Trinity is not only mirrored in its created image but where it is given according to the divine likeness. We shall return to this topic later.

For the moment it suffices to better understand, in light of Scripture and Tradition, what John Paul II affirms in his *Letter to Families*: "In the light of the New Testament it is possible to glimpse the original model of the family which is sought in God himself, in the Trinitarian mystery of his life" (LF 6). The unveiling of the creative "We" in the beginning was possible only in the light of Christ's divine personhood and his communion of love with the Father in the unity of the Holy Spirit. Once the revelation of the intimate life of the Trinitarian "We" is achieved, a new view on the original doctrine of the *imago Dei* becomes possible. Not only an exegetical view but also a theological one, yielding a more complete understanding of the mystery of the creation of man as man and woman, starting from the Trinitarian mystery and from the covenant between God and humanity in Christ. This is what John Paul II took as his task, drawing inspiration from Genesis, Vatican II, and the theological tradition re-read and renewed by contemporary exegesis and philosophy. The fruits of his thought on the *imago Dei* are clearly visible in the progression that leads from *Familiaris Consortio* to the *Letter to Families* by way of *Mulieris Dignitatem*. These official texts, interpreted against the background of his Wednesday catecheses to the faithful,[31] make official in some way the posi-

---

31. John Paul II, *The Theology of the Body: Human Love in the Divine Plan* (Boston: Pauline, 1997).

tive conclusions of several current theologians concerning the family analogy of the Trinity.[32] John Paul II brings to it his original contribution, especially at the level of a theology of the body and the sexual complementarity of man and woman as image of God.

Finally, may it suffice to briefly consider *Mulieris Dignitatem* in order to appreciate John Paul II's breakthrough on the theme of image-likeness. He starts by joining together the two narratives of creation, following the example of the exegesis mentioned earlier: "The text of Genesis 2:18-25 helps us to understand better what we find in the concise passage of Genesis 1:27-28. At the same time, if it is read together with the latter, it *helps us to understand even more profoundly* the fundamental *truth* which it contains *concerning man* created as man and woman in the image and likeness of God" (MD 6). Beforehand, he had stated the perfect equality between man and woman as persons created in the image and likeness of the personal God. But here it is the man-woman complementarity which is targeted and attributed to the *imago*. A little further on, he adds, "*The woman is another 'I' in a common humanity.* From the very beginning they appear as a 'unity of the two.' . . ." Thus, the difference between the sexes seems here, to all appearances, to be part of the original characteristic of the *imago Dei.* The end of the paragraph confirms this in stating that according to the book of Genesis, the man-woman difference is intended for their marriage with a view to "the transmission of life to new generations, the transmission of life to which marriage and conjugal love are by their nature ordered . . ." (MD 6).

The following paragraph, no. 7, continues with the explanation of the *communion of persons* of man and woman as a reflection of the communion of love in the uni-trinitarian God: "The fact that man 'created as man and woman' is the image of God . . . also means that man and woman, created as a 'unity of the two' in their common humanity, are called to live in a communion of love and in this way to mirror in the world the communion of love that is in God, through which the three Persons love each other in the intimate mystery of the one divine life" (7). We must recognize, along with Angelo Scola, that herein lies an exceptional revaluing of sexuality, a

---

32. Cf. Pierre Adnès, "Dimensions trinitaries et ecclésiales du mariage," *Dictionnaire de Spiritualité,* vol. X, 372-75; Paul Evdokimov, *The Sacrament of Love* (Crestwood, N.Y.: St. Vladimir's Seminary Press, 1985); B. de Margerie, *The Christian Trinity in History;* Jürgen Moltmann, *The Trinity and the Kingdom: The Doctrine of God* (San Francisco: Harper & Row, 1981); E. C. Muller, *Trinity and Marriage in Paul* (New York: Peter Lang, 1990).

statement of the eminently personal and relational character of human beings and a "significant expansion of the classical doctrine of the *imago Dei*."[33]

This approach coincides in all but a few details with the vision of Hans Urs von Balthasar, who includes the man-woman difference within the image of God, while avoiding identifying the sexual complementarity too exclusively with the image. He differs from Karl Barth on this point and rather falls in with E. Przywara, who maintains that the image of God is found both in and beyond the man-woman duality: "On the one hand, we cannot regard sexuality as a closed circle, as if a man cannot be human except within the sexual relationship between man and woman. On the other hand, however, the spiritual side of the 'image of God' is not isolated from the creature's internal cosmic sexuality, as if man cannot be human except in the spiritual and personal 'interiority of the image of God.'"[34] The dimension proper to the family appears with the gift of fertility, which establishes an immediate relationship with God, as Balthasar notes: "Adam can beget offspring 'in his own likeness, after his image' (Gen 5:3), but when Eve holds her first-born son in her arms, she cries: 'I have gotten a man with the help of the Lord' (Gen 4:1). She understands that the human child is not a mere gift of nature but a personal gift of God."[35]

Notwithstanding this "personal" dimension in the transmission of life, which links the couple to the Creator, it remains the case, for Balthasar, that the sexual dimension of the image of God is still an enigma because of the painful reciprocity between sexual generation and death.[36] "Where death is, there is marriage; and where there is no marriage, there is no death either," said John Chrysostom.[37] This enigma is cleared up only in Christ, who takes upon himself and goes beyond the limits of sexual fe-

---

33. A. Scola, "L'imago Dei e la sessualità umana: A proposito di una tèsi originale della 'Mulieris Dignitatem,'" *Anthropotes* 1 (1992), p. 63. See also M. Séguin, "The Biblical Foundations of the Thought of John Paul II on Human Sexuality," *Communio* (Summer 1993), pp. 266-89.

34. E. Przywara, *Mensch* I (1959), p. 134, quoted by Balthasar, *Theo-Drama*, vol. II, p. 370. See also Karl Barth, *Kirchliche Dogmatik*, III.1, pp. 329-77; III.2, pp. 344ff.

35. H. U. von Balthasar, *Theo-Drama*, vol. II, p. 372.

36. H. U. von Balthasar, *Theo-Drama*, vol. II, p. 374.

37. John Chrysostom, *De Virginitate* 14.6, quoted in Balthasar, *Theo-Drama*, vol. II, p. 375.

cundity in his suprasexual yet not asexual relationship with the Church.[38] That is why sexuality cannot be understood in its deeper meaning outside this unforeseeable integration in the nuptial relationship between God and man by the grace of Christ. In the natural, pre-Christian sphere, sexuality remains in tension between dionysian exaltation which propels it into God and, on the contrary, a depreciation which expels it from an authentic spiritual sphere. "Sexuality . . . is in danger of being suppressed ascetically in favor of the spiritual or depreciated as inferior or demonic. Not infrequently the two extremes turn into their opposites — as in Gnosticism, for example."[39] It is therefore essential to keep in mind the link of the first Adam with Christ if one wishes to understand how the *imago Dei* gives a basis to the family analogy of the Trinity, while at the same time not limiting itself to this context.

Theological Meaning of the Family Analogy of the Trinity

In the light of Scripture and Tradition, it thus seems legitimate to affirm an authentic analogy between the Trinity and the family. John Paul II confirms it officially while remaining prudent and measured in his statements. The family "we" would be in the image of the Trinitarian "We" in a way that goes far beyond the simple metaphor and which is situated in the sphere of analogical knowledge. We should not forget here the commonly held doctrine of analogy which he recalls in no. 8 of *Mulieris Dignitatem,* according to which all resemblance between the Creator and his creature is limited by an always-greater dissimilarity.[40] Even though man is created in God's image and likeness, which gives foundation to an authentic knowledge of God, "God does not cease to be for him the one who dwells in unapproachable light" (1 Tim. 6:16). We must be conscious at all times of the

---

38. H. U. von Balthasar, *Theo-Drama*, vol. II, p. 413: "The suprasexual (and not sexless) relationship between the incarnate Word and his Church is a genuinely human one; human beings can be enabled to participate in it. Consequently the sexual man/woman fruitfulness need be no longer the exclusive model of human fruitfulness. On the contrary, this form of fruitfulness is seen to be the purely worldly metaphor of a unique fruitfulness that burst through the cycle of successive generations and of which Christ says: 'He who is able to receive this, let him receive it' (Mt. 19:12)."

39. H. U. von Balthasar, *Theo-Drama*, vol. II, p. 382.

40. DS 806.

limits of analogy, especially when Scripture attributes masculine and feminine qualities to God and theology seeks to situate within the Trinity the difference of the sexes. "God is spirit (Jn. 4:24) and possesses no property typical of body, neither 'feminine' nor 'masculine'" (MD 8).

Having said this, let us re-examine the question, by asking what specifically constitutes the family analogy of the Trinity? On what precisely does it hinge? On the correspondence between the persons or the communion of persons? A recurring expression in the writings of John Paul II guides us towards the second hypothesis: the *communio personarum* is the common meeting place of the deeper reality of the family and of the mystery of the Trinity: "In the words of the Council, the communion of persons is, in a certain sense, deduced from the mystery of the Trinitarian 'We,' and therefore 'conjugal communion' also refers to this mystery" (LF 8). A little further in this same *Letter to Families,* the Pope draws the conclusions of this likeness: "When they are united by the conjugal covenant in such a way as to become 'one flesh' (Gen 2:24), their union ought to take place 'in truth and love' and thus express a maturity proper to persons created in the image and likeness of God" (LF 8). The historical outline earlier allowed us to evoke two types of family analogy: one typically within the family, proposed by Gregory of Nazianzen and opposed by Augustine; the other primarily social, initiated by Augustine, developed by Richard of Saint Victor, and solidly established by Bonaventure. "It seems that it is this latter social and family analogy that John Paul II proposes when he speaks of the Holy Trinity and of the human family as a 'communion of persons.'"[41] This analogy is based fundamentally on the interpersonal love which, by means of gift and reception, engenders persons, maintains them in relation, and allows them to fulfill themselves as persons "by a sincere gift of self." "Human fatherhood and motherhood . . . contain in an essential and unique way a likeness to God which is the basis of the family as a community of human life, as a community of persons united in love *(communio personarum)*" (LF 6). The specificity of the analogy is centered on communion, a communion of personalizing love that is found analogically in the family and the Trinity.

The theological meaning of this analogy appears to be twofold. On one hand, it offers an anthropological starting point for human knowledge of the Trinity, a revealed starting point which allows theology to deepen the mystery of God as love from the perspective of human experience and

41. L. Gendron, *La famille*, p. 144.

in more accessible language than that of the intrasubjective analogy. On the other hand, it helps Christians to understand and to live the deeper meaning of the family reality, beginning with the Trinity as its source and model. This second perspective, katalogical in style, looks at the communion of created persons as a reflection and participation in the communion of Trinitarian Persons. This participation translates itself existentially by a sincere and free self-giving of the persons, in love: "Man created in the image and likeness of God can find himself fully only in the unselfish gift of himself" (LF 13); "The persons are thus relational and, we might even say, relations; for they are in the image and likeness of the divine Persons which Saint Thomas defined in terms of Subsistent Relations."[42] "The family is the environment in which man can exist 'for himself' by the unselfish gift of himself" (LF 11). Hence the stress put by John Paul II on existential relations "of love and truth" which shape the personal identities and the family unity in the image and likeness of the Trinity.

The family analogy of the Trinity illustrates therefore its fruitfulness in explaining "the genealogy of the person" (LF 9) from love and self-giving and "the family as an environment for human growth"[43] with its eternal dimension. But its roots in the *imago Dei* give it an even wider scope. Indeed, the fundamental anthropological meaning of Gen 1:27, interpreted along with Gen 2:18ff, is the establishment of a partnership, man-woman, blessed by fecundity at the heart of their communion, so that creation in the image of God may serve as a basis for the *common fecundity* between God and man. By the mutual gift of man and woman, which alleviates man's original solitude, the living God and source of life gives fecundity to their union and joins them to himself in the very transmission of the image of God to other human persons (LF 8). Despite the immeasurable distance between the divine and the human, there exists sufficient likeness between the image and its divine Model so that a community of mutual gift joins the Creator and his creature in transmitting life. The child is welcomed as a personal gift from God in answer to the mutual gift of the spouses. "I have gotten a man with the help of God" (Gen 4:1). In other words, the family analogy of the Trinity unveils the basis for the first nuptial relation between the Creator and his creature.

42. L. Gendron, *La famille,* p. 144.

43. C. Cafarra, "La famiglia come ambiente di crescita umana," *Anthropotes* 2 (1994), pp. 217-25.

The common fecundity of the divine "We" and the human "we" must not be seen exclusively from the angle of fertility. It is no doubt its most creative moment but it also expands to the many relationships of education, sharing, and affection that make up the community life of persons committed one to another and one "for" another in the family's framework. Within these horizontal relations "in love and truth," the living God blesses the developing persons with his Presence. He envelops them in his own personalizing communion which heals, raises, transforms, and deifies their human and family relations. The grace of the Holy Spirit has a clear influence in this respect, particularly by virtue of the Sacrament of marriage which links sacramentally the spouses' union and the union of Christ and his Church. Hence the emergence of a new likeness, properly supernatural, which crowns the first creation by offering the family the status of domestic Church. In this regard, the family, in its experience, is both crowned and surpassed. It is crowned because the new and eternal Covenant in Christ broadens the family's natural fruitfulness by allowing it to participate in the very fruitfulness of the Spirit. It is surpassed because Christ as eschatological Spouse calls some of his disciples, man and woman, to a consecration in virginity and so to a higher spiritual fecundity based on relations of virginal love. As regards this New Testament fulfillment, the family as a reality belonging to the first creation, without losing any of its own quality, takes on the meaning of a promise, a prophecy, a "sign" of a greater mystery: that of the fruitful union of Christ and the Church.

Conclusion

Today, the family analogy of the Trinity is witnessing significant developments at the level of exegesis and dogmatic theology. These developments, which we have only briefly described here, allowed John Paul II to give this analogy an almost official status in magisterial teaching, despite the reservations to which it has been subject throughout the history of theology. We have underlined the prudence with which John Paul states it and the limits which he acknowledges in interpreting it at the level of the communion of persons. While requiring a deeper critical examination to determine its definitive validity, this analogy already offers a fresh and fruitful start to understanding more fully the Trinitarian mystery and the mystery of man and woman as partners of the God of Love. It also serves as a major component of a Trinitarian anthropology, built on a covenant theology.

For the purposes of this critical review, it would be worth considering on the one hand the relationship between Person and Love in the Trinity and in the family, in order to determine how and to what extent Christ's mediation allows them to be identified in each of the two cases. In the same vein, it is worth pursuing further the analysis of the concept of divine unity as a unity of Love. How does the unity of Love of the uncreated Persons, absolutely distinct and correlative, enter into harmony with the unity of love of created persons within the family? Also, one must clarify the theological scope of the man-woman, masculine-feminine, male-female complementarities, inscribed in the image of God, in relationship with Him who, while founding and modeling these differences, remains nevertheless, the totally Other one, a pure Spirit. What consequences follow for the family analogy, considered both on a conceptual level and on the level of the existential Trinity-family relationship?

Current theological thought on the Christian family, icon of the Trinity, should produce much spiritual and pastoral fruit when the results of a renewed Trinitarian theology have been assimilated by theological anthropology. A "metaphysics of being as love" would be the indispensable philosophical counterpart because understanding man, in the light of revelation, comes through a deeper understanding of being as gift.[44] What can be expected from a Trinitarian anthropology of the family built on these foundations? Theoretically, it would mean deepening the category of person as relation in the Trinity's image; practically, it means a positive appreciation of human love, sexuality, woman's dignity, and the sacramentality of the family.[45] In other words, the theological foundation of the civilization of love.

44. Cf. Ferdinand Ulrich, *Homo Abyssus: Das Wagnis der Seinsfrage*, 2d. ed. (Freiburg: Johannes Verlag, Freiburg, 1998).

45. Botero, *Per una teologia della famiglia*, pp. 66ff.; Blanca Castilla y Cortàzar, "La Trinidad como familia: Analogia humana de la procesiones divinas," *Annales teologici* 10 (1996), pp. 381-416.

.

CHAPTER III

The Covenant of the Trinity and the Family: The Domestic Church

More than ever before, the present hour of the Church is marked by the battle for human dignity. The defense of human life from the womb to the tomb has become a paramount duty for the Church in the face of the "scientifically and systematically planned threats" which John Paul II denounces as a "conspiracy against life."[1] Nor does the Church respond to these errors and abuses by mere denunciation; she sets forth a "Gospel of Life" which combats the "culture of death" prevalent in contemporary societies by proposing a civilization of love and of life. The Church's response is contained in two correlative themes, the Trinity and the family, which form the essential content for and path of the New Evangelization. The principal challenge is to explicate these two realities, the created image and the uncreated Archetype, so as to give to the men and women of our time a new sense of belonging to the mystery of the Church. This challenge demands a deeper meditation on the Trinity-family relationship from the perspective of the family's participation in the mystery of the Church.

The Second Vatican Council quietly restored the notion of the family as domestic Church to contemporary discussion.[2] Paul VI took up this initiative, which also gave rise to enthusiastic developments in ecclesiology.

1. John Paul II, *The Gospel of Life: Encyclical Letter on the Value and Inviolability of Human Life* (Rome: Libreria Editrice Vaticana, 1995), no. 17.
2. *Lumen Gentium* no. 11; *Apostolicam Actuositatem* no. 11.

John Paul II, in turn, made it a key to the future of evangelization: "As domestic Church, the family is called to proclaim, celebrate, and serve the Gospel of Life" (EV 92). The search for a Trinitarian anthropology of the family passes through the theme of the domestic Church, which concretizes, as it were, a new dimension of the relationship between the Trinity and the family, namely, the dimension of grace or, in patristic terms, the dimension of the divine likeness in view of which the image was created. If it is legitimate to affirm an authentic analogy between the creative Trinity and the created family, this affirmation is only the portico of an immense cathedral, housing a covenantal mystery which unfolds into the many dimensions of participation and fruitfulness. We must now enter into that "sanctuary of life," the family, to discover the "Presence" which gives to each person and to the communion of persons a sacred and inviolable character.

John Paul II speaks abundantly of the family as "a community of love and of life" which is called to become what it is, a domestic Church committed at the very heart of the Church's mission. Is this merely pastoral rhetoric, or are we in the presence of an authentic theology of the family? What is the role of the domestic Church in God's covenant with his people? What is the basis of the family's ecclesiality and its participation in the mission of the Church? These questions require a fundamental theological reflection which demonstrates the foundations of the ministries of the Christian family in today's world.

The Family, Domestic Church

Since Vatican II granted the term citizenship in theology,[3] it has become increasingly common to speak of the family as the domestic Church. The expression was borrowed from the tradition stemming from St. John

---

3. The first mention of the "domestic Church" occurs in the Constitution on the Church: "In hac velut ecclesia domestica. . . ." "[The family] is, so to say, the domestic Church, in which the parents, both by word and example, have to be the first preachers of the faith for their children . . ." (LG 11). The second reference is found, in a slightly different form, in the Decree on the Apostolate of the Laity: "tamquam domesticum sanctuarium Ecclesiae se exhibeat": "[The family] must present itself as a domestic sanctuary of the Church" (AA 11); Cf. M. Fahey, "La famille chrétienne, Eglise domestique à Vatican II," *Concilium* 260 (1995), pp. 115-23.

Chrysostom,[4] but it has deep roots in the Bible. In fact, the idea of "house" (*oikos*), which is its remote source, occupies an important place in both the Old and the New Testaments.[5] In the Old Testament it designates the house of God, his earthly sanctuary (Gen. 28:17-19; Judg. 17:5). On the other hand, "in the New Testament the Christian community is called the *naos tou Theou* and the *oikos tou Theou*, the earthly sanctuary of God: Hebrews 3:6; 1 Peter 4:17; 1 Timothy 3:15."[6] Michel writes that "the primitive Christian communities were organized into families, groups of families, and houses";[7] they gathered in houses to celebrate their assemblies, which comprised the broader family, along with slaves and neighbors. The head of the family played a specific role in these assemblies (1 Cor. 4:15; Gal. 4:19; 1 Tim. 3:5), as did couples, if we go by the reference to Prisca and Aquila in Romans 16:3-5. However, we must beware of identifying the "Ecclesia domestica" described by the New Testament, especially in Paul and Acts, with the nuclear family, which the Magisterium has in mind in its contemporary use of this term.[8] The expression *kat'oikon ekklēsia*, which we find in St. Paul, does not mean "the house as Church, but rather the local Church which meets in the house of a particular Christian."[9] This broader meaning nevertheless remains the basis for the later tradition, which will evolve towards a narrower sense of family.

St. John Chrysostom, whose homilies extend the teaching of Clement of Alexandria, a pioneer of the patristic theology of the married couple, is the great catechist of the "domestic Church." Chrysostom exhorts fathers to make their homes into a little church where the Word of God is meditated and passed on: "On returning home [from Church], let us prepare two tables, one for food and one for the Word of God, whereupon the man should repeat the things that were said in Church. Let the wife learn and

4. P. Evdokimov, "Ecclesia Domestica," *L'Anneau d'Or: Cahiers de spiritualité conjugale et familiale* 107 (1962), pp. 353-62.

5. R. De Vaux, *Les Institutions de l'Ancien Testament* (Paris, 1960); O. Michel, "Oikos, oikia," *GLNT* VIII, pp. 337-449.

6. José Silvio Botero, *Per una teologia della famiglia* (Rome: Borla, 1992), p. 68.

7. O. Michel, "Oikos, oikia," p. 366.

8. On the interpretation of the *Ecclesia domestica*, see the study of J. P. Audet, *Mariage et Célibat dans le service pastoral de l'Eglise* (Paris, 1967), pp. 59-103. See also H. J. Klauck, *Hausgemeinde und Hauskirche im frühen Christentum* (Stuttgart, 1981); R. Aguirre, "La casa como estructura base del Cristianismo primitivo," *Estudios Eclesiasticos* 59 (1984), pp. 27-51.

9. N. Provencher, "Vers une théologie de la famille: l'Eglise domestique," *Eglise et Théologie* 12 (1981), p. 17.

the children hear; nor should the servants be deprived of this reading. Make of your home a church, because you are accountable for the salvation of your children and servants."[10] Corresponding to this paternal responsibility is the commitment of all to live according to the Spirit of the Church: "All, even the smallest ones, must feel actively committed to seeking the message of the Word of God and to living it together. . . . Make your home into a church. For where we find psalmody, prayer, and the inspired songs of the prophets, there is certainly no mistake in calling such a gathering a 'church.'"[11] In addition to these ecclesial traits of the family, St. John Chrysostom also cites domestic concord, openness to strangers and the poor, welcome and hospitality as its essential virtues. He remains, among the numerous Fathers who spoke on the Church in the home, an inexhaustible source of familial spirituality.

It was Paul VI who popularized the expression, "the family, domestic Church." His best-known public statement on the subject is his talk to the Equipes Notre-Dame on May 4, 1970. In this allocution, Paul VI speaks of the mission of the Christian home, which he defines as "a veritable cell of the Church,"[12] whose members live a life of tenderness, hospitality, and irradiation of the Gospel. In his apostolic exhortation, *Evangelii Nuntiandi,* Pope Paul dwelt once more on the action of the family in evangelization, noting in this context a fundamental criterion of the family's ecclesiality: "The family has certainly deserved throughout the Church's history the beautiful definition 'domestic Church' ratified by the Second Vatican Council. This means that in each Christian family we should find the various aspects of the entire Church." Drawing his inspiration from this principle, one author has defined the ecclesial character of the family in the following terms: the family is a presence of Christ, a locus of evangelization, and a place of prayer and charity.[13]

What Paul VI began, John Paul II has energetically carried on, most

10. John Chrysostom, *Homilies on Genesis* 6.2, Patrologica Graeca 54, p. 607.

11. John Chrysostom, *Exp. in Ps* 41:2, PG 55, p. 158.

12. Paul VI, "Allocution aux équipes Notre-Dame" in *Documentation catholique* (1970), n. 1564, p. 504. Here he cites John XXIII's previous use of the same expression: "La famille chrétienne: Allocution pontificale aux 'Equipes Notre-Dame,'" *Documentation catholique* (1959), n. 1304, col. 649 (our translation from the original text in French).

13. N. Provencher, "Vers une théologie de la famille: L'Eglise domestique," *Eglise et théologie* 12 (1981), pp. 9-34. See also D. Tettamanzi, *La famiglia via della Chiesa* (Milan: Massimo, 1991).

notably in *Familiaris Consortio,* which contains multiple references to the "domestic Church."[14] These references can be grouped into three categories. The first, comprising numbers 21, 38, 48, and 49, relates to the basis for the affirmation that the family is a domestic Church: by the Word, the sacraments, and its own unity, the family is a particular actualization of ecclesial communion. Numbers 51, 52, 53, and 54 underline the family's mission in evangelization, which is based on its participation in the mission of the Church: "the evangelization of the future depends in large part on the domestic Church" (52). Finally, numbers 55, 59, and 61 refer to life within the family as a domestic sanctuary where prayer and worship are offered. In these three categories we find the reflection, or rather, incarnation, of the principal characteristics of the Church — communion, mission and worship — at the level of the family. It follows from this analysis that the family is more than a field for the implementation of the Church's pastoral ministry; it is also an authentic manifestation of the Church. John Paul II has given powerful expression to this point in terms of mission: "the essence and role of the family are in the final analysis specified by love. Hence the family has the mission to guard, reveal and communicate love, and this is a living reflection of and a real sharing in God's love for humanity and the love of Christ the Lord for the Church His bride" (FC 17).

Taking their cue from John Paul II, who grounds the mission of the family in its identity as Church, a number of theologians have shown that the family is not just an "image of the Church," but an "ecclesial reality."[15] The conjugal and familial community "not only makes the Church present and active, but constitutes the Church itself — a 'little Church,' to be sure, yet a Church in a proper and specific sense, a real Church, an 'Ecclesia domestica.'"[16] Paul Evdokimov vigorously emphasizes this central affirmation: "It is not merely a question of *resembling* the Church; as a reality of grace, the community of the spouses is an organic part of the ecclesial community: *it is the Church*."[17] This conviction finds its basis in Ephesians 5:21ff., which states that the Christian couple participates in an authentic sense in Christ's love for his Church, a participation that is rooted in the

---

14. D. Tettamanzi, "La famiglia cristiana 'velut Ecclesia domestica' nell'Esortazione 'Familiaris Consortio,'" *La Scuola Cattolica* 111 (1983), pp. 107-52.

15. A. Peelmann, "La famille comme réalité ecclésiale," *Eglise et Théologie* 12 (1981), pp. 95-114.

16. L. Gendron, "Le Foyer chrétien, une église véritable?" in *Communio* XI, 6, p. 77.

17. P. Evdokimov, "Ecclesia Domestica," *L'Anneau d'Or* 107 (1962), p. 357.

order of created things and which blossoms in the order of grace. This conviction also rests, as we saw earlier, on the fact that the fruitful couple is a created image of the Trinity, called to reflect and make present the communion and distinction of the divine Persons: "Having become an 'icon' in the order of the 'new creation' thanks to the saving intervention of the Father and the Son in the Spirit, it (the family) proclaims that a baptized couple's communion of love is a revelation and a life-giving realization of the eternal communion of the Father and the Son in the Spirit."[18]

This supernatural participation in the Trinitarian communion is the ultimate basis of the family as an ecclesial reality. It is also emphatically underscored by the Eastern tradition. Evdokimov, for example, explains this participation in the following way.[19] Referring to its Christological foundation, he writes: "The icon of the Wedding at Cana mystically represents the nuptials of the Church and of every soul with the divine Spouse. By virtue of the sacrament of matrimony, *every couple marries Christ.* Therefore, in loving each other, the spouses love Christ."[20] The same author adds what he calls the pentecostal foundation, that is, the gift of the Spirit, who seals the unity of the conjugal and familial "we" in a real and not merely symbolic manner. This pneumatological perspective is echoed by *Familiaris Consortio:* "The Holy Spirit who is poured out during the celebration of the sacrament commits to the Christian spouses the gift of a new communion, a communion of love that images in a living and real way the altogether unique unity which makes the Church the indivisible mystical body of Christ" (FC 19). Could it not be said that the Holy Spirit is in some sense the sacramental marriage bond which links the spouses at the very heart of their self-giving to each other in Christ? This pneumatological question, to which we will return later, poses from a new viewpoint the problem of a Trinitarian anthropology of the family. How does the sacramental covenant between Christian spouses participate in the relations among the divine Persons? What level of communion do we need to address in order to give a theological and anthropological account of the foundation of the family as domestic Church?

18. L. Gendron, "Le Foyer chrétien, une église véritable?" p. 77.

19. P. Evdokimov, "Ecclesia Domestica," 353-62. See also the same author's *Sacrament of Love: The Nuptial Mystery in the Light of the Orthodox Tradition* (Crestwood, N.Y.: St. Vladimir's Seminary Press, 1985).

20. P. Evdokimov, "Ecclesia Domestica," p. 358.

The Anthropological Foundation
of the Ecclesiality of the Family

The subject of the domestic Church, such as we have outlined it through its biblical and patristic origins, certainly merits deeper reflection along the lines suggested by John Paul II in *Familiaris Consortio:* "Family, become what you are" (FC 17). Theological investigation can already appeal to achievements in the area of biblical studies, as well as to reliable findings in Christology and Pneumatology, which justify an authentic participation of the family in the Trinitarian communion. Yet, despite these advances, the impression remains that talk of the family as an integral part of the being and mission of the Church expresses a theological intuition that has yet to achieve the status of a profoundly coherent systematic ecclesiology. Earlier, we remarked that *Familiaris Consortio* had not yet achieved the personalist integration which emerges more clearly in *Mulieris Dignitatem* and the *Letter to Families.* The document still lacked an interpretation of the family as *imago Trinitatis* (image of the Trinity), which would free up the category of relation as a basis for deepening the notion of the person as created in the image of the uncreated Persons.[21] In this regard, it is useful to reflect on Cardinal Ratzinger's rather harsh criticism of Augustine's anthropological orientation towards the intrasubjective analogy, for "as a result, the Trinitarian concept of person was no longer transferred to the human person in its immediate impact."[22] "In fundamental ways it influenced both the concept of the Church and the understanding of the person which was now pushed off into the individualistically narrowed 'I and you' that finally loses the 'you' in this narrowing."[23]

In light of this criticism, it is necessary to attempt a more precise account of the missionary and ecclesial identity of the family, from a starting point which simultaneously underlines the relationship between person, mission, and communion. The basic question can be formulated as follows: How can we understand the membership of married persons in the Church's communion and their committed involvement in the Church's mission as proceeding from the couple's inmost being? How do we avoid

---

21. On the notion of person, see the article by J. Ratzinger, "Concerning the Notion of Person in Theology," *Communio* 17 (Fall 1990), pp. 439-54.

22. J. Ratzinger, "Concerning the Notion of Person in Theology," p. 447.

23. J. Ratzinger, "Concerning the Notion of Person in Theology," p. 454.

representing the missionary identity of the Christian family as something added from the outside to persons who have already been constituted independently of it? Can we imagine an identity of person and mission that allows us to understand the Church (and consequently the Christian family) as an essentially missionary reality? Hans Urs von Balthasar's "dramatic theology" ventures just such an identification and represents a shift towards a radically Trinitarian and personalist anthropology. We shall now proceed to set forth Balthasar's view, which, in my opinion, adds an element otherwise missing from the theological anthropology of the family.

While classical thought defines the person from the starting point of nature, Balthasar opts for a formal determination of the person from the starting point of grace, that is to say, from the starting point of Christ. God elects, calls, and blesses his spiritual creature, giving him a new name "in Christ"; this is the starting point for Balthasar's "theological" conception of the person. Balthasar maintains a descending, typically Ignatian perspective which defines man from Christ instead of defining grace from nature.[24] He "gave first place to the theology and anthropology that think in terms of descending *agape,* and he gave the subordinate place to the theology and anthropology of ascending *eros.* . . . It is important, however, that the line of *eros* is not simply dropped, but integrated into the whole."[25] At the basis of this reversal of perspective is a theology of election elaborated upon a metaphysics of the *analogia entis* (analogy of being), interpreted as an *analogia libertatis* (analogy of freedom). "In the analogy of freedom between God and the creature, [man] chooses 'what God our Lord gives us to choose, spontaneously and voluntarily cooperating in that particular choice which, in the eternal freedom of God, has been chosen for us.'"[26] The person responds to his vocation by living "for the praise, reverence and service" of God and by letting himself be sent with Jesus to serve oth-

---

24. It is not possible here to elaborate on the background of this Christocentric vision, which extends the shift effected by Henri de Lubac in the manner of conceiving the relation between nature and grace. Cf. A. Scola, "Nature and Grace in Hans Urs von Balthasar," *Communio* 18 (Summer 1991), pp. 206-26; M. Ouellet, "Paradox and/or supernatural existential," *Communio* 18 (Summer 1991), pp. 259-80.

25. W. Löser, S.J., "The Ignatian Exercises in the Work of Hans Urs von Balthasar," *Hans Urs von Balthasar: His Life and Work,* ed. David Schindler (San Francisco: Ignatius, 1991), pp. 103-20; here, p. 115.

26. H. U. von Balthasar, *The Glory of the Lord V: The Realm of Metaphysics in the Modern Age* (San Francisco: Ignatius, 1992), p. 105.

ers. The Balthasarian conception of the person thus emerges against this metaphysical and theological backdrop, wherein the primacy of Christ radically determines the horizon of theological anthropology.

In order to understand better the concept of person which results from this reversal of perspective, we must now complete the discussion, begun earlier, of the family as image of the Trinity. Following the personalist philosophers, Balthasar sees the constitution of human subjectivity in terms of the interpersonal relations "I-Thou-We." He shows that on the natural plane the awakening of the conscious and free "I" depends upon the love which it receives from the "Thou." The child's subjectivity awakens in response to its mother's smile. Self-consciousness blooms in communion. Balthasar penetrates more deeply into this dialogical structure of human freedom in light of Thomistic "*esse,*" which mediates the subject's access to self, to the other, and to the totality of Being: "The opening up of the person to its archetype can only be such if it is simultaneously a surpassing of its limits toward the whole community of beings, if it is freedom as communion."[27]

Human freedom is by nature intersubjective. It exists in giving and receiving. The author of the *Theo-Drama* maintains that a purely individual freedom is unthinkable. The deepest reason for this impossibility is the very nature of the infinite Freedom which finite freedom images. Now, infinite Freedom is essentially a Freedom in communion, a Freedom which engenders the Other in order to be One with him in Love. Accordingly, infinite Freedom can offer finite freedom, in Christ, a space of giving and receiving where it, finite freedom, can be fulfilled in love: Finite freedom "can only be what it is, that is, an image of infinite freedom, imbued with a freedom of its own, by getting in tune with the (trinitarian) 'law' of absolute freedom (of self-surrender): and this law is not foreign to it — for after all it is the 'law' of absolute Being — but most authentically its own: 'This freedom is to find delight in the law of God: for freedom delights. If you do something as a slave, even if it be something right, it is not God who is delighting you. . . . Let him become your delight and then you will be free!'"[28]

27. H. U. von Balthasar, *Theo-Drama: Theological Dramatic Theory,* vol. II: *Dramatis Personae: Man in God* (San Francisco: Ignatius, 1990), pp. 270-71 (the translation is our own, based on *Theodramatik,* II, 1, p. 246: "die Eröffnung der Person auf ihr Urbild kann nur zugleich ihre Entschränkung auf alles Mitseiende, Freiheit als Kommunion sein").

28. H. U. von Balthasar, *Theo-Drama,* vol. II, p. 259; Balthasar's citation from Augustine, *In Ioan. Evang.,* 41.8.10 has been translated from the Latin, PL 35 (1968).

Furthermore, this freedom-as-communion is not only a matter of horizontal intersubjectivity, but is at the same time transcendental-dialogical, inasmuch as it rests upon a "gift" of being bestowed by infinite Freedom for the sake of an essentially supernatural nuptial covenant: "[T]he finite, since it is subject, already constitutes itself as such through the letting-be of Being by virtue of an *ekstasis* out of its own closed self, and therefore through dispossession and poverty becomes capable of salvaging in recognition and affirmation the infinite poverty of the fullness of Being and, within it, that of the God who does not hold on to Himself. Only on this level and in this medium can the event take place which the Bible describes as the process from (God) person to (man) person: predestination, election, vocation, justification, sanctification, glorification (Rom 8:28-30), for all these are *modi* of radiant and universal love. . . ."[29]

This very dense text contains several key elements underlying Balthasar's conception of the person. The first is the subject's openness to the fullness of being, which is the condition of access to the other and to oneself as a spiritual subject. Second, there is the mediation of being *(esse)*, a mediation that Balthasar expresses in terms of wealth and poverty: *"esse"* as such, in fact, is "nothing," and yet it is the "act" which permits the existent *to be*. Third, this act conceals and contains the "Act" of infinite freedom — with its simultaneity of infinite wealth and poverty — which does not cling to itself, but gives itself kenotically. Finally, Balthasar affirms that this transcendental-dialogical structure is the basis of every Person-to-person relationship between God and man. In Balthasar's reading, this Person-to-person dialogue is fully realized only in the fulfillment of humanity in Christ, yet the desire for it is inscribed in the very essence of man as image of the Trinity. In saying this, Balthasar champions, alongside Henri de Lubac, an interpretation of the nature-grace relationship in terms of paradox. Man has only one finality, which is supernatural, yet he is incapable of attaining it on his own. Therein lie the paradox and the nobility of man according to Saint Thomas Aquinas, who expresses it in terms of *desiderium naturale visionis* (the natural desire to see God). As image of God, man is a freedom in search of a Freedom. From the very beginning, creation, and therefore nature, is intrinsically oriented to the grace of Christ. Vatican II expressed this paradoxal truth in the following

29. H. U. von Balthasar, *Glory of the Lord, A Theological Aesthetics*, vol. V: *The Realm of Metaphysics in the Modern Age* (San Francisco: Ignatius, 1989), p. 627.

words: "in reality, the mystery of man is truly illuminated only in the mystery of the incarnate Word" (GS 22). Balthasar gives this paradox of man a dramatic twist which culminates in a Christocentric and Trinitarian conception of the person.

"It is when God addresses a spiritual subject, tells him who he is and what he means to the eternal God of truth and shows him the purpose of his existence — that is, imparts a distinctive and divinely authorized mission — that we can say of a spiritual subject that he is a person."[30] Balthasar draws a distinction between the "spiritual subject," which coincides with what classical theology calls person, and the "theological" person, which designates the same subject enriched with the supernatural mission which it receives from the Word of God. "'Person' is the 'new name' by which God addresses me (Rev. 2:17) and which comes from 'the beginning of the creation of God' (Rev. 3:14); it always implies a task, namely, to be a 'a pillar in the temple of my God' (Rev. 3:12).[31] Christ is the archetype of the event in which the Word comes to personalize a subject. Christ's humanity is assumed into the Person of the incarnate Word, which is identical with his universal mission. This identity of person and mission is an *a priori* identity in Christ by reason of the hypostatic union. It is an *a posteriori* identity in all other spiritual subjects, inasmuch as they receive their supernatural determination in time, following the election and the call of God. Consequently, persons find their theological identity "in Christ," in a progressive and dramatic identification with the Word-mission which defines their role in the body of Christ.

This radically Christocentric vision of the person has a corresponding ecclesial dimension. Every participation in the universal mission of Christ simultaneously implies a relationship to the community of the Church in one of an infinite variety of modalities. "When a human being becomes a person, theologically, by being given a unique vocation and mission, he is simultaneously de-privatized, socialized, made into a locus and a bearer of community."[32] The person and the community penetrate and sustain each other without confusion. Balthasar gives a phenomenological description of these realities using biblical figures who participate in the communion

---

30. H. U. von Balthasar, *Theo-Drama: Theological Dramatic Theory,* vol. II: *Dramatis Personae: The Persons in Christ* (San Francisco: Ignatius, 1992), p. 207. In our text "conscious subject" has been rendered as "spiritual subject."

31. H. U. von Balthasar, *Theo-Drama,* vol. III, p. 208.

32. H. U. von Balthasar, *Theo-Drama,* vol. III, p. 271.

of the Church through mission. The group of theological persons who incarnate original and permanent missions in the Church he terms the "Christological constellation."[33] Peter incarnates the pastoral charism of unity and Paul embodies the charism of freedom in the Spirit; James represents the principle of Tradition, while John incarnates "the love which abides." The "Twelve" find their center of gravity in these "pillars" (Gal. 2:9; Acts 3:12), who are themselves preceded and enveloped by the archetypal mission of Mary, the mother without spot or wrinkle.[34] In this context, Balthasar takes an in-depth look at the issue of the personhood of the Church. The Church, in fact, appears as the unity of a multiplicity of "qualitative missions," which, together with numberless other more or less anonymous missions, make up the *communio sanctorum* (communion of saints), whose inchoative subjectivity is Mary.[35] The relationships between these person-missions in the heart of the communion that is the Church reflect and incarnate by way of analogy the laws of circumincession governing the relations among the Persons of the Trinity. The Christian family participates in this mystery thanks to the fact that the interpersonal relations between the spouses are elevated by grace to the dignity of a sacramental sign of Christ's love for his Church. We shall return to this point later on. Let us simply add, before we conclude this section, that persons, families and communities which do not belong to the domain of the visible Church are not necessarily excluded from sharing in the status of theological persons. This is due, once again according to Balthasar, to the scope of Jesus' eschatological work and to the universality of the gift of the Spirit, which authorize us to say that every man is associated in one way or another with the Paschal Mystery. Although it is difficult to know *how* non-Christians participate in the Trinitarian communion apart from the sacramental dimension of the Church, the *fact* that they do is nevertheless beyond doubt; we often catch a glimpse of it in the quality of their fraternal relations.

---

33. H. U. von Balthasar, *Theo-Drama*, vol. III, pp. 279ff. See also H. U. von Balthasar, *The Office of Peter and the Structure of the Church* (San Francisco: Ignatius, 1986), pp. 131-62.

34. H. U. von Balthasar, *Theo-Drama*, vol. II, pp. 183-225.

35. H. U. von Balthasar, "Who Is the Church?" *Explorations in Theology II: Spouse of the Word* (San Francisco: Ignatius, 1991), pp. 143-91. We cannot enter here into a more detailed analysis of the perichoresis of Mary and the Church, which brings out in a manner at once real and symbolic the mutual immanence of person and community. See also *The Office of Peter and the Structure of the Church*, p. 196.

This vision of the person, at once Christocentric and ecclesial, does affect the ecclesiology of communion developed at the Second Vatican Council and therefore its application to the domestic Church. It allows us to express in anthropological terms the essentially missionary nature of the Church and the family. By affirming that the person finds his deepest identity "in Christ," Balthasar defines the person by his belonging to Christ, hence, by his membership in the body of Christ, the Church. By identifying this relationship to Christ with the ecclesial mission to be lived out in the Spirit (charism), Balthasar simultaneously achieves a radical integration of the person into the community. As a result, we are led to speak not only of an ecclesial dimension of the person, but of the *ecclesiality* of the person. Balthasar states this explicitly in the context of a discussion on the Eucharist, where the essentially relational and missionary nature of the person is most evident: "Everyone who participates in the pneumatic body of Christ, shared out in the Church, not only becomes a member of the Church community: he actually acquires an intrinsically ecclesial quality."[36]

In this view, ecclesiality and mission are no longer dimensions or qualities added to persons in an exterior fashion, but constitute the very identity of these persons. Conversely, persons who are in communion by virtue of their mission constitute the very identity of the Church. In such a perspective it becomes highly significant and even theologically justified to speak of the ecclesiality of the family and of its participation in the mission of the Church. The strict correlation of grace, mission and person brings to light the anthropological foundation that etches the communion and mission of the Church upon the very heart of the family. In this view, there is simply no place for the impression that mission is merely an extrinsic addition to the family. In the act of faith that animates their "sincere gift of self" (LF 11) through love, the members of the familial-ecclesial community are constituted as persons, who at the same time constitute the communion and mission of the Church. Their gift thus manifests the essentially relational and missionary nature of "persons in Christ." At the same time, this confirms that created persons possess a likeness to the Persons and missions of the Trinity which establish the Church's communion as an *Ecclesia de Trinitate* (Church from the Trinity) and the Christian family as an *Ecclesia domestica.*

36. H. U. von Balthasar, *Theo-Drama*, vol. III, p. 281.

The Sacramentality of the Domestic Church

The Trinity's self-communication to man in Christ bestows a new likeness to God. This likeness, which is ecclesial in nature, entails a mutual inclusion of the person and the community analogous to the circumincession within the Trinity. As domestic Church, the family participates in this likeness in a way that places familial relationships at the service of the Church's mission. Consequently, the family participates in the Church's sacramentality, that is to say, in its nature as sign and instrument of the intimate union between the Trinity and humanity in Christ (LG 1). Hence the question of the domestic Church as a *"sacramentum Trinitatis"* (sacrament of the Trinity). Does the family really possess such a sacramentality? If so, what are its nature and scope? Is it merely a more or less "aesthetic" reflection of the Trinity in the world? Or are we dealing with something deeper, with a genuine participation of the family in God the Savior's presence in the world. An adequate answer to these questions would require explanations, which are only begun here and to which we will return further on. Suffice it to indicate a direction for deepening our understanding of the covenant between the Trinity and the family from the sacramental perspective.[37]

The sacramentality of the family, taken in a broad sense, is rooted in the sacraments of Christian initiation: "For by baptism, the man and the woman are definitively inserted into the new and eternal covenant, which is Christ's nuptial covenant with his Church. It is by reason of this indestructible insertion that the intimate community of life and conjugal love established by the Creator has been raised and assumed into the nuptial charity of Christ, as well as sustained and enriched by his redemptive power" (FC 13). Baptism signifies and creates a person's relationship of ecclesial membership in Christ. It ratifies, by the sacrament of faith, the personal bond of subjects with Christ, Head of the Church of which these same subjects are members. As members of Christ's Body in virtue of the Paschal Mystery, the baptized no longer belong to themselves, but to Christ: "No one who is baptized lives for himself or dies for himself; whether in life or in death we be-

---

37. Cf. José Silvio Botero, *Per una teologia della famiglia,* esp. Chapter III, "La sacramentalità della famiglia," pp. 121-46; I. Sanna, "Sacramentalità della famiglia: nota sui presupposti antropologici," *Lateranum* 45 (1979), pp. 304-19; G. Colombo, "La teologia della famiglia," *Chiesa e famiglia in Europa* (Brescia: Morcelliana, 1995), 45-75.

long to the Lord" (Rom. 14:7-8). In consequence, the baptized and confirmed live and die "in the Lord," sharing in the life and in the sentiments of the Lord: "It is no longer I who live, but Christ who lives in me" (Gal. 2:20). For this reason, the love of baptized spouses is not merely blessed by Christ, but taken up into Christ's love for the Church. In fact, their love already belongs to him because of baptism and confirmation. This is where the importance of the celebration of the sacrament of marriage comes from: the act by which this love is humanly exchanged in an offering to Christ which he welcomes and ratifies in return. What the sacrament of marriage adds, therefore, is participation as a couple, so much so "that the primary and immediate effect of marriage *(res et sacramentum)* is not supernatural grace per se, but the Christian marriage bond, a communion which is typically Christian, representing as it does the mystery of Christ's incarnation and the mystery of his covenant" (FC 13).

The essential theme of this passage of *Familiaris Consortio* is that the sacramentality of the family entails a primary dimension which we could term "institutional": the seal of the sacrament of marriage on the mutual consent of the spouses. This dimension concerns the primary effect of marriage, that is, the conjugal bond, which indissolubly unites two persons in Christ, through a common decision of mutual gift which goes beyond the emotional ups and downs of their limited and sinful human subjectivity. The indissolubility of the institution of marriage is a precise expression of the fact that conjugal love belongs radically to the greater mystery of Christ and the Church. This means, paradoxically, that at the very moment the spouses vow to love each other, they are, as it were, blessed and expropriated. The fact that they make their pledge in faith, and therefore "in Christ" signifies that Christ is both the ultimate Master and the Mediator of their union. With Evdokimov, we said that "by the sacrament [of matrimony] every couple marries Christ." Consequently, the pledge of each spouse vis-à-vis the other is first and foremost a pledge to Christ, who, in return, becomes the guarantor of their love by his Paschal Mystery and by the gift of the Spirit. Christ's nuptial mediation, which is symbolized at Cana,[38] signifies that the authentic love of the spouses is taken up into Divine Love (GS 48) and into the Trinity's relation to the world. In virtue of

38. Cf. I. de la Potterie, "Le Nozze messianiche e il matrimonio cristiano," *Lo Sposo, la Sposa*, Parola Spirito e Vita no. 13 (Bologna, 1986), pp. 87-104; D. Tettamanzi, *La famiglia della Chiesa*, esp. Chapter II, "Come a Cana di Galilea: Cristo incontra gli sposi," pp. 31-51.

the hypostatic union, which is both the foundation and the framework of the covenant between the spouses, their interpersonal love is taken up into the exchange between the divine Persons, becoming from that moment on a function of this exchange. From this comes a broader understanding of the sacramentality of the family. Therefore, the love of Christian spouses and the richness of their family relationships become a sacred sign, a vehicle and sanctuary of a greater Love, the love of the Trinitarian, incarnate God, who enters into a humble and indissoluble bond with their community of life and love.

This theological and sacramental perspective can seem too beautiful and idealistic, or on the contrary provoke reservations, for example concerning the spouses' freedom. Would not this freedom be excessively "constrained" by God's closeness? Is the sovereign dignity of the human person, desired and created for his own sake, compatible with a sacramentality understood such that human love is placed in the service of another Love? In a number of significant ways this inverts our usual perspective of sacramentality, envisaged from the viewpoint of the nature of conjugal and family love. We move away from a vision of God blessing from on high a human love which, though remaining a "worldly reality," is elevated "supernaturally." Instead the central focus is a Trinitarian vision in which the divine Persons are implicated in the exchange of gifts by the couple who marry. The spouses are no longer the principal agents and owners of their conjugal and family love; rather they are "ministers" of a greater Love which expresses and pledges itself sacramentally through their love and their communal life. At the very heart of the exchanges of love between the spouses, Christ and the Church exchange divine Love personified, the Holy Spirit. At the heart of the mystery of the Christian family, it is the very event of the Trinity which is actualized sacramentally; it is the Father and the Son who exchange their eternal love in a created manner in the Holy Spirit. For this reason, the love of the Trinity becomes the personal and sacramental norm which governs the total mutual gift of the spouses, their openness to life and their fecundity. This is why, finally, the domestic Church is the "sanctuary of life" (LF 11), the locus of that Presence which makes of the communion of persons a sacred and sacramental reality. This perspective is in accordance with the Catholic idea of sacraments and sanctification, but it might provoke a reflex of rejection from Protestant authors who fear a sort of idolatry of sanctification, or who strongly emphasize the obstacle of sin to the existence of such a sacramentality. Despite these fears, it seems necessary to me to maintain this opening for the family towards the gift of Trinitarian communion because the grace of this communion, without endangering human freedom, constitutes the pre-supposition of an authentic fulfillment of persons in the truth of love.[39]

Conjugal and familial love is not, then, merely an image of the love of Christ and the Church, but its living, sacramental reality: "By their mutual belonging, they represent in a real manner, by the sacramental sign, Christ's relation to his Church" (FC 13). This means that the conjugal and parental love of the spouses implicates infinitely more than themselves; "it is the visible sign of the very love of God" (FC 14). By the sacrament of marriage, the spouses acknowledge the grace of their love, the Author and Spouse of this love, and its transcendent finality. The spouses find themselves involved in a divine plan which "implies not only their future, but the future of humanity, and even the future of God."[40] Their complete mutual self-gift implies by its very nature an openness to the third, the child. Yet at an even deeper level it implies openness to a divine third, the Spirit, who gives himself to the spouses as the source and the fruit of this mutual love. The very personalizer of the fruitfulness of love within the Trinity likewise crowns the unity of the spouses by his own unifying and personalizing gift. This points to a *spiritual* fecundity of Christian marriage which always accompanies authentic conjugal love, whether or not a new human creature can actually result from this love. This spiritual fecundity bears witness to the presence of the Trinity in the sanctuary of the family and to its involvement in human history through the domestic Church. We can already sense that the covenant between Trinitarian love on the one hand and conjugal and family love on the other is not confined to relations of a purely "aesthetic" nature, but carries with it an authentic "drama," that is to say, the ethical requirements of unity, faithfulness, and fecundity. We shall have to return to these requirements in order to spell out in detail the Trinitarian mission of the family in today's world.

39. Cf. the objection made by Karl Barth against the sacrament of marriage in *Kirchliche Dogmatik*, 3d ed., vol. III/4 (Zurich, 1969), pp. 137ff.

40. Philippe Delaye, "La Pastorale familiale dans l'optique de 'Familiaris Consortio,'" *Esprit et Vie* 42 (October 21, 1982), p. 566.

Conclusion

Taking the notion of the domestic Church as our starting point, we set off in search of the foundations of the ecclesiality of the family and of the participation of the Christian family in the mission of the Church. Largely presupposing the biblical and patristic bases of the domestic Church, we have tried to lay out in detail the anthropological foundation of the ecclesiality of the family using the theological concept of person developed by Hans Urs von Balthasar. His Christocentric vision of the person considers mission as the means by which the baptized and confirmed are inserted "into Christ" and into the Trinitarian communion. In this perspective, the very "personhood" of the Church assumes a theo-dramatic visage, because it is defined by its participation in the Trinitarian missions of the Word and the Spirit. The family as domestic Church thus finds itself at the heart of, indeed, at the service of, these Trinitarian missions, which constitute the identity of the Church and its sacramentality in relation to the world.

We could sum up the results of our study by saying that the communion of persons at the heart of the domestic Church reveals not only a new likeness between the Trinity and the family, but above all a mutual immanence of the two realities, a sort of circumincession which involves the family in the Trinitarian relations. The communion of persons based on the "sincere gift of self" (LF 11) creates more than a "resemblance" to the communion of the Trinity; it sacramentalizes in some sense the gift of the divine Persons to the world, and even the exchange "between" the divine Persons. A covenant mystery takes place under the "sacramental species" of the fidelity, unity and fecundity of the spouses. The covenant of the Trinity and the family, the domestic Church, thus engenders new creatures, sons and daughters of God in the order of nature and the order of grace. These creatures, brought to baptism, bear witness that divine love and human love are capable not only of mutuality, but also of a common divine-human fecundity. The spousal dignity of the person and the sacramental fecundity of the family, the image of God, appear here in all their splendor. This still remains to be seen in relation to the spiritual fecundity of consecrated persons, who incarnate in a particular way the eschatological fecundity of the Spirit, towards which, in time, Christian spouses are journeying.[41]

41. See Antonio Sicari, *Breve Catechesi sul matrimonio* (Milan: Jaca, 1994); Piero Coda, "Famiglia e Trinità," *Nuovo Umanità* XVII (1995), pp. 2, 13-45.

We have thus added a component to the ongoing search for a Trinitarian anthropology of the family: a relational and missionary vision of the family which issues, finally, from the identity between Person and Love in the Trinity. While there remains the task of critically validating this proposal, we can already perceive how a more thorough articulation of the Trinity-family relation on the basis of the correspondences between person, mission and communion allows, indeed, demands a vital and dynamic participation of the Christian family in the mission of the Church. At stake in this participation are not only the spiritual health of families and the establishment of a civilization of love, but nothing less than the renewal of the Church's mission from the ground up.

CHAPTER IV

The Trinitarian Mission of the Family
at the Dawning of the Third Christian Millennium

"The whole of our history could be described as the continually revised
sketch of a community among human persons in the image of the Trinitarian communion and as the progressive realization of a community among
human and divine persons."[1] This perspective of communion evoked by
Canon Philippe Delaye contains the whole practical program which a Trinitarian anthropology of the family ought to develop. We thus stand before
the task and the challenge of sketching out a spirituality and ethic of the
family. Our previous reflections concerning the ecclesiality of the family
have identified mission as the path of unity between the Trinity and the
family. We must now explore this path, what we might call the Trinitarian
mission of the family at the dawning of the third Christian millennium.
John Paul II expresses it thus in *Familiaris Consortio:* "The family finds in
the plan of God the Creator and Redeemer not only its *identity,* what it *is,*
but also its *mission,* what it can and should *do*" (FC 17). The pope adds to
this a call urging the family to responsibility in order that it realize its vocation to communion and to mission: "Family, 'become' what you are!"

The path that we have followed up to now confirms and even radicalizes this call to mission. For, in the light of a Christocentric and Trinitarian
theology of the person, it has become clear that mission is not something

1. Philippe Delaye, "La pastorale familiale dans l'optique de 'Familiaris Consortio,'" *Esprit et Vie* 17 (29 April 1982), p. 562. See also *Gaudium et Spes,* no. 12, and the decree on lay
apostolate, *Apostolicam Actuositatem,* no. 11.

added to the domestic Church's identity; mission coincides with the domestic Church. We recall, in effect, that the Trinitarian mission of the family has its roots, as we have seen, in its identity as image of the Trinity by virtue of creation, and in its identity as ecclesial icon of the Trinity by virtue of the covenant of Christ and the Church, of which the family is a realization in miniature.[2] This identity of the Christian family requires a corresponding praxis, that is, a specific spirituality and ethic, of which we must present at least the outline.

The Search for a Spirituality of the Family

The first thing we ought to be aware of is the denial of a need for a spirituality of the family. Cardinal Daneels of Brussels made an intervention that attracted much notice at the 1981 synod, in which he echoed a critique of the current pastoral approach to the family: "Too much morality and not enough spirituality!" It is true that from the historical perspective a systematic reflection on the spirituality of the family is still in its early stages.[3] It was first necessary to experience the awakening of the lay state in the twentieth century, validated by the Second Vatican Council, in order for conditions to be favorable for such a development. There are many causes for this delay. On one hand, we could mention that, especially since the Middle Ages, the monastic and religious ideal in a certain sense monopolized "the state of perfection," as if the lay life were an inferior form of Christian existence. On the other hand, there has been "insufficient theological development at the level of ecclesiology and a theology of the sacraments,"[4] which has not allowed the charism proper to marriage and family to be given its

2. L. Gendron, "Le Foyer chrétien, une Eglise authentique?" *La mission des Laics* (Montreal: Bellarmin-Cerf, 1987), pp. 249-69. See also M. Emynian, "The Family: Domestic Church," *Theology of the Family* (Malta: Jesuit Publications, 1994).

3. We lack systematic studies on the developments of the spirituality of the family in the history of Christianity. Besides a few considerations in general studies (cf. L. Bouyer, *Histoire de la spiritualité chrétienne*, 3 vols, [Paris, 1960, 1961, 1966]), one finds useful information concerning the ancient and patristic periods in J. MacAvoy's article "Famille" in *Dictionnaire de la Spiritualité*, vol. V, col. 61-72; concerning the modern period see Pierre de Locht, "La spiritualité conjugale entre 1930 et 1960," *Concilium* 100 (1974), pp. 33-45.

4. Gianna and Giorgio Campanini, "Famille," *Dictionnaire de la vie spirituelle*, ed. Stefano di Fiores and Tullio Goffi, trans. Francois Vial (Paris: Cerf, 1983), p. 415.

true worth. The beginning of a veritable movement of familial spirituality only appears with the promulgation of *Casti Connubii* (Pius XI, 1930). This spirituality has gradually inscribed itself within an ecclesiology of communion, centered less exclusively on the hierarchical ministry and religious orders, and becoming more aware of the plurality of vocations, charisms and ministries in the Church. It was to receive an extraordinary confirmation from the ecclesiology of the Second Vatican Council, and in particular from the doctrine on the universal call to holiness.

The need for a specific spirituality of the family is moreover experienced and demanded by the present conditions of modern secularized society. The Christian ideals of unity, fruitfulness, and indissolubility in marriage have been undermined by the values of individual autonomy, the technological mastery of fertility, and love freed from every institutional constraint. It is difficult to safeguard the traditional values of marriage and the family in this secularized context, more favorable to a "culture of death" than a "culture of life." The influence of the secular media, combined with a concerted resistance within the Church herself, creates an unfavorable climate for the blossoming of families. The practical triumph of contraception, the increasingly common recourse to sterilization, and the trivialization of abortion introduce confusion in the consciences of spouses and their children. This confusion becomes all the greater when theologians present the Church's ethical demands as excessive, merciless, and even contrary to Christian freedom. We will not defeat cultural and ideological resistance through a simple repetition of traditional moral instructions. We must develop a positive vision of domestic values, a "personalist" family spirituality which truly grounds conjugal and familial relationships within the Trinitarian communion incarnated and revealed in Jesus Christ.

"There is a constant in any authentic Christian spirituality of the family, independent of any conditioning from the various sociological 'models' (the patriarchal families of yesterday, and the more communitarian families of today). This constant is a radical relationship with Christ who makes the family a *locus* of salvation, grace, and service."[5] Without any doubt, a radical relationship with Christ constitutes the most adequate response to the need for a Christian spirituality of the family. From this perspective the Christocentric orientation effected by Vatican II is still await-

---

5. G. & G. Campanini, "Famille," p. 414.

ing a corresponding praxis adapted to the reality of the family. This praxis is in the process of being developed with the help of John Paul II's Magisterium, whose encyclicals *Veritatis Splendor* and *Evangelium Vitae* mark an evolution of Church doctrine in a Christocentric perspective.[6] Spirituality of the family can receive stimulus and confirmation only from this perspective: teaching to take inspiration from the Word of God rather than from contemporary cultural models. Thus a spirituality of the family can escape the danger of sociologism, for "it effects a decisive transition from the category of 'model' to the theological category of 'image.'"[7] In this way, the spirituality of the family is called to effect a "theological turn," which means nothing other than following Christ; he is the "Image of God" *par excellence* who incarnates the supreme norm of the communion between the divine Persons and human persons. In following Christ, the family does not isolate itself from the anthropological and sociological reality in which it lives; on the contrary, the family finds precisely that "path" which allows it to integrate all of its relations into its mission.

Consequently, it is the duty of a spirituality of the family to cultivate the "theological" consciousness of the family members, that is, the consciousness of a personal relationship with God which constitutes the foundation of their dignity and the source of their capacity for gift in Christ's image. We ought to emphasize, however, along with Mr. and Mrs. Campanini, that a conjugal and familial spirituality must be lived in a very concrete way according to the specific condition of marriage and family: "not *beyond* it, or even merely *by making use of it,* but purely and simply *in* the family."[8] Little by little, there will emerge an original and specific spirituality, whose fundamental characteristics will be those of being a spirituality of the couple, in which the two are called to become one flesh (Gen. 2:24); a lay and incarnate spirituality which is lived in the family, at the heart of the world of love, sexuality, and fruitfulness; an ecclesial spirituality which, by virtue of the sacramental meaning of conjugal love, bears witness to an even greater mystery.[9] We must now sketch out a few of its components, in function of the love which has become, as John Paul II says, its central axis of integration.

6. Cf. J. Servais, S.J., "'Si tu veux être parfait . . . Viens suis-moi,' Le Christ, norme concrète et plénière de l'agir humain," *Anthropotes* 1 (1994), pp. 25-38.

7. G. & G. Campanini, "Famille," p. 414.

8. G. & G. Campanini, "Famille," p. 413.

9. G. & G. Campanini, "Famille," pp. 416-17.

Love: The Essence of a Spirituality of the Family

"The essence and role of the family are in the final analysis specified by love. Hence the family has the *mission to guard, reveal, and communicate love,* and this is a living reflection of and a real sharing in God's love for humanity and the love of Christ the Lord for the Church His bride" (FC 17). The personalist revolution that today's world needs is contained in embryonic form in this solemn declaration by John Paul II, which introduces the third part of *Familiaris Consortio.* The pope thus extends the line of *Gaudium et Spes,* which defined marriage as a personal union in which the spouses reciprocally give and receive each other (GS 48). In defining the essence and the mission of the family by love and not first by procreation, the pope is not making a questionable concession to the modern mentality. He claims to be returning to "the very roots of reality" (FC 17). This position marks an important step toward the personalist recasting of the Christian doctrine of marriage and the family. It places the three traditional values of marriage — procreation, faithful love, and sacramental signification — in the line of fruitful conjugal love and no longer in that of procreation as a distinct end.[10] We must take note of this doctrinal development and situate it within the framework of the Trinitarian mission of the family.

If the mission of the family is love, an integral spirituality of the family must be developed on the basis of the components of love which the family lives. We can group these around three principal focal points: (1) love as the total personal gift of the spouses; (2) love as openness to life; and (3) love as a sacrament of the gift of Christ for the Church. These three components of conjugal and familial love are strictly connected and interdependent. Their articulation represents one of the major challenges of contemporary theological reflection, especially at the level of conjugal ethics in the face of the contemporary hedonistic and liberal mentality. The Church's Magisterium has taken a firm position in this regard, with its refusal of contraception, a refusal which was founded on natural law in *Humanae Vitae;* then further developed in *Familiaris Consortio* from a personalist point of view, and definitively confirmed from the viewpoint of fundamental moral theology in *Veritatis Splendor.* This is therefore a firm Church doctrine which validates a deep reflection on human love in

10. W. Kasper, *Teologia del matrimonio cristiano,* 2d ed. (Bologna: Queriana, 1985), p. 18.

God's image. Without entering into this ethical debate, which goes beyond the scope of our current reflection, we must nevertheless touch upon this question in the perspective of a Trinitarian anthropology.[11]

Love as the Total Gift of Self

The Trinitarian mission of the family begins with what constitutes the very foundation of the relationship between Christian spouses: conjugal love as a total and exclusive self-gift. This love was very well described in *Humanae Vitae*: "Conjugal love comprises a totality involving all aspects of the person — the call of the body and instinct, the force of emotion and affectivity, the aspiration of the spirit and the will; it aims at a profoundly personal unity, one which, beyond the union in one flesh, leads spouses to become one heart and one soul; it demands indissolubility and fidelity in the definitive reciprocal gift; and it opens into fruitfulness."[12] This description is taken up in *Familiaris Consortio* in which the two ends of marriage, union and procreation, are unified from the starting point of love. "In its most profound reality, love is essentially a gift; and conjugal love, while leading the spouses to the reciprocal 'knowledge' which makes them 'one flesh', does not end with the couple, because it makes them capable of the greatest possible gift, the gift by which they become cooperators with God in giving life to a new human person. Thus the couple, while giving themselves to one another, give not just themselves but also the reality of children, who are a living reflection of their love, a permanent sign of conjugal unity and a living and inseparable synthesis of their being a father and a mother" (FC 14).

Conjugal love such as we have just described it is irreconcilable, according to the Church, with modern techniques of contraception. These are judged "intrinsically bad,"[13] first for reasons of respect for the natural

---

11. Klaus Hemmerle, "Matrimonio e Famiglia in un'antropologia trinitaria," *Nuova Umanità* 6 (1984), pp. 3-31. The most accessible and objective study I know concerning this question is that of Michel Séguin, *La Contraception et l'Eglise, Bilan et Prospective* (Montreal: Ed. Pauline & Mediaspaul, 1994). See also G. Grisez, W. E. May, J. Boyle, and J. Finnis, "Every Marital Act Ought to Be Open to New Life: Toward a Clearer Understanding," *The Thomist* 52 (1988), pp. 365-426.

12. Paul VI, *Humanae Vitae*, no. 9.

13. Paul VI, *Humanae Vitae*, no. 14.

law; but the most profound reasons are drawn from the very nature of conjugal love: "Thus the innate language that expresses the total reciprocal self-giving of husband and wife is overlaid, through contraception, by an objectively contradictory language, namely, that of not giving oneself totally to the other. This leads not only to a positive refusal to be open to life but also to a falsification of the inner truth of conjugal love, which is called upon to give itself in personal totality" (FC 32). What the Church seeks to safeguard in rejecting contraception is, ultimately, the image of God in the conjugal relationship between man and woman. For the couple to be image of God requires love as a total personal gift of the spouses, "two in one flesh," which places created persons in communion with the divine Persons. Those that oppose it accuse this doctrine of biologism because it seems to make the freedom of persons subject to the contingencies of a biological law. The Church's response to this objection recalls the intrinsic connection between body and person, which modern anthropology, essentially dualist, tends to separate excessively. Rejecting this connection represents an anthropological option with vast consequences, the effects of which we observe in the moral drift toward a culture of death.

Klaus Hemmerle sheds a noteworthy light on this doctrine, in a way which is at once Trinitarian and phenomenological. During a remarkable intervention in Warsaw in 1983, he confirmed the inseparability of the "I" and "thou" in the act of love by which the spouses give themselves to each other and simultaneously give each other a future in the person of the child: "What indisputably belongs to the sexual communion is the relation between the 'I' and 'thou' as equals, and both brought to each other and ordered in a bipolar fashion toward a *personal* gift: as a personal gift, the gift is absolutely other and equal at once to both, and it is, as a gift, a reciprocal gift of the partners and an inalienable gift to them."[14] In conjugal life, Hemmerle adds, one does not give some *thing,* one gives oneself. To love another in the total and exclusive language of the body means: "you alone, you for always! With you, only with you, I wish to have the whole of my future and the whole of yours."[15] An openness to the child belongs intrinsically to this unity and indissolubility of love: "You alone — with you forever — with you, beyond ourselves."[16] This openness is required not only

14. K. Hemmerle, "Matrimonio e Famiglia in un'antropologia trinitaria," pp. 18-19.
15. K. Hemmerle, "Matrimonio e Famiglia in un'antropologia trinitaria," p. 19.
16. K. Hemmerle, "Matrimonio e Famiglia in un'antropologia trinitaria," p. 19.

as a total attitude, but precisely within each act. The reason for this is the very nature of sexuality, in which "man expresses himself and gives himself as a whole."[17] That is why a contraceptive intrusion makes a lie of the corporal language of love. It blocks *a priori* the openness to the possible third which the language of the flesh expresses naturally. The responsible choice of having conjugal relations only during the infertile periods of the menstrual cycle, is a moral choice that respects the objective meaning of the act of love and does not sin against the fecundity of love, unless, of course, the choice is motivated by mutual selfishness. This choice instead signifies a respect for the partner and a respect for time as an existential component of conjugal love, revealing to the couple that they are a gift to each other, and that they must receive themselves from an Other, from God. The moralist Michel Séguin arrives at the same conclusion at the end of a thorough study of this thorny question. He writes: "After twenty-five years, we have come to understand better why, on an objective level, contraception is an evil *against love:* because it systematically attacks the procreative power implicit in human love; it attacks, at the same time, the very love of the couple insofar as it is a mystery of communion, a total and reciprocal gift of self."[18] The Trinitarian mission of Christian spouses thus begins with love as a total self-gift which accepts being in the image and likeness of God. That is why John Paul II states that the first task of the family's mission is the formation of a community of persons: "to live with fidelity the reality of communion in a constant effort to develop an authentic community of persons" (FC 18).

Love as the Mystery of Fruitfulness

"Since there is a creative act of God at the origin of all human life, contraception, in contrast to the natural regulation of birth, appears objectively as a closure of the couple to the possibly creative presence of the divine Partner."[19] The experience of numerous couples confirms this point of view. Many of those who have accepted recourse to natural methods of family planning have seen their love grow and blossom in learning to prac-

17. K. Hemmerle, "Matrimonio e Famiglia in un'antropologia trinitaria," p. 20.
18. M. Séguin, *La Contraception et l'Eglise*, p. 302.
19. M. Séguin, *La Contraception et l'Eglise*, p. 303.

tice periodic continence. They have experienced the spiritual fecundity of this attitude and its effect on the human quality of their love.[20] The profound reason for this fact is the openness to God which is inscribed in the way in which the spouses manage their fertility. Contraception signifies a closure to the divine Partner, an exclusion of him who provides the first and most important fecundity of marriage: spiritual fecundity.

One of the urgent tasks of a spirituality of the family is a deepened reflection on this point. It ought to shed more light on the Trinitarian nature of love which first involves a spiritual fruitfulness. The "third" that phenomenology speaks about is not first the child as the possible and essentially unforeseeable fruit of love, but love itself as the objective spirit of the total gift of the partners. Klaus Hemmerle confirms this, drawing from St. Bonaventure, who considers the Trinitarian Archetype of human love as *bonum diffusivum sui.* He refers in particular to the Person of the *Condilectus,* who is the fruit of the mutual love between the originating Father and the originated and co-originating Son: "It is precisely the third Person who is decisive for a complete understanding of this originating event and for understanding it as an event stemming from God's absolute goodness. A love which wills only its own partner, equal to itself, and does not open itself with him and beyond him, is not the love that abandons itself totally in thus fulfilling itself as love."[21] Love is essentially Trinitarian. It confers on all that proceeds from it a Trinitarian stamp. Human love is the reality which most explicitly bears the mark of the Trinitarian character of love. When two spouses are united, while respecting their being the image of God, they embrace the movement of the self-transcendence of the Trinitarian Persons toward the unity of the Spirit of Love. They are, in a sense, drawn to and measured by the "objective spirit" of their love — its spiritual fecundity — even before the child appears as a concrete possibility.

Hans Urs von Balthasar is one of the authors who has particularly emphasized the meaning of the spiritual fruitfulness of marriage. His approach draws from Ephesians 5 where St. Paul speaks of marriage as the sign of Christ's love for the Church. In a still more explicit way than

20. Marie and Benoît Grenier, "L'impact de la régulation naturelle sur l'amour conjugal," *La famille chrétienne dans le monde d'aujourd'hui,* Coll. Communauté et Ministères (Paris: Bellarmin, 1995), pp. 105-14; See also Scott and Kimberly Hahn, *Rome Sweet Home* (San Francisco: Ignatius, 1993), pp. 25-42.

21. S. & K. Hahn, *Rome Sweet Home,* pp. 27-28. The authors refer to Bonaventure, *Hexaemeron,* XI, 12.

Hemmerle, he interprets the mutual gift of the spouses as a kenotic movement of total gift which points essentially toward a third: "The personal coming together of the two self-emptying partners is only possible in terms of the third factor, which — long before the arrival of the child — is that objective of the meeting of their two freedoms."[22] He specifies this "objectivity" of the mutual love of the spouses by speaking of "the spirit of the loving covenant" or of "the covenant itself as institution transcending both of them"[23] and protecting them from the fluctuations of their fragile and sinful subjectivities. This objective third term may even be the Holy Spirit who inspires moments of reserve and abstinence in spouses seeking holiness in order that they may attend more freely to the service of God: "Do not deprive each other except by mutual consent and for a time, so that you may devote yourself to prayer. Then come together again" (1 Cor. 7:5). In this perspective, Balthasar demonstrates that love, as a movement of self-transcendence in the image of Christ, expresses the body's belonging to the Spirit: "Do you not know that your body is a temple of the Holy Spirit, who is in you, whom you have received from God? You are not your own; you were bought at a price. Therefore honor God with your body" (1 Cor. 6:19-20).

The price of the body's belonging thus to the Spirit is the total gift of Christ on the cross. For Christ, by his obedience of love until death, "merited" that his body be transfigured in the Spirit and through the Spirit. By being raised from the dead, he did not abandon the corporal condition; rather, he brought it to its fulfillment. Indeed, he became available, eucharistically, for a relationship of both "physical" and "spiritual" love between the Head of the mystical body and all of his members. That is why Christ's total gift has become the model *par excellence* of the fruitful self-gift of the spouses; and this self-gift has become the sacrament of the union between Christ and the Church. "For von Balthasar, the spouses' abandonment to each other in marriage is a vivid witness to Christ, because the fidelity expressed in the marriage promise reflects the radicality of the love expressed once and for all on the cross of Christ. Moreover, the fruitfulness of their physical union reflects not only the incommensurable

---

22. H. U. von Balthasar, *Explorations in Theology IV: Spirit and Institution* (San Francisco: Ignatius, 1995), p. 218; see also J. O'Donnel, "Hans Urs von Balthasar sulla teologia del matrimonio," *La Civiltà Cattolica* III (1988), pp. 483-88.

23. H. U. von Balthasar, *Explorations in Theology IV*, p. 219.

fruitfulness of Christ's death for his people, but also the infinite fruitfulness of the Trinitarian communion."[24] The kenotic gift of Christ would obviously remain an inaccessible and inimitable model, if it were not at the same time a source of the Spirit. The Spirit makes possible not only an "imitation" but a "sacramental participation" in his gift, a gift which becomes inwardly immanent to the mutual gift of the spouses, and combines his fruitfulness to theirs. The spouses' mission is thus to bear witness to an openness to God and to life, which allows the fecundity of the Trinity to be poured out spiritually, physically, and socially in the family.

Love as Sacrament

This openness to the divine Partner leads us now into the sacramental dimension of love, which most explicitly reveals the Trinitarian mission of the family. When God communicates himself to his image in Jesus Christ, in the context of the Covenant, the internal laws of his being combine, so to speak, with the dynamic structure of human love — that is, with the three dimensions of being-in-itself, being-with, and being-for. Human life and Trinitarian Life are thus wedded in a veritable reciprocal love-story between God and man, between the Trinity and the family. That is why we can say with Hemmerle that "phenomenology discloses the vocabulary of human existence, theology reveals it as Trinitarian. But only the common act with the Trinitarian life that is open to us renders it and us 'speakers' in our own life."[25] The challenge of a spirituality of the family is to insure that the Word of God to the world and the word of the family manage to maintain the same discourse, the discourse of divine love incarnate in human love.

The sacramental mission of the family is to mediate Christ's love for the Church, that is, the Trinitarian love for the world. The material of this mediation is the multiplicity of the daily relationships of life together, sharing, education, and the service of society. The form of this mediation is human love insofar as it incarnates, through words, gestures, and faithfulness, the Christic form of Love. The sacramental content of this mediation is the Trinitarian communion, in which the spouses are offered a spe-

---

24. J. O'Donnel, "Hans Urs von Balthasar sulla teologia del matrimonio," p. 488.
25. K. Hemmerle, "Matrimonio e Famiglia in un'antropologia trinitaria," p. 30.

cific gift through the Holy Spirit, who is poured out in the ecclesial celebration of their marriage (FC 19). When the Spirit of Love is not excluded from their communion by sin, it immerses the conjugal, parental, and familial relationships in the very relationships of the Holy Trinity. Paul VI joyfully expressed this profound truth: "Through the parents who love their child in whom Christ lives, emerges the love of the Father which is poured out into his beloved Son (cf. 1 Jn. 4:7-11). Through their authority, his authority is exercised. Through their devotion his providence is manifest as the 'Father from whom all paternity draws its name, in heaven and on earth' (cf. Eph. 3:15)."[26] That is why the parents in communion with Trinitarian love participate in the salvific mission of the Church: "they not only *receive* the love of Christ and become a *saved* community, but they are also called upon to *communicate* Christ's love to their brethren, thus becoming a *saving* community" (FC 49). This salvific ministry of the family is a specific realization of Christ's unique priesthood, which is exercised according to the threefold modality of prophet, priest, and king. *Familiaris Consortio* makes this explicit by presenting the Christian family as (1) a community that believes and evangelizes; (2) a community in dialogue with God; and (3) a community at the service of man (FC 50-65).

Conjugal and familial spirituality is called to support this salvific ministry by being rooted in an authentic theology of the family. This implies a deeper reflection on the ultimate sacramental meaning of the communion of persons. In taking up the exhortation of St. John Chrysostom, "Make your home a Church," we ought to cultivate more the sacramental or "iconic" consciousness of the family, that is, a consciousness that family relationships truly serve the greater Mystery of Christ and the Church. This sacramental consciousness, of course, goes hand in hand with a life of prayer, dialogue, and regular contact with the Lord's Eucharistic offering. The mystical body of Christ draws nourishment from its sacramental body. The domestic Church cannot blossom sacramentally without regular participation in the Eucharist, the sacrament *par excellence*. The awakening of this sacramental consciousness in the family should, moreover, lead to an increased respect for the human person, a more adequate promotion of the dignity of the woman, and a rediscovery of the sacred character of conjugal and familial love. This love is sacred because it is sacra-

---

26. Paul VI, "Allocution aux Equipes Notre-Dame," *La Documentation Catholique* (1970), no. 1564, p. 504 (our translation).

mental, because it bears within itself the greater Love of Christ and the Church, of which the Holy Spirit is the nuptial bond and fecundity. In this sacramental perspective, the requirements of unity, indissolubility, and fecundity in marriage and the family no longer appear as more or less arbitrary laws of an institution culturally behind the times. They are the logical consequences of the Trinitarian Mystery which gives itself in participation, in elevating man, that is to say the family, to the dignity of a partner in the covenant.

The sacramental consciousness of the Christian family, consequently, blossoms into a sense of familial relations' belonging to the Trinitarian Mystery. Conjugal and familial love, being "in Christ" by virtue of the sacraments of baptism and marriage, belong radically to the sphere of Trinitarian relations. St. Thomas Aquinas teaches that the divine Persons are pure subsistent relations of knowledge and love. Hans Urs von Balthasar shows that these Person-relations are open and constitute the space of the fulfillment of human persons. The divine Persons effectively create and sanctify conjugal and familial relations "in Christ"; it is through him, with him and in him that these created relations are assumed into the Trinity's own uncreated relationality in order to be sanctified and transfigured. That is why Trinitarian love, governed by a law of "appropriation as expropriation,"[27] becomes the inspiration and the norm of a familial communion in the image of the Trinity. The more the spouses conform themselves to the archetype of their love, the more they are "expropriated" by God and for God, and the more they become the *locus* where divine superabundant fecundity flows. The first fruit of this participated divine fecundity is the divine Spirit himself who seals their mutuality in his own and who allows himself to be "co-spirated" by them into the very heart of their prophetic, kingly and priestly ministry. The family, the domestic Church, thus becomes an authentic sacramental mediation, a free-flowing spring of life, growth, education, and service; it becomes a sacrament of divine paternity and divine filiation in the fecundity of the Spirit. St. Thomas compared the sublime character of the Christian parents' ministry of education to that of priestly ministry, thus: "Some only propagate and guard spiritual life by a spiritual ministry: this is the role of the sacrament of *Orders;* others do this for both corporal and spiritual life, and this is brought about by the sacra-

---

27. Balthasar, *The Glory of the Lord, A Theological Aesthetics,* vol. VII, *Theology: The New Covenant* (San Francisco: Ignatius, 1989), pp. 399-414.

ment of marriage, by which a man and a woman join in order to beget off-spring and bring them up to worship God."[28]

The covenant between the Trinity and the family, in Christ, thus signifies a wondrous exchange of human and divine love in which the spouses give their nuptial love to Christ and in exchange Christ gives them the very Love of God under the nuptial modality of the Gift of the Spirit. Such an exchange entails the demands of fidelity and fecundity. The Trinitarian law of Love henceforward regulates the exchanges of the spouses and all of their familial and social relationships. Openness to the "third," the necessity of which we saw above, therefore includes not only an openness to the Spirit and an openness to the child but also the missionary openness to society. The sacramental mission of the family thus implies a missionary projection. This is first and above all realized in the being of the family itself, in the communion of persons, the gift of life and the education of children. This mission naturally extends to an apostolate for other families or to any other positive impact on society, compatible with the primary mission. We will return later to the different characteristics and implications of this mission.

A complementary light on the family's participation in Trinitarian fecundity can be drawn from the Christian vocation to virginity. John Paul II has clearly stated that "Christian revelation recognizes two specific ways of realizing the vocation of the human person, in its entirety, to love: marriage and virginity or celibacy" (FC 11). We have seen that the fruitfulness of marriage includes a spiritual and a physical dimension. Consecrated virginity replies to a specific call of Christ, inviting a more direct participation in his spousal love for the Church and therefore in its eschatological fecundity. Consecrated virginity flows directly from Christ's *agape* manifested on the cross and receives, through the sacrifice of conjugal and familial fecundity, a particular and superabundant participation in the infinite fecundity of the cross. "By virtue of this witness, virginity or celibacy keeps alive in the Church a consciousness of the mystery of marriage and defends it from any reduction and impoverishment" (FC 16). In their encounter with consecrated persons, spouses and their families have a foretaste of the eschatological fulfillment towards which their own lives are leading. They receive from this encounter a powerful support for their own faithfulness and an encouragement to intensify their relationship with God, source of all fecundity.

28. Thomas Aquinas, *Summa contra Gentiles*, IV, 58 (FC 38).

The Family at the Service of the Glory of God

We have seen that the Trinitarian mission of the family begins with the formation of an authentic community of persons based on the total and open gift of the spouses. It extends into the mysterious spiritual and human fruitfulness of this love. It reveals its sacramental depth in the kenotic love of the spouses which incarnates the love of the crucified Christ for his Church. Thus the theology of "God's plan for marriage and the family" reaches a culmination that we can further detail in the chapters to come. Before concluding this first part of our reflection, however, it is necessary to take a further step in discovering the eschatological meaning of a Trinitarian spirituality of the family. We have already mentioned that a Trinitarian anthropology of the family opens a new horizon of meaning for conjugal and familial love, situating it already in an eschatological perspective, as a service to the Glory of God understood as an exchange between the divine Persons. Let us now set this perspective out in detail, extending a reflection made by John Paul II in his *Letter to Families*.[29]

In speaking of the parents' cooperation in the transmission of the gift of life, that is, in the communication of the image of God to their children, the pope explains that the genealogy of the person is linked on one hand to biology but also and above all to the divine will which "wills man to be a being in his likeness, to be a person" and consequently wills him "for his own sake." Considering moreover that the human person is created for eternal life, John Paul II is led to ask a very interesting question: "Does affirming man's ultimate destiny not conflict with the statement that God wills man for his own sake?" (LF 9). He responds with Augustine that the conflict is merely apparent and that the human heart finds the fulfillment of its longing in the fullness of divine life. But an explanation is not given and the reader remains unsatisfied. The pope nevertheless draws from this a very important implication for the way in which the parents are called to give testimony: "they must want the new human creature in the same way as the Creator wants him: for himself" (LF 9).

The Trinitarian perspective that we have begun to explore allows us to complete this reflection. It helps us to overcome the apparent contradiction between wanting the person for his own sake and making him destined for divine life. By situating the creature concretely within the exchange between

29. John Paul II, *Letter to Families* (Rome: Libreria Editrice Vaticana, 1994).

the divine Persons, as a reciprocal gift from the Father to the Son and from the Son to the Father in the unity of the Holy Spirit, we see more clearly that while being wanted for his own sake, the human person is wanted for God, for the service of his glory. The novelty here is that this glory is henceforth seen, in the light of the New Testament, as Trinitarian glory. This means that the human person is called to express the mutual love of the Divine Persons, the uncreated love that eternally unites them and that constitutes their beatitude. This ultimate horizon further extols the eminent dignity of the person, about whom the Council has said that he is "the only creature on earth that God wanted for its own sake" (GS 24) The human person is henceforth seen as being worthy of being loved not only for his own sake, but also for the super-eminent service that he gives to God. In loving his creature for Himself, in a Trinitarian manner, God loves him even more than in merely loving the creature for the creature's own sake. For he bestows upon him not only the reality of being loved and of loving in return, but also, through a completely gratuitous grace of love, the opportunity to contribute to his own Trinitarian beatitude, in a certain sense.

The reversal of perspective which we spoke of at the beginning here reaches its culmination in this vision, a vision that could prove to be surprisingly fecund and full of promise for theological anthropology. This is so because the ultimate end of the human creature appears thus to be theologically defined not only by the desire for beatitude in God but by the deeper perspective of being of service to the beatitude of God.[30] "Father, I wish that where I am they also may be with me, that they may see my glory that you gave me, because you loved me before the foundation of the world" (Jn. 17:24). If it is true that the Divine Persons glorify each other mutually with the very mutual gift of the creatures, must we not conclude that the "sincere gift of self" of created persons participates not only in God's love for his creatures, but also in God's love for God? Do we not find in this an ultimate Trinitarian horizon of meaning which allows us to surpass a certain latent anthropocentrism which modern transcendental theology only radicalizes? For, the traditional ascending perspective of Augustine's *cor inquietum* certainly illuminates the fact that God means everything for man's beatitude, but it does not illuminate the astonishing fact that the creature has some part in God's beatitude. Without in any way compromising the freedom of

---

30. Cf. Marc Ouellet, *L'existence comme mission: L'anthropologie théologique de Hans Urs von Balthasar* (Rome: Pontifical Gregorian University, 1983), pp. 97-146.

creation and the gratuitousness of divine life, it is possible to deepen the reflection of theological anthropology and so to understand the mission of the Christian family as a service to the glory of God. Thanks to its open and differentiated relations with the divine Persons, made possible by the mystery of the incarnation and of the Holy Family, the Christian family becomes the locus for the sacramental expression of divine paternity, of divine filiation and of divine mutuality, according to an infinite variety of modalities which bear witness to the unfathomable richness of Trinitarian Love. Its primordial mission is to be a reflection, a wellspring, and a living and blossoming presence of Trinitarian love in the world and for the world.

Allow me, in conclusion, to cite the testimony of the French poet Charles Péguy (1873-1914), who played a prophetic and liberating role, albeit a little-known one, in the spiritual renewal of France in the twentieth century. Poet and peasant, journalist and soldier, he converted to Catholicism at the age of 34 after a long and difficult journey. Married to a militant socialist unbeliever with whom he had four children, he was never able to participate in the sacramental life of the Church because of his irregular matrimonial situation. This is why he intensified his relationship with God on the basis of his literary art, helped by the most common prayers of Tradition: the *Pater,* the *Gloria,* the *Ave Maria,* the *Salve Regina.* He inaugurated modern pilgrimages to the cathedral of Chartres in order to entrust to Mary his family, in danger of disintegration and struck by illness and poverty. His poetic song was raised in unison with his witness of heroic conjugal fidelity in the midst of conditions of poverty, solitude, and public misunderstanding of his work. He died in combat on the fifth of September 1914, while defending his country. He was 41 years old. His wife and his children were baptized shortly afterwards.

Today, Péguy's witness retains all of its relevance because, by his conversion, his art and his limited situation in the Church, he proclaims the priority of the "theological" and the "incarnate" in a Christocentric and Trinitarian spirituality of the family. At the heart of Péguy's spiritual poetry,[31] one

---

31. *Le Mystère de la charité de Jeanne d'Arc, Le Porche de la deuxième vertu,* and *Le Mystère de Saints Innocents,* are the major poetic works containing Péguy's theological vision. The great biblical poem *Eve* is an epic synthesis of the history of salvation; it is necessary to go back to Dante's *Divine Comedy* to find something similar. See *Oeuvres Poétiques complètes* (Paris: Bibliothèque de la Pléiade, 1975). In English see: *The Mystery of the Charity of Joan of Arc* (New York: Pantheon, 1950); *The Portal of the Mystery of Hope* (Grand Rapids: Eerdmans, 1996); *Mystery of the Holy Innocents* (New York: Harper, 1956).

finds, as with St. Thérèse of Lisieux, the mystery of the Person of Jesus, incarnate Word of God, which focuses spirituality anew on the incarnation, childhood, and hope.[32] From this flows a deeper understanding of the mystery of the Church and of the communion of saints enveloped by the tenderness of the Mother of God:

> Lay them to rest on four young heads,
> those graces of gentleness and consent,
> and weave for their foreheads, O queen of the pure wheat,
> Some sheathes picked in the harvest of celebration.[33]

Conclusion

At the end of this first sketch of a Trinitarian anthropology of the family, it is still too early to draw clear conclusions, for there remains too much to do in order to complete and *critique* the perspectives that we have opened for discussion. This Trinitarian theology of the family suggests several fundamental questions which it presupposes, and which condition its development. In the first place, for example, the renewal of Trinitarian theology on the basis of Christology must still deepen its understanding of the relation between the immanent and economic Trinity; this would allow us to articulate better the relation of the Trinity to the history of the world. Secondly, a theological notion of the person as relation, applicable both to God and to creatures, remains yet to be explored in a critical fashion on the basis of a theological vision of the transcendentals. Person and love would thus be revealed as more fundamental categories than those of nature and substance.[34] Third, much remains to be discovered with regard to the dimension of the family in the Bible, and the model of the Holy Family could shed much light on ecclesi-

32. H. U. von Balthasar, *The Glory of the Lord: A Theological Aesthetics*, vol. III: *Studies in Theological Style: Lay Styles* (San Francisco: Ignatius, 1986), pp. 400-517.

33. Charles Péguy, "Prière de report," taken from *Cinq prières dans la cathédrale de Chartres*, Oeuvres Poétiques complètes, p. 921 (our translation). "Veuillez les reposer sur quatre jeunes têtes/Vos grâces de douceur et de consentement/Et tresser pour ces fronts, reine du pur froment/Quelques épis cueillis dans la moisson des fêtes."

34. Cfr. Klaus Hemmerle, *Thesen zu einer trinitarischen Ontologie* (Einsiedeln: Johannes Verlag, 1992); *Tesi di ontologia trinitaria* (Rome: Città Nuova, 1996).

ology.[35] Fourth, the relation between the states of life in the Church,[36] especially the complementarity between marriage, virginity and hierarchical ministry, as well as the questions of conjugal and family morality which are progressively being re-cast in a Christocentric perspective, all require to be thought through from the starting point of a Trinitarian anthropology of the family. Each one of these points invites patient, fundamental, and multidisciplinary study, without neglecting the contribution that can come from the concrete experience of couples and families.

Some will judge the approach we have sketched here to be abstract, utopian, and foreign to modern sensibilities. Others will reproach it no doubt for conceding too much to the "personalist" concerns of a modern thought which are difficult to harmonize with the metaphysical tradition. Some will find, perhaps, a few stones still rough and in need of being shaped and polished in the light of Tradition. For my part, at the end of this first part of this reflection, I draw the following conclusion: systematically putting into relation the Trinity and the family contains a surprising potential for the future of the Church's theology and mission. At a time when theology risks being dissolved into anthropology under the pressure of an anthropocentric culture, God's plan for marriage and the family brings theological reflection back to the terrain of the real and dramatic history of human persons grappling with love, sexuality, and fecundity. The family resituates theology at the center of revelation, serving God's covenant and his human partner, whose body as nuptial and sacramental, bears witness to the incarnation of Love. In this way, theological anthropology better understands the supreme dignity of the human person in the light of the family's participation in the Trinitarian missions of the Word and the Spirit. And it is reconciled with real history, corporal realities, intersubjectivity and the cosmic rooting of humanity, from which modern dualism and individualism had unfortunately turned into alienation.

At a time when secularized societies are degenerating into a "culture of death" without a future, the Church proposes a realistic alternative which is attractive and full of hope: a civilization of love based on the values of the Christian family. The total gift of the spouses, and the unity and

---

35. V. Liberti & E. Dehoniane, eds., *La famiglia nella bibbia* (Rome, 1989); Piero Coda, "Famiglia e Trinità," *Nuova Umanità* XVII, 2 (1995), pp. 13-45 with an abundant bibliography.

36. Cf. H. U. von Balthasar, *Christlicher Stand* (Einsiedeln: Johannes Verlag, 1977); *The Christian State of Life* (San Francisco: Ignatius, 1983).

fecundity of the family proclaim to the world that Trinitarian Love is at work in history. The Christian family is a witness to the fact that the Glory of Trinitarian communion, which shines on the face of Christ and his Bride, already dwells within the simplest and most concrete realities of life. That is why the "communion" of the domestic Church is increasingly affirmed as the path for the Church and the new evangelization. It invites the cultures of "having" and "doing" to transcend themselves toward a civilization of love and of life.

In these first years of the third Christian millennium, a new missionary spirit and a true missiological orientation should have the family as its catalyst and great promoter. Evangelizing the family's various relationships in the image of the Trinity, cultivating its sacramental life and consciousness, and revealing to the family the divine missions in which it participates; all this could have a planetary impact on the mission of the Church and the future of humanity.

PART 2

Perspectives of Trinitarian Spirituality for Marriage and Family

CHAPTER V

The Holy Spirit:
Seal of the Conjugal Covenant

"Marriage in Christ is marriage in the Spirit." I welcome this opportunity to contribute to the theological reflection on the gift of the Holy Spirit to Christian spouses, a theology which, in the opinion of Carlo Rocchetta, "is only in its initial stages."[1] I would like to begin with *Gaudium et Spes* and its perspective of salvation history: Christ the Lord "encounters Christian spouses through the sacrament of marriage" and "abides with them" in such a way that "authentic married love is caught up into divine love and is directed and enriched by the redemptive power of Christ and the salvific action of the Church"; thus Christian spouses are "as it were, consecrated," in "the Spirit of Christ and their whole life is suffused by faith, hope, and charity" (GS 48).

The objective of this reflection is to sketch out a systematic presentation of the relation between the Holy Spirit and marriage within the context of a Trinitarian theology of the covenant. The Holy Spirit, "seal" of Trinitarian love, is given to the spouses as the "seal" of their conjugal covenant, in prolongation of his spousal gift as the "seal" of the covenant between God and humanity in Christ.[2] This comprehensive perspective is

---

1. Carlo Rocchetta, preface to Moisés Martinez Peque, *Lo Spirito Santo e Il Matrimonio* (Bologna: EDB, 1993), 13; by the same author, *Il sacramento della coppia* (Bologna: EDB, 1996), 255-75.

2. G. Fitzer, "Sfragís," *Grande Lèssico del Nuovo Testamento*, vol. 7 (Brescia: Paideia, 1967), 377-418; C. Lesquivit and M.-F. Lacan, "Sigillo," *Dizionario di Teologia biblica*, 1202-1203.

not simply intended to overcome a certain classical formulation that overlooked the particular gift the divine Persons make to the couple. Its aim is to understand the sacrament of marriage and therefore the exchange of love between man and woman within the horizon of the *imago Dei*, as the couple's participation in the exchange of "gifts"[3] between the divine Persons. This presentation should lay the foundation for a Trinitarian and missionary spirituality of married couples and the family.

The Holy Spirit, Seal of the Covenant between God and Humanity in Christ

Three moments permit us to follow the progressive involvement of the Holy Spirit in the history of the covenant between God and his people. Those which stand out are the preparation, celebration, and fulfillment of the covenant. A premise and presupposition of our reflection is a nuptial interpretation of all of salvation history.[4] God's covenant with Israel and humanity is the story of a wedding. The symbol *par excellence* of biblical revelation is conjugal love. A couple stands at the beginning of salvation history and another at its conclusion: Adam and Eve set the history of humanity in motion, while the Lamb and his Bride, who descends from God in heaven, conclude the adventure of historical time. In the span of time between the initial couple and the eschatological couple, the Holy Spirit implores and summons; he prays for the final fulfillment together with the Bride whom he has called: "The Spirit and the Bride say, 'Come.' And let him who hears say, 'Come.' And let him who is thirsty come, let him who desires take the water of life without price" (Rev. 22:17).

In the interest of brevity, we will only touch upon the theology of the covenant and the nuptial symbolism which marks it. It will nonetheless constitute the foundation and framework of the following dramatization. Salvation history is a spousal drama of Trinitarian revelation: A God who is Bridegroom seeks after his unfaithful bride, he regenerates her in the

---

3. A. Mattheeuws, *Les "dons" du mariage: Recherche de théologie morale e sacramentelle, Culture et Vérité* (Brussels, 1996); Hans Urs von Balthasar, *The Christian State of Life*, trans. Sr. Mary Frances McCarthy (San Francisco: Ignatius, 1983), *Explorations in Theology*, vol. 4, *Spirit and Institution* (San Francisco: Ignatius, 1995), 217-24.

4. Cf. Giorgio Mazzanti, *I Sacramenti, simbolo e teologia* (Bologna: EDB, 1997), 153ff.; Luis Alonso-Schökel, *I nomi dell'amore: Simoboli matrimoniali nella Bibbia* (Piemme, 1997).

suffering of humbled love and lifts her up in his glory. The Father sends his Son as the Bridegroom, accompanied by the Holy Spirit, who prepares the bride for the encounter with the Bridegroom and the fulfillment of the eschatological wedding. The limited purpose of this reflection is therefore to follow the unfolding of God's nuptial adventure with humanity from the point of view of the Holy Spirit, as witness, "seal," and fecundity of the eschatological wedding.

The Holy Spirit and the Preparation for the Wedding

In the Old Testament, the story of the relationship between God and his people Israel is presented as the story of God, the Bridegroom who unites himself to Israel, the bride.[5] Also in the New Testament, Christ is described as the one who espouses humanity destined to be nuptially united to him for eternity in the home of the Father and in the loving power of the Spirit. Some references will suffice to demonstrate the Old Testament's preparation for the wedding.

The message of the prophets is rather illustrative in this regard. The prophet Hosea (in the second half of the eighth century B.C.) describes God as *Ish* and Israel as *Ishah,* relying on the texts of Genesis: "She shall be called Woman, because she was taken out of Man" (Gen. 2:23). He alludes to the adultery of the bride, an event that fractures the love affair which had endured since the time of the exodus (Hos. 2:2-23). Notwithstanding her betrayals, her prostitution, Yahweh will continue to be united to Israel, transforming her into a faithful bride forever (Hos. 2:19-20).

Isaiah (in the second half of the eighth century B.C.) sings the lamentation of the beloved *(dôd)* for his vineyard Israel and presents God as the Bridegroom (Is. 5:1-7). Jeremiah (between 622 and 587 B.C.) sees Israel as the unfaithful bride and adulteress, but God does not repudiate her: "I have loved you with an everlasting love; therefore I have continued my faithfulness to you" (Jer. 31:3). God will make a new covenant with the house of Israel: "I will put my law within them, and I will write it upon their hearts; and I will be their God, and they shall be my people" (Jer. 31:33). The novelty of the covenant is based on three points: (1) divine initiative in forgiving

---

5. For a brief presentation of this, see C. Pellistrandi, *Jérusalem épouse et mère* (Paris: Cerf, 1989).

sins (v. 34; Ezek. 36:25, 29; Ps. 51:3-4); (2) personal responsibility and retribution (v. 29; Ezek. 14:13); and (3) interiorization of religion: the law ceases to be only an external code in order to become an inspiration that touches the "heart" of man (v. 33) under the influence of God's Holy Spirit, who gives man a new heart (Ezek. 36:26-27; Ps. 51:12; Jer. 4:4).

This new and eternal covenant is proclaimed once again by Ezekiel (36:25-28), and Isaiah in the last chapters (Is. 55:3; 59:21; 61:8). "A new heart I will give you, and a new spirit I will put within you; and I will take out of your flesh the heart of stone and give you a heart of flesh. And I will put my spirit within you and cause you to walk in my statutes and be careful to observe my ordinances" (Ezek. 36:26-27). "Like a young man marrying a virgin, your re-builder will wed you, and as the bridegroom rejoices in his bride, so will your God rejoice in you" (Is. 62:5).

Also, Zechariah (a priest in Jerusalem after the Babylonian exile around 520 and 518 B.C.) speaks in spousal terms about the relationship between God and Israel: "Thus says the Lord of hosts: I am exceedingly jealous for Jerusalem and for Zion. . . . I have returned to Jerusalem with compassion" (Zech. 1:14, 16); "I am jealous for Zion with great jealousy, and I am jealous for her with great wrath . . . they shall be my people and I will be their God, in faithfulness and in righteousness" (8:2, 8). The message of the prophets therefore appears pervaded by nuptial symbolism and completely cloaked in a passionate tone, which will then be availed of and developed in another mode of expression by the Wisdom tradition.

The summit of the spousal tradition is without a doubt the Song of Songs. Few books have had the fortune of the Song of Songs, not only in the tradition of the Fathers and mystics, but first and foremost in the Hebrew tradition. Rabbi Aqiba (†135 A.D.) asserts that "the entire world was not equal in value to the day in which the Song of Songs was given to Israel. All of Scripture is in fact holy: but the Song of Songs is the Holy of Holies."[6] In the Hebrew tradition, the canonical legitimization of its erotic

---

6. *Mishnah Jadajim, III,* 5; cited in Elena Bartolini, "La storia dell'amato e dell'amata come epifania dell'Eterno nel Cantico dei Cantici," in Renzo Bonetti (ed.) *Verginità e Matrimonio* (Ancora, 1998), 103-26, esp. 109; See the book of Alonso-Schökel already cited above. See also Hans Urs von Balthasar, *The Glory of the Lord: A Theological Aesthetics,* vol. 6, *Theology: The Old Covenant,* trans. Brian McNeil, C.R.V., and Erasmo Leiva-Merikakis (San Francisco: Ignatius, 1991), 130-37; J. P. Sonnet, S.J., *Le Cantique, entre érotique et mystique: sanctuaire de la parole échangée,* NRTh 199 (1997), 481-502; Gianfranco Ravasi, *Cantico dei Cantici* (Milan: San Paolo, 1987).

content would have been due to its allegorical interpretation. Modern Christian exegetes tend to recover the literal sense of the Song of Songs.[7] In fact, the description of an intense universal human experience, stronger than man, an uncontrollable fire, became the most adequate literal-allegorical language for expressing the spousal mystery between God and humanity, between God and the individual soul. In the wake of Origen, the tradition continued endlessly to address the allegorical sense of the Song, but often forgot the value of the literal sense presupposed by the great Alexandrian. "The whole ancient economy," writes Alonso-Schökel, "enters into a relationship of love like that of the gift of a bridegroom to his promised bride."[8]

A very significant feature of the Song of Songs is the fact that, "although in other texts the man is the one who falls in love, in the Song of Songs the woman also falls in love; and with such intensity and clarity she says to him from the very beginning *'Let him kiss me with the kisses of his mouth!'*"[9] In fact, according to von Balthasar, the song celebrates "but one thing: the beautiful, resplendent, and awesome glory of the *eros* between man and woman."[10] "*Eros* hovers freely about its own house, without any other purpose than loving and being loved: nowhere is there talk of marriage, or indeed of children"; "*eros* is self-sufficient" in its dreamed-of and desired existence, detached from the historical circumstances of sin and guilt; "this is a supralapsarian *eros,* as it were."[11] It is as if the Holy Spirit had wished to express in this canticle something absolute, ahistorical, with

---

7. "The theological sense of the Song of Songs lies precisely there, in the tranquil affirmation of the positive value that sexuality and its use possess, in accordance with the vision of the Creator" (P. Grelot, "Le sens du Cantique des cantiques d'après deux commentaires récents," *Revue Biblique* 71 [1964], p. 46); John Paul II refers to this modern exegesis of the Song of Songs in his catechesis on human love: cf. John Paul II, *The Theology of the Body: Human Love in the Divine Plan* (Boston: Daughters of St. Paul, 1997), pp. 368-75.

8. Alonso-Schökel, *I nomi dell'amore,* p. 62.

9. Alonso-Schökel, *I nomi dell'amore,* p. 48.

10. H. U. von Balthasar, *The Glory of the Lord: A Theological Aesthetics,* vol. VI: *Theology of the Old Covenant,* trans. Brian McNeil, C.R.V., and Erasmo Leiva-Merikakis (San Francisco: Ignatius, 1991), p. 131.

11. Balthasar, *The Glory of the Lord,* vol. VI, pp. 131-33: "No poet who intended to express something else — namely, Yhwh's love for his people — would have written in so totally profane and areligious a fashion and with such wholehearted abandon to the joys of the senses. Such an allegorical interpretation emerged only after the translation of the Septuagint (250-150 B.C.)."

the lyrical tone of blazing images; to in some way foretell of "the couple which will realise for all time what had been intimated for an instant in paradise and could not be made to last: the couple formed by the second Adam and the second Eve. This will no longer be a suspended idea, but the full, historical incarnation of the absolute love between man and woman, which is an end in itself and is no longer subject to any law of genealogy."[12]

As a poem of conjugal *eros* that attains to the sacred sphere of the divine, the Song of Songs became the chosen poem of the burning love of God for his people and of humanity for its God. Origen marked the beginning of an ingenious allegorical reading that applies such language to the relationship between individual souls and the Logos: "We must consider now the actual words with which the Bride first voices her prayer: *Let Him kiss me with the kisses of His mouth.* Their meaning is: 'How long is my Bridegroom going to send me kisses by Moses and kisses by the prophets? It is His own mouth that I desire now to touch; let Him come, let Him come down Himself!' So she beseeches the Bridegroom's Father, saying: 'Let Him kiss me with the kisses of His mouth.' And because she is such that the prophetic word, *While thou art yet speaking, I will say, 'Lo, here am I!'* can be fulfilled upon her, the Bridegroom's Father listens to the Bride and sends His Son."[13]

Some exegetes have held the opinion that in the prophetic message, the nuptial symbolism oscillates between two perspectives: *remembrance* and *expectation*. The first is manifested as Israel's nostalgic longing to re-create the past accord she had with her God; the second is living in anticipation that something totally new is about to occur that will re-create the relationship between the people and Yahweh. Baten believes that the past may refer to the betrothal of God and his people, while the messianic day may coincide with their wedding.[14]

---

12. Balthasar, *The Glory of the Lord*, vol. VI, p. 137. Thus, Balthasar observes that the numerous ecclesial commentaries on the Song of Songs that interpret it as pertaining to Christ and his Bride the Church are also correct.

13. Origen, "The First Homily," in *The Song of Songs: Commentaries and Homilies,* vol. 23, Ancient Christian Writers, trans. R. P. Lawson (New York: Paulist, 1992), p. 269.

14. R. A. Baten, *New Testament Imagery* (Leiden: Brill, 1971), p. 10, cited in G. Mazzanti, 169. For what follows, I draw my inspiration from pp. 153-78.

The Holy Spirit and the Celebration of the Wedding of the Lamb

"The Bridegroom is coming!" is the cry of the Holy Spirit to the bride so that she may welcome the mystery of the Incarnation. The allegorical interpretation of the Song of Songs brings out the presence of the Holy Spirit, whom the Tradition also calls "the substantial Kiss" between the Father and the Son. Now this kiss is "in act" between the Father and the *Incarnate* Son. In this sense, "the patristic-ecclesial Tradition always considered two New Testament events together: the wedding feast at Cana and the descent of the Spirit at Pentecost."[15] In fact, the presence of the Holy Spirit, symbolized by the wine at Cana and the inebriation of the apostles, is connected with the realization of the nuptial union between the Creator and his creatures.

The Holy Spirit who overshadows the unfolding of cosmic life reappears over the Virgin Mary at the moment of the incarnation, which marks the beginning of the new creation: the Spirit as *shekinah,* as divine shadow-presence, rests upon Mary so that she may conceive Christ (Lk. 1:35). The same Spirit, in the form of a dove, descends upon Christ, who comes out of the Jordan baptized; he then leads him into the desert where he is tempted in order to prepare him to fulfill, in humility and obedience, the mission entrusted to him by the Father. The Spirit then appears under the veiled form of the wine of inebriation during the wedding feast at Cana, preparing "the Hour" of the Cross, the Hour of the messianic wedding with a nuptial "first sign."

Prepared by the Holy Spirit since the beginning of creation, the messianic wedding is celebrated on the altar of the Cross. It is precisely there that the nuptial chamber receives the *sacrum commercium et connubium.* In his representation of all men, Christ "through the eternal Spirit offered himself without blemish to God" (Heb. 9:14); his personal offering is the decisive "yes" of the Bridegroom, pronounced in obedience to the Father (2 Cor. 1:20) once and for all. This "yes" of Christ the Bridegroom is not only the merciful "yes" of God who forgives sins; it is precisely the "yes" of the covenant, the "yes" of both God and man, of the Bridegroom and the Bride, brought about and confirmed by the Holy Spirit. To be sure, offering himself to the Father, Christ gives up his Spirit for all men: "And he bowed his head and gave up his spirit" (Jn. 19:30).[16] Mary is

---

15. G. Mazzanti, *I Sacramenti, simbolo e teologia,* p. 170.
16. Cf. Ignace de la Potterie, *Il mistero del cuore trafitto* (Milan: EDB, 1988), pp. 89-120.

there to receive it, the Woman of the Apocalypse (Rev. 12:1ff.), the New Eve who is born from the bath of regeneration (Eph. 5:26), from the water and blood of the New Adam's pierced heart. Thus the couple of the messianic wedding, which was desired and prepared for so long, is united on the altar of the unique sacrifice with the seal of the eternal Spirit of God.

The gift of the Spirit therefore marks the fulfillment of the nuptial covenant between God and humanity in Christ. The event of the resurrection is truly baptism of fire,[17] followed by the confirmation of Pentecost. The beginning of the *Letter to the Romans* solemnly affirms that Jesus Christ was "designated Son of God in power according to the Spirit of holiness by his resurrection from the dead" (Rom. 1:4). Thus, the Risen One can re-create humanity as the holy bride, insufflating into her the Spirit of sanctification. On Easter evening, after greeting the apostles with peace, "he breathed on them and said to them, 'Receive the Holy Spirit'" (Jn. 20:22). The Risen One effuses the Spirit of the covenant, the Spirit of reciprocal Love who thus becomes the new protagonist of the history of the Church and humanity.

The Holy Spirit, Seal and Fecundity of the New and Eternal Covenant

At this point we shall offer some preliminary remarks about the symbol of the seal. In the biblical world the seal was not only an art-engraved jewel (Sir. 32:5ff.), but a symbol of the person and of his authority (Gen. 38:18; 41:42). To affix a seal attested to the fact that a certain object belonged to oneself (Deut. 32:34); affixing it upon a document guaranteed its validity (Jer. 32:10), and indicated its completion (Rom. 15:28). The seal of God is a poetic symbol of his sovereignty over his creatures and history. God seals the book of his plans (Rev. 5:1-8), and no one deciphers their secret, except the Lamb who fulfills them.

Such symbolism assumes a new value when Christ speaks of being marked with the seal of God, his Father (Jn. 6:27); "in fact this seal of the

---

17. Cf. Piero Coda, "Evento pasquale, dono dello Spirito e battesimo nella prospettiva del vangelo di Giovanni," *Uno in Cristo Gesù: Il battesimo come evento trinitario* (Rome: Città Nuova, 1996), pp. 166-94.

Father placed upon the Son of man is not simply the power he confers upon him to fulfill his work (cf. Jn. 5:32, 36), but is also the consecration that makes him the Son of God (Jn. 10:36)."[18] In his sovereign action, God destined the Son of man for this — confirming him, as it were, with his own seal — to give men food for eternal life. This confirmation-consecration is connected to the anointing-consecration mentioned elsewhere in the New Testament: "God anointed Jesus of Nazareth with the Holy Spirit and with power" (Acts 10:38).

In the Pauline letters, the gift of the Spirit is tied to the image of the seal. "He has put his seal upon us and given us his Spirit in our hearts as a guarantee" (2 Cor. 1:22). God, marking believers with his seal, made them his possession; a guarantee is the Spirit of God in their hearts (cf. Rom. 5:5). The concept in Ephesians 1:13ff. and 4:30 is different than that of 2 Corinthians 1:22: "Now the seal is the Holy Spirit as a pledge of inheritance; with it the believer is marked, established, and guarded for redemption, so that he may become God's own again on the day of the redemption."[19] The importance of this for Paul is to emphasize that both in justifying and sealing it is God who acts.

The sovereign action of God, the signature of his powerful name, is precisely the resurrection of Christ as the fulfillment of the Paschal Mystery. This event is the culmination of salvation history. It is the Trinitarian event *par excellence,* signed and effected by the Holy Spirit as a gift from the Father (Jn. 15:26) in response to the Son's obedience of love. The paschal event therefore contains at once a *Trinitarian* and *spousal* meaning: a Trinitarian meaning, since the resurrection seals in the economy the unity of love which was sealed by the Holy Spirit's procession in the immanent Trinity; a spousal meaning, because this anointing-confirmation seals the fecund gift of the Risen One as the eschatological Bridegroom who generates his bride. In effect, in the power of the Spirit of love entrusted to him, the dead and risen Christ (the New Adam) lets flow from his pierced heart the body, faith, beauty, and fecundity of his bride. Hence, the spousal meaning of the resurrection reveals that the "Person-Gift of the Father and Son" in God, the seal of their consubstantial unity, becomes the spousal bond between God and man in the Crucified and Risen One. Thus the Holy Spirit henceforth freely carries out in the Church, until the final ful-

---

18. C. Lesquivit and M.-F. Lacan, *Dizionario di Teologia biblica,* p. 1203.
19. G. Fitzer, "Sfragis," pp. 407-8.

fillment, the role of the fecund "seal" of Love, which he eternally performs in the immanent Trinity.[20]

In conclusion, it is necessary to point out that the Holy Spirit in Person is the fulfillment of the new and eternal covenant between God and humanity.[21] Salvation history assumes its spousal profile precisely because it is the event and result of the dramatic exchange between the divine Persons. The Creator Father created everything for his Son, "through him and for him" (Col. 1:15-16); Christ received and redeemed everything out of love for the Father; and the Holy Spirit glorifies everything by the fact that he seals in creatures the unity and freedom of Love that constitutes the Trinitarian beatitude. Thus the divine plan of salvation, by virtue of the fact that it assumes creatures into the glory of the Holy Spirit, is nothing other than the participation in the mutual glorification of the divine Persons.

The Holy Spirit, Seal of the Conjugal Covenant in Christ

The mystery of the covenant between God and humanity appears in history under a spousal profile thanks to the engagement of the Holy Spirit as the agent, confirmation, and seal of Trinitarian love, both within the economy of salvation and within the immanent Trinity. Now this consideration naturally blossoms in the sacrament of marriage, which is a "great mystery" precisely "in reference to Christ and the church" (Eph. 5:32). Marriage symbolizes the union between Christ and the Church, a union sealed by the Holy Spirit. Therefore, the spousal involvement of the Holy Spirit in marriage-sacrament must be understood. In the interest of brevity, we shall simply illustrate how the divine Persons accompany and transform the couple's love story into the Trinitarian story. In fact the couple's love is an *imago Dei* and is called to be a *likeness,* that is, to be taken up into and enriched by the exchange of "gifts" between the divine Persons. Our reflec-

20. Cf. M. Ouellet, "The Spirit in the Life of the Trinity," *Communio* 25 (Summer 1998), pp. 199-213; John Paul II, *Dominum et Vivificantem,* p. 10.

21. "The purpose of the whole economy of Christ is the descent of the Holy Spirit" (Simeon the New Theologian, Homily 38:1); "The Word assumed flesh so that we could receive the Holy Spirit" (Athanasius, PG 26:996C). "Where the Holy Spirit is, there also is the Church" (Ignatius of Antioch and Irenaeus); cited in Giorgio Mazzanti, *I Sacramenti, simbolo e teologia,* pp. 171-72.

tion will focus on the sacramental celebration. As well as being a precise event in time, the wedding celebration is also a symbolic event that in a certain sense assumes and recapitulates the whole life of the couple and the family. Obviously we shall turn our attention in large part upon the role the Holy Spirit plays in the Trinitarian work of the *benediction* and *sanctification* of the couple and family within the horizon of the Trinitarian relations.

The Holy Spirit Leads the Couple to Christ, the Redeemer

In addressing the marriage of two baptized persons, the first fact to be underscored is the Holy Spirit's engagement in the birth and development of the couple's love. If the Holy Spirit who inspires Scripture considered the Song of Songs to be a celebration of human eros in God's plan, we must conclude that despite the wound of sin, God considers the union of man and woman to be very good and worthy of the greatest praise and sacrifice. This is inferred from the literal sense of the Song; but it is also evident that in light of all of Scripture, the idyllic atmosphere of the Song of Songs nevertheless sinks its theological roots into the gift which the Creator Father makes of the original couple to the eschatological couple. As we have already alluded to, the relationship of conjugal love between the bridegroom and the bride, which is affirmed and celebrated as desire, union, and joy beyond the wound of sin, is already in the mind of the Author of Scripture referring to Christ and the Church.[22]

The Spirit of God is therefore truly involved *("partie prenante")* in this celebration of natural *eros*.[23] He neither disdains nor disregards it, since such love was created "in Christ" to be given to him and fulfilled in him. "All things were created through him and for him" (Col. 1:16). The Holy Spirit thus operates from within creation itself, driving the couple in love towards their aim and archetype: Christ. Nevertheless, his creative action in service

---

22. The fulfillment of the Old Covenant in the New Covenant of Christ, who died and rose from the dead, authorizes this retrospective theological reading of the Song of Songs, obviously presupposing also the theological value of the literal sense. Cf. Henri de Lubac, *Scripture in the Tradition*, trans. L. O'Neill (New York: Crossroad, 2000); see also Luis Alonso-Schökel, "*Cantico dei cantici*, Introduzione," in *La Bibbia, Parola di Dio scritta per noi*, official text of the Italian Episcopal Conference (CEI), vol. 2 (Turin: Marietti, 1980), pp. 425-27.

23. A. Mattheeuws, *Les "dons" du mariage*, pp. 401-31, esp. p. 424.

of the Father does not end on the creaturely plane. The Holy Spirit also stirs up a love lived in faith, namely, the response to the gift received in Baptism. Two baptized persons cannot separate their love for one another from their belonging to Christ. Assumed by Christ as members of his body, they are already marked with his seal and made participants in his life and mission. Therefore, faith in Christ requires the baptized person to offer Christ the love received from the Creator Father. Thus the Holy Spirit guards the Christocentric sense of conjugal love, calling the couple to invoke God's blessing upon their love, inspiring them to be faithful to the Father's will, and moving them to consecrate their marital life to Christ.

Fidelity to the Creator Spirit therefore normally results in the celebration of the sacrament of matrimony. This public gesture expresses with liturgical language the couple's will to mutually give themselves to one another for their whole lives "in faith," that is, "in Christ." In this regard, we must stress the Christological, spousal meaning of the celebration of the "exchange of consent" offered in faith. When theological doctrine affirms the spouses to be the "ministers" of the sacrament of matrimony, it does not mean that they are the principal agents of the sacrament. The principal agent of the sacrament is Christ, who acts through the mediation of the couple. Of the "human act by which the partners mutually surrender themselves to each other" (GS 48), one must say in fact that it is an act of Christ who receives them and gives them to each other.[24] In this way marriage becomes a sacramental reality, that is, a "divine gift" hidden within a "human gift"; this gift of Christ is an act of spousal love which blesses the couple and entrusts them with a sacramental mission.

Christ Assumes the Couple into His Self-Offering to the Father in the Holy Spirit

The couple's act of faith, made in the Church, sacramentally introduces their love into Christ's offering to the Father. Thus, as in the days of his earthly life, Christ "offered himself without blemish to God" (Heb. 9:14), so too does he assume the couple's marital relationship within his sacrificial love offered to the Father for the Church. The act of offering the couple to the Father is thus returned without measure. Christ is devoted to re-

---

24. Cf. C. Rocchetta, *Il sacramento della coppia* (Milan: EDB, 1996), pp. 213ff.

deeming their love, healing its wounds, and coming to its aid when it is subject to falling; as *Gaudium et spes* affirms, "authentic conjugal love is caught up into divine love and is directed and enriched by the redemptive power of Christ and the salvific action of the Church" (48). In Christ's redemptive sacrifice all the couple's sins are already expiated and absolved; obstacles are removed, thus calling to mind the communication of Christ the Bridegroom's redemptive love in the life of the couple through the sacrament of Reconciliation. It is precisely the Holy Spirit's task of remembrance that reminds the couple of this through the Church, and communicates the redeeming gift of Christ to their wounded and weak love.

The encounter with Christ in the sacrament further communicates a new sense of gratitude to the couple for their love. Matrimonial grace primarily consists in participating in the spousal love of Christ and the Church. This spousal love is essentially salvific and eucharistic; it expresses the Father's love for humanity and the Son's gratitude for the Father's love. Hence, it is from this love that matrimonial grace receives its imprint and exigency. Thus, once the sacramental act of marriage has been accomplished, the Church proceeds normally in the eucharistic offering of Christ who assumes the entire life of the couple into his sacrificial gift offered to the Father. In this way Christ returns to the Father with the created gift received from him; he re-presents and re-gives the redeemed couple to the Father, enriched by his spousal love for the Church. The Holy Spirit is the witness and objective guarantee of this, since he is precisely the one who has glorified Christ's spousal love, raising him from the dead.

The Father Seals the Couple's Union "in Christ" with the Gift of the Holy Spirit

"In the epiclesis of this sacrament the spouses receive the Holy Spirit as the communion of love of Christ and the Church (Eph. 5:32). The Holy Spirit *is* the seal of their covenant, the ever-available source of their love and the strength to renew their fidelity" (CCC 1624). The *Catechism* links the gift of the Spirit-Communion with the symbol of the seal. "He is the seal, the source, the strength of their covenant." The Holy Spirit as the bond of love, the "intratrinitarian seal," therefore crowns the Trinitarian gift given to the couple. The Father is its source because the Spirit proceeds from him (Jn. 15:26); the Son is the co-source *(Filioque procedit)* in a certain derived mode, since it is his grateful counter-gift of consubstantial Love which awakens and provokes the so-called gushing forth of the Holy Spirit from the heart of the Father. The exchange between the divine Persons culminates, therefore, in sharing with the new spouses the joy of the divine "Third." This joy of the Spirit of Love, who eternally kindles the mutual ecstasy of the Father and Son, now becomes the source of the mutual ecstasy of the sacramental couple.

The symbolic logic of the seal invites us to deepen our understanding of the implications of the exchange between the divine Persons that reaches and penetrates the exchange between the human persons. The gift of the Spirit as the bond of Trinitarian love signifies, among other things, a belonging, a guarantee of validity, a security, and an intangibility. Therefore, in the figurative language of love and faith, "personal belonging in its strictest sense and highest value"[25] is signified. "Set me as a seal upon your heart, as a seal upon your arm" (Songs 8:6). This song-prayer of the bride in the Song of Songs comes together precisely where the two "passions" encounter each other: the passion of human love strong as death and tenacious as Sheol and the passion of divine *agapē* stronger than both death and Sheol. This wedding reaches its summit in the spousal gift of the Holy Spirit. By virtue of this gift, the spouses find that they are lifted up above themselves, for they are involved in the substantial kiss of the Father and the Son. The grandiose encounter of the two fires of heaven and earth is the feast *par excellence*. It cannot but summon men of every culture to celebrate the most beautiful symbol of the eschatological wedding with the inebriation of wine, the joy of dance, and the song of creation.

The moment of celebration, the culmination of the "aesthetic" sense of created reality, nevertheless does not conceal the "dramatic" moment of the event. The solemn consecration of the couple "to Christ, in Christ, and in the Holy Spirit" naturally involves the commitment to the unity, indissolubility, and fecundity of marriage. Otherwise God would not be involved. The Holy Spirit seals the "Christian conjugal bond" (FC 13), that is, he takes possession of the couple in the name of the most Holy Trinity. The personal seal or tri-personal seal, inscribed from this point onwards in the "one flesh" of the spouses, "guarantees, elevates, and perfects" their natural love. However, it imports much more than this. In assuming human *erōs* up into the spousal *agapē* of Christ, the Holy Spirit draws with him the

25. Cf. G. Fitzer, "Sfragis," pp. 396, 405-6.

longing of God, his "jealously," his desire for expansion *(diffusivum sui)* and universal nuptiality. That breath of love overflows into humanity, inflaming hearts in the conjugal Pentecost. It endlessly effuses joy, security, and freedom of love with tongues of fire and fruitful gestures. As a result, the conjugal *communio,* blessed and sanctified by God himself, supernaturally opens up into sacramental *missio,* that is, into the irradiating energy, beauty, and life that proceeds from the Father and flows from the heart of Christ the Bridegroom to humanity, his bride. The "great mystery" is rooted in this, as is the great responsibility of Christian marriage.

In this way the sacramental event seals the couple's vocation to matrimonial sanctity. The "great mystery" in which the couple participates calls them to the total gift of self, in openness to the Holy Spirit and to his present and future gifts. The spouses are primarily called to participate in the unity of the Holy Spirit, who draws with him the unity and the fecundity of the whole Trinity. The first fruitfulness of Christian marriage is therefore spiritual and supernatural. It consists in the unifying gift of the Holy Spirit who joins man and woman in the ecstasy of love: "This at last is bone of my bones and flesh of my flesh" (Gen. 2:23). In this sense, the primary end of sacramental marriage is supernatural: it consists in the sanctity of conjugal love called to reproduce and incarnate the spousal love of Christ and the Church (Gen. 2:24; Eph. 5:21-23). The blessing of children is inserted within this horizon of faith, which is totally entrusted to God and expects to receive from him "the unexpectable: the fruit of his grace."[26] The "most precious gift of children" does not appear, therefore, as a merely natural process, but is viewed from within the spiritual fecundity of the couple. The openness of faith can certainly mean forgoing the gift of children in view of a superior spiritual fruitfulness.[27]

"The ultimate reason for this," writes von Balthasar, "is that their faith participates in the grace of the cross, whose fruitfulness is open to the infinite"; "in this fecundity of the Lord's crucified love, *the very law of Trinitar-*

---

26. H. U. von Balthasar, *The Christian State of Life,* trans. Sr. Mary Frances McCarthy (San Francisco: Ignatius, 1983), p. 246.

27. H. U. von Balthasar, *Teologica,* vol. III, *Lo Spirito della Verità* (Milan: Jaca, 1992), p. 276: "Starting from a full awareness of this participation one grasps more clearly the Christian possibility — which can become a divine exigence — of renouncing the use of marriage, and in the natural absence of marriage of living entirely the pneumatic love (which would be nothing at all without a body) between Christ and his Church, in order to take part in his more than natural fecundity."

ian love has become manifested, which is not exhausted between the Father and the Son, but has for its fruit the third, the Spirit, to whom belongs therefore, in a special manner, love in God."[28] That intratrinitarian "third" becomes the "third" of the believing couple, poured out between them as the Spirit of their love, who inspires, directs, sustains, nourishes, and moves their love along the path of Christ's *agape.*[29] That "third" is not only the subjective "we" of their love, but also the objective "you" who calls the couple to a total and reciprocal gift of self which is open to life. This objective gift is truly a consecration, that is, a definitive seal which signifies the couple's exclusive belonging to Christ (precisely as a couple) with the unrenounceable commitment to be a sacramental sign and symbol of his love for the Church. The official texts of the Church still speak of *"veluti consecrantur,"*[30] "as it were consecrated," but the deeper pneumatological understanding now being proposed should cause the "as it were" to be dropped for a fuller recognition of the matrimonial charism of the people of God (1 Cor 7:7; LG, 11).

The Holy Spirit thus appears in the wedding celebration and in the life of the couple as a spousal Spirit, an objective and irreversible gift (seal), a perennial source of sanctification, a "communional" breath poured out into the heart of the couple (FC, 13, 18) as the bond of Trinitarian love. After having collaborated with the Creator Father in forming man and woman in the image of God; after having collaborated with the Redeemer Son in redeeming fallen love in need of healing, the Holy Spirit lets himself be given to the couple and the family as the royal seal of Trinitarian Love imprinted in the "one flesh" of the *"imago Dei."* With this tri-personal seal are communicated the joy of shared love, the Eucharist for the love bestowed, and the surprise of being fruitful in God, with God and of God himself. With this also comes the challenge, which may at times be either a cross or a joy, for the couple to exist and live with and for each other, and together for the divine "Third" and human "third." From this pneumatological mystery, in which the conjugal charism and matrimonial grace participate, flows an authentically conjugal and family spirituality.

28. Balthasar, *Teologica,* vol. III, p. 214.

29. Cf. H. U. von Balthasar, *Explorations in Theology,* vol. IV, *Spirit and Institution* (San Francisco: Ignatius, 1995), pp. 221ff.; see also his *Teologica,* vol. III, pp. 275-76. Cf. also Ouellet, "The Spirit in the Life of the Trinity," pp. 204ff.

30. "Spouses, therefore, are fortified and, as it were, consecrated for the duties and dignity of their state by a special sacrament" (GS 48; cf. Pius XI, *Encyclical Letter, Casti connubii: AAS* 22 (1930), p. 583).

The Holy Spirit, Source of a Trinitarian Spirituality
for the Couple and the Family

The Holy Spirit unites man and woman within the spiritual fruitfulness of Christ who joins the Church to his eschatological fecundity. In this sense we have emphasized that natural fruitfulness is subordinate to and integrated into the fecundity of faith. The end, good, or primary gift of sacramental marriage is the seal of the Holy Spirit himself, who is given from the beginning as a pledge for the couple's entire life. This Gift-Person assumes the natural ends and goods of marriage into his gift, and requires the couple to be available and unconditionally faithful to Love. This already defines the meaning of conjugal and family spirituality, which "is none other than the development of a theological and ecclesial life, in the image of the Most Holy Trinity, within the specific context of the family cell."[31] At this time, we will neither offer an overview of this nor a spiritual itinerary for spouses, but only some fundamental points upon which every couple can develop and discover their own path to sanctity.

A Spirituality of "Giving and Receiving" in Faith,
the Spirit of Trinitarian Love

"So we know and believe the love God has for us. God is love, and he who abides in love abides in God, and God abides in him" (1 Jn. 4:16). We shall take as our point of departure this Johannine passage which roots the most fundamental Christian attitude in having faith in love. It may seem paradoxical to place faith in love at the basis of conjugal spirituality. Love appears, in fact, to the couple as an anthropological given to be cultivated rather than a mystery to be believed. Perhaps it would be better to base it on the anthropological reality of conjugal love and suggest some means of living it spiritually. If so, it would run the risk of overlaying conjugal love with a spirituality imported from without. We therefore start with the grace of the Holy Spirit which envelops conjugal

---

31. Joseph Mac Avoy, "Famille," *Dictionnaire de Spiritualité*, vol. V (Paris: Beauchesne, 1964), p. 73; cf. P. Adnès, *Mariage et vie chrétienne, Dictionnaire de Spiritualité*, vol. X, pp. 355-87; Costante Provetto, "Il cammino della spiritualità coniugale," in *Nuova Enciclopedia del matrimonio* (Brescia: Queriniana, 1988), pp. 377-424; Tullo Goffi, *Spiritualità del matrimonio* (Brescia: Queriniana, 1996).

love, with all of its components and dimensions, in the mystery of Trinitarian Love.

The Holy Spirit's first gift to the spouses is precisely the gift of faith in love: "No man has ever seen God; if we love one another, God abides in us and his love is perfected in us. By this we know that we abide in him and he in us, because he has given us of his own Spirit" (1 Jn. 4:12-13). The Holy Spirit teaches us to see God in the other and in communion with him or her. To believe in love means to see with the eyes of the Spirit, who makes us enter into Jesus' own mode of vision. This way of seeing in love allows one to discover the infinite value of the other and of oneself as the image of God, from whence flows the mystery of "giving and receiving" divine Love in human love. The spouses are involved in a special way in that exchange because the sacrament configures them to the love of Christ and the Church. In their reciprocal self-giving and receiving, they give and receive one another from God; still more profoundly they mutually give and receive God himself.[32] To believe in Love means, therefore, to enter into the dance of the three Persons, in their giving, receiving, and sharing Love.

"The Spirit, which the Lord pours forth, gives a new heart, and renders man and woman capable of loving one another as Christ has loved us," that is, of loving with "the very charity of Christ who gave Himself on the Cross" (FC 13). "Matrimonial love," comments Martinez Peque, "is far from being a mere elevation of natural love, even if it were the highest, for conjugal love that flows from the sacrament is the Holy Spirit, the love of the Father and the Son given to the spouses so that they may love one another with the same love with which Christ loves the Church."[33] The love of the Holy Spirit, designated in the New Testament as *agapē*, is described by Saint Paul as patient, merciful, humble, and respectful (1 Cor 13:4ff); it neither disregards nor replaces natural love in its sexual *(erōs)* or personal (friendship) dimensions, but integrates and perfects it "in Christ" for the service of God.

In a beautiful address given in 1982, John Paul II pointed out that "The new covenant abides in and transfigures the reality of Christian marriage. The covenant not only inspires the life of the couple, but is fulfilled in them, in the sense that the covenant pours out its energies into the life of

---

32. Cf. Philippe Delaye, "La pastorale familiale dans l'optique de 'Familiaris Consortio,'" *Esprit et Vie* 42 (21 October 1982), pp. 36ff.

33. M. Martinez Peque, *Lo Spirito Santo e il Matrimonio* (Rome: Edizioni Dehoniane, 1993), p. 182.

the spouses: it shapes their love from within. Thus they love one another not only as Christ loved, but already — mysteriously — in the very love of Christ, for his Spirit is given to them."[34] In this way, the spouses "not only imitate and are a sign of the love *(agape)* of Christ for the Church, but they also really participate in it thanks to the gift of the Spirit."[35]

A Spirituality of Joy and Gratitude
for Participating in the Gift of God

To believe in love means, therefore, to become aware of the presence of the divine "Third" in the life of the couple and the family. Now, that divine Third, the Spirit of Love, is joy, surprise, gratitude, and freedom which is open to the future. This mode of being is offered and given to the couple as a grace and a responsibility. It signifies the gushing forth of a spring of gratitude.

From this perspective, the Holy Spirit teaches the couple to thank God for their vocation. The vocation to Christian marriage is an authentic call to holiness founded by Christ on the sacrament which consecrates the spouses. The consecration of the spouses is a source of sanctity and joy in a world that has lost the sense of a definitive commitment to love. John Paul II reaffirmed that "marriage and virginity or celibacy are two ways of expressing and living the one mystery of the covenant of God with His people" (FC 16). To affirm the full value of marriage as a way to holiness and an inseparable source of spiritual fecundity, we must focus upon its consecratory character. As early as 1962, Carlo Colombo wrote that "This aspect of consecration belongs to the initial act (marriage *"in fieri"*), and is not repeated again; but along the whole course of life all the successive acts of love, which continue and develop the initial commitment, preserve the same meaning and the same supernatural value, the same sanctifying capacity."[36]

34. John Paul II, "Se tu conoscessi il dono de Dio" ["If you knew the gift of God"], speech given to Foyers des Equipes de Notre Dame, September 23, 1982. Published in T. Barberi and D. Tettamanzi, eds., *Matrimonio e famiglia nel magistero della Chiesa* (Milan: Massimo, 1986); cf. *Familis Consortio,* 63.

35. M. Martinez Peque, *Lo Spirito Santo e il Matrimonio* (Rome: Edizione Denoniane, 1993), p. 183.

36. Carlo Colombo, "Il matrimonio, sacramento della nuova legge," *La Scuola Cattolica,* Year XCI, 1963; cf. C. Rocchetta, *I sacramenti della fede,* 7th ed. (Milan: EDB, 1998), pp. 333-41.

Sacramental consecration signifies, therefore, a taking possession of, a belonging, that requires an availability without calculation: "Set me as a seal upon your heart, as a seal upon your arm" (Songs 8:6). As Adrienne von Speyr notes, "when love is in us, we do not possess it, it possesses us; we become a function of this love."[37] The spouses are consecrated to love; they belong to Christ and their love belongs to the Holy Spirit, a "third." "There is a trinity in love," writes Saint Augustine: "the lover, the beloved, and love"; the Holy Spirit is Love who unites the Lover and the Beloved in and beyond themselves. Sealed by this consecratory gift, the spouses can always draw from the font of sacramental grace for nourishment, purification, and the renewal of their union.

An aspect of belonging to the objective love of the Spirit which must not be overlooked is precisely the openness to fecundity, the reception of children, and then the daily devotion to their education. These dimensions of conjugal and family "ministry" are not duties extrinsic to love, as if they were a submission to the laws of nature. Lived in matrimonial grace, they appear as concrete services of the one love that embraces and involves their mutual and sincere gift of self. A grace for our time would be the humble and distressing awareness of Francis of Assisi that "Love is not loved." Neither the divine nor the human "third," neither the Holy Spirit nor the child, is sufficiently loved.

If the couple senses the spiritual and divine meaning of their conjugal and family relationships, they will also understand the value of interpersonal dialogue nourished by prayer, worship, eucharistic life, return to the baptismal font through sacramental forgiveness, and the daily self-surrender to the other in God and to God in the other. Thus sacramental grace effects a gradual transformation in the being of the couple, and inscribes in their flesh the likeness to the one eucharistic flesh of Christ and the Church. Their fecund communion becomes a mission, that is, a sign, a point of reference, an icon of the Church, a source of grace for the family, the Church, and the world.

37. Adrienne von Speyr, *Le Cantique des cantiques* (Brussels: Culture et vérité, 1995), p. 86.

A Spirituality of Dialogue and Openness to Radiate the Gift of Trinitarian Fecundity in the Church and the World

The Holy Spirit, effused during the sacramental celebration, brings the infinite dynamism of Trinitarian love within the natural dynamism of human love. Taken up into the Trinitarian relations by virtue of the covenant, conjugal and family relationships cannot close themselves within the restricted circle of the nuclear family. Being a "little Church" or "domestic Church" throws open the doors of the family home to the local ecclesial community and the whole of humanity. The spousal breath of the Holy Spirit does not at all stop with the couple's primordial and inseparable task of unity and fecundity, but extends to the broader area of family hospitality, celebrated by St. John Chrysostom; the union of families and the family apostolate encouraged by Pius XII; as well as the new evangelization, both of the family and by the family, as proposed by John Paul II.

In this light, conjugal and family spirituality is called to an epochal turn. Undeveloped for centuries because of greater attention to the spirituality of virgins, it now emerges as a providential remedy and a way out of the Church's missionary crisis. In the wake of the Second Vatican Council and the Church's new sacramental consciousness, the hour is coming to pass from the situation of crisis to the missionary awareness of cultural regeneration. In fact, the emergence of the *kairos* of matrimonial holiness, thanks to the witness of holy couples and to post-conciliar doctrinal development under the impetus of John Paul II, allows us to catch a glimpse of a new springtime of the Church's mission. Becoming more deeply aware of the matrimonial charism *(res et sacramentum)* and the grace of the Holy Spirit moves the evangelized couple and family from this point onwards to become the evangelizing "subject," that is, the agent, bearer of grace, indwelt temple of the divine presence, radiant icon of Trinitarian Love.

Conjugal and family spirituality, growing in the committed and faithful couple, thus reaches the maturity of a mission consciously and joyfully assumed. The sacramental mission of the couple and the family is not an addition *ad libitum* for those who have time to help out in the parish or diocesan organization. The mission is inscribed in the being of the couple as a *communio personarum* sealed by the Holy Spirit. This seal of marital holiness is a supernatural work of art, which shines in the midst of society as a real symbol of the Church indissolubly united to Christ. The witness of united families, who live according to the model of the "Holy Family," at one time called the "earthly trinity,"[38] carries with it a creative breath of culture and civilization.

Conclusion

The hour of conjugal and family spirituality is therefore the hour of the transcendence of self into the image of the Trinity, the hour of becoming a "house of God," a home of the Most High, an icon of the Trinity, memory and prophecy of the wonders of salvation history. When God had finished the work of the six days of creation, after the masterpiece of man created as man-woman in his image, he exclaimed: "It is very good!" Yes, it is very good, the mutual gift of man and woman as a sacrament of Christ, the Bridegroom, and the Church, his Bride. If it is very good for God, it must also be very good for us and a reason for praise and thanksgiving. Man's vocation to love flourishes precisely as praise of God's grace (Eph. 1:1ff.), that is, as holy service to the mystery hidden for endless ages, but revealed now in the life of the spouses and the family.

The reawakening of this sublime vocation is nourished by prayer, by living the gospel in sacrifice, and by belonging to the eucharistic community. In this way the Church, the Bride, becomes fruitful in the domestic Church, and God himself is grateful to the family for being not only an "object" of his grace, but for being with him, in him, and through him, a "subject" of the exchange of love between the divine Persons.

This is the ultimate horizon opened up by *Gaudium et Spes* in number 48 when it affirms that "authentic married love is caught up into divine love and is directed and enriched by the redemptive power of Christ and the salvific action of the Church, with the result that the spouses are effectively led to God and are helped and strengthened in their lofty role as fathers and mothers . . . fulfilling their conjugal and family role by virtue of this sacrament, spouses are penetrated with the spirit of Christ and their whole life is suffused by faith, hope, and charity; thus they increasingly further their own perfection and their mutual sanctification, and together they render glory to God."

Participation in the glorification of God is precisely the gift of the

---

38. I. Noye, "Famille (Dévotion à la sainte Famille)," *Dictionnaire de Spiritualité*, vol. V (Paris: Beauchesne, 1964), p. 85.

Holy Spirit as the seal of the glory of God imprinted in the flesh of the risen Christ, and in the "one flesh" of Christ the Bridegroom and his Bride the Church. This same seal marks the Christian couple and family with belonging and service to the truth of absolute Love. The horizon of that service is the glory of God, believed, celebrated, and translated into daily gestures. The glory of Trinitarian Love does not distract the couple from earthly reality and the daily problems of love, fruitfulness, and education. Rather, it immerses them more deeply in these realities with the grace of the Holy Spirit, because Love is made flesh to remain among us as the source and pledge of eternal life.

CHAPTER VI

Fathers and Mothers . . . as Your Heavenly Father

"Saint Joseph was called by God to serve the person and mission of Jesus directly *through the exercise of his fatherhood.* It is precisely in this way that, as the Church's Liturgy teaches, he 'cooperated in the fullness of time in the great mystery of salvation' and is truly a 'minister of salvation.'" Thus Pope John Paul II writes in his apostolic exhortation *Redemptoris custos,* dedicated to the figure of Saint Joseph, patron of the universal Church: "His fatherhood is expressed concretely 'in his having made his life a service, a sacrifice to the mystery of the Incarnation and to the redemptive mission connected with it; in having used the legal authority which was his over the Holy Family in order to make a total gift of self, of his life and work; in having turned his human vocation to domestic love into a superhuman oblation of self, an oblation of his heart and all his abilities into love placed at the service of the Messiah growing up in his house.'"[1]

The call to holiness in marriage, so wonderfully lived by Saint Joseph, is rooted in the plan of the heavenly Father, who together with the Son and the Holy Spirit, wished to share his fecundity with his creatures. For this reason he created man in his image, man and woman, and he bestowed upon them the blessing of fruitfulness in view of Christ and the Church. "This mystery is great!" exclaims the Apostle of the Gentiles (Eph. 5:32), contemplating the spousal love of Christ and the Church, which is prolonged sacramentally in Christian spouses and the family. Today, this mys-

1. John Paul II, *Redemptoris custos* 8.

102

tery is found at the center of the Church's dramatic fight for life. The Holy Father, John Paul II, made it the banner of his pontificate, calling everyone, churches, societies, and cultures, to rediscover the human and sacramental value of marriage and family.

Notwithstanding John Paul's vigorous magisterial and pastoral impetus in the wake of conciliar renewal, nor the notable development of lay spirituality in the twentieth century, the call to holiness in marriage and the family is not yet fully recognized and lived in the Church. It is also undergoing, in an ever more aggressive form, the trials of a secularized culture. In fact, the loss of Christian roots is accompanied by the collapse of the family and a disregard for the sacredness of life. Therefore, a new evangelization, not only of the family, but also by the family, is urgent in order to bring to light an "adequate anthropology,"[2] capable of reconstructing the unity of the human family around the heavenly Father who shared his paternity with "Joseph, the husband of Mary, of whom Jesus was born, who is called Christ" (Mt. 1:16).

With this chapter we hope to contribute to the quest for a "theology" of matrimonial and family sanctity. We proceed on the basis of the methodological proposal of K. Hemmerle, who suggests that one begin from the Trinitarian mystery in order to understand, from above, the mystery of the human family here below.[3] Taking as our point of departure therefore the Mystery of the Father who creates everything *in Christ*, we shall see how the Holy Spirit gives the gift of sanctity to married couples and the family. The Spirit urges the spouses to live and to understand the mystery of their fatherhood and motherhood in faith, so that they will allow themselves to be shaped by the divine Child given to the Holy Family of Nazareth. Our reflection will develop as follows: (1) the vocation of fathers and mothers to the perfection of love; (2) the growth of persons in the community of life and love according to the image of God; and (3) the Holy Family, model of sanctity by virtue of its availability to receive the fecundity of the heavenly Father.

2. John Paul II, *The Theology of the Body: Human Love in the Divine Plan* (Boston: Daughters of St. Paul, 1997). See in particular C. Caffarra's "General Introduction" to the Italian version, *Uomo e donna Io creò: Catechesi sull'amore umano* (Rome: Libreria Vaticana, 1995), pp. 5-24.

3. "By starting from God who reveals himself, that is, from originality and inaccessibility, from the outward love that he is in himself and which is communicated beyond himself, we look at the world, men and revelation itself in a new way," K. Hemmerle, "Matrimonio e famiglia in una antropologia trinitaria," *Nuova Umanità* 6 (1984), n. 31, p. 4.

The Vocation of Fathers and Mothers
to the Perfection of Love

"You, therefore, must be perfect, as your heavenly Father is perfect" (Mt. 5:48). The evangelist St. Matthew places this powerful exhortation at the conclusion of the solemn Sermon on the Mount. Chapter five of his gospel begins with the proclamation of the beatitudes which Jesus, the new Moses, true Teacher of the New Law, announces to the disciples who are gathered around him: "Blessed are the poor in spirit . . . Blessed are the merciful . . . Blessed are those who are persecuted, for the Kingdom of heaven is theirs." Jesus compares these traits to the justice of the pharisees and scribes. He thus affirms the new justice of the Kingdom that gives glory to the Father. His message concerns the fulfillment of the Law through a religious attitude of justice of heart, which surpasses that of the Old Law.

Nevertheless it is worth noting how Jesus, even though emphasizing the novelty of the Kingdom, places himself within the tradition of Israel. In fact, his discourse takes up again the law of sanctity proclaimed in detail by the book of Leviticus: "You shall be holy; for I the Lord your God am holy" (Lev. 19:2). In the Old Law, this commandment appears after a list of ritual prescriptions and sexual prohibitions, followed by moral precepts, the first of which resounds: "Every one of you shall revere his mother and his father, and you shall keep my sabbaths: I am the Lord your God" (Lev. 19:3). Despite the numerous moral and religious observations, the predominant accent of the text is on the holiness of God, who calls on the Israelites to behave in a manner conformed to the dignity of the covenant. The same emphasis on God's holiness prevails in the passage in Matthew's gospel regarding the sanctity of Christian marriage.

Marriage: A Christian Vocation

There was a time in which marriage had been considered a "common" state for Christians, while the term "vocation" was reserved for religious and priestly life. Today, the concept of vocation concerns every state of life in the Church. To be sure, the Second Vatican Council applies it explicitly to marriage (LG 35; GS 49, 52).[4] The constitution *Lumen Gentium* speaks

4. P. Adnès, "Mariage et vie chrétienne," *Dictionnaire de Spiritualité*, vol. 10, 355-87, esp. 380.

of the universal vocation to holiness in these terms: "It is therefore quite clear that all Christians in any state or walk of life are called to the fullness of Christian life and to the perfection of love" (LG 40). It goes on to say that fathers and mothers are called to manifest an "unfailing and generous love, . . . [to] build up the brotherhood of charity, and . . . [to] stand as witnesses and cooperators of the fruitfulness of mother Church, as a sign of, and a share in that love with which Christ loved his bride and gave himself for her" (LG 41). The question: "Does there exist a vocation to marriage?"[5] therefore requires an unequivocal response in the affirmative. Nonetheless, it must be pointed out that practically speaking the value of Christian marriage as a path to holiness remains yet to be truly recognized. Thus it is worth briefly recalling its New Testament foundations.

Christ inaugurated a radical novelty in calling some of his disciples to virginity or to the apostolic ministry, but this fact, conspicuously attested to in the gospels, does not eliminate the vocation to marriage, which is expressed differently, but decisively and clearly, through his attitude, gestures, and words. In the gospel of Matthew, after the discussion about divorce, the disciples express their perplexity to Jesus: "If such is the case of a man with his wife, it is not expedient to marry." He responds to them saying: "Not all men can receive this precept, but only those to whom it is given" (Mt. 19:10-11). The same idea is taken up again by Saint Paul in the first letter to the Corinthians: "I wish that all were as I myself am. But each has his own special gift from God, one of one kind and one of another" (I Cor. 7:7). Marriage therefore is not a purely "worldly affair" as Luther thought, but a vocation accompanied by a specific "gift"; in fact according to Ligier, a "charism of consecration," which Vatican II confirmed in the wake of Pope Pius XI's encyclical *Casti Connubii*.[6]

Other New Testament passages illustrate the sacramental foundation of the Christian vocation to marriage. The presence of Jesus at Cana of Galilee for the first of his signs holds a sacramental meaning of unsurpassed importance in the gospel of John (Jn. 2:1-12). The sign of Cana, in

5. D. Tettamanzi, "Esiste una vocazione al matrimonio?" *La Famiglia* (1973), n. 38, pp. 125-41.

6. "They will be fortified, sanctified and as it were consecrated *(roborati, sanctificati et quasi consecrati)* by so great a sacrament," Pius XI, *Insegnamenti pontifici: Il matrimonio,* n. 304 (221), AAS 22 (1930), p. 583. Cf. LG 11, GS 48. Cf. L. Ligier, *Il matrimonio: Questioni teologiche e pastorali* (Rome: Città Nuova, 1988), pp. 114ff. "We shall distinguish in conjugal life the *"charism of consecration"* and the *"grace of sanctification."*

fact, proves to be a key for reading all the other signs since it elevates human marriage to the dignity of a figure-symbol of the eschatological fulfillment of the Kingdom of God in the Hour of the Cross. Also, Jesus' decisive Word on marriage "in the beginning," presented within the context of the ecclesiastical discourse in Matthew, clearly emphasizes God's intervention in instituting marriage. "What therefore God has joined together, let no man put asunder" (Mt. 19:6). Finally, the paschal sacrifice of Jesus is explicitly linked to marriage in St. Paul's letter to the Ephesians: "This is a great mystery, and I mean in reference to Christ and the Church" (Eph. 5:32).[7] Thus, the Church understood the sacramentality of marriage based on these scriptural foundations, which John Paul II has commented on at great length, emphasizing in an absolute way the "prototypical" value of marriage in relation to the other sacraments.[8]

The Christian vocation to marriage proceeds then from the mystery of the covenant which God has sealed with humanity in Christ, making marriage its sacramental symbol: "The communion between God and His people finds its definitive fulfillment in Jesus Christ, the Bridegroom who loves and gives Himself as the Savior of humanity, uniting it to Himself as His body. He reveals the original truth of marriage, the truth of the 'beginning,' and, freeing man from his hardness of heart, He makes man capable of realizing this truth in its entirety" (FC 13). This vocation consists in following Christ the Bridegroom who loves the Church and sacrifices himself for her on the Cross. Christ assumes the man-woman relationship, symbol *par excellence* of the first creation, within his spousal relationship with the Church. Thus he calls the spouses to live in his love and by his love, in a properly Christian "state of life," founded on matrimonial consecration. From this comes a commitment of faith to live a faithful, indissoluble, and fruitful love as an authentic *sequela Christi*.

The vocation to marriage therefore is rooted not only in the creation of man and woman in the image of God (Gen. 1:26-27; FC 11), but in the "gift" of the sacrament, which communicates to the spouses a specific participation in the spousal love of Christ and the Church. "Authentic married love is caught up into divine love and is directed and enriched by the redemptive power of Christ and the salvific action of the Church, with the

---

7. Cf. K. H. Fleckenstein, *"Questo mistero è grande": Il matrimonio in Ef. 5:21-32* (Rome: Città Nuova, 1996).

8. John Paul II, *The Theology of the Body*, pp. 333-41.

result that the spouses are effectively led to God and are helped and strengthened in their lofty role as mothers and fathers" (GS 48). By virtue of this participation the spouses fulfill their own mission in the Church; "penetrated with the spirit of Christ . . . their whole life is suffused by faith, hope, and charity; thus they increasingly further their own perfection and their mutual sanctification, and together render glory to God" (GS 48).

The Sanctity of Fathers and Mothers:
In the Image of Their Heavenly Father?

If conjugal sanctity consists in union with Christ the Bridegroom, who sacrifices himself on the Cross, how does its specific dimension of fatherhood and motherhood come about? As the result of a natural event blessed by the Creator? Or as something more essential which is brought about by the sacrament? What is the relation between God's fatherhood and the fatherhood-motherhood of Christian parents? Saint Paul points us towards a solution in his letter to the Ephesians evoking the mystery of divine Fatherhood: "I bend my knee before the Father, from whom every fatherhood in heaven and on earth takes its name, . . . from the Spirit in the interior man" (Eph. 3:14-16).

The apostle emphasizes that every fatherhood, both heavenly and earthly, takes its name from the One and Only Father revealed by Our Lord Jesus Christ as his Father and the Father of us all. "That Christ may dwell in your hearts through faith; that you, being rooted and grounded in love, may have the power . . . to know the love of Christ which surpasses knowledge, that you may be filled with all the fullness of God" (Eph. 3:17-19). The relation between divine and human fatherhood cannot be understood by a simple analogy between the human and the divine, moving in an ascending direction from below. If so, our temptation would be to think of divine fatherhood based on the model of human fatherhood, when in fact the divine Father owes his creating act to no one other than himself. By contrast, every fatherhood in heaven and on earth takes its name from Him, the Father of Our Lord Jesus Christ. The analogy must, therefore, pass through the descending mediation of Jesus Christ, the only begotten Son who has revealed to us the Trinitarian mystery of divine fatherhood. Our point of departure therefore is Jesus Christ, who reveals the mystery of the Father; human fatherhood and motherhood therefore will be illuminated from above.

"Holy Father, keep them in thy name, which thou hast given me, that they may be one, even as we are one" (Jn. 17:11). Jesus lifts this prayer up to his Father in the solemn and decisive moment that precedes his sacrifice. He asks that his disciples may be one, as the Father and the Son are one in Love. Jesus says, "Holy Father, consecrate them in truth"; the truth of love, so "that the love with which thou hast loved me may be in them, and I in them" (v. 26). The abyssal depth of this prayer should open wide the doors of Christian spirituality in general, and conjugal and family spirituality in particular. We are called to be holy as God is holy, that is, to be one as God is one in Love. We shall dwell upon the mystery of God's holiness which proceeds from the Father and is unfolded in the Trinity of Persons.

Jesus describes the holiness of God as a mystery of unity in Love. God is Holy because he is Three in One, that is, Triune. John confirms this when he says that "God is Love" (1 Jn. 4:8). He is not only thinking of God's love for us, but is foremost referring to his existence as three Persons in Love. John speaks of the Father *(ho theos)*, the first to love, who sent the "only begotten Son" (v. 9) into the world so that we may have life through him, and who gave us the "gift of his Spirit" (v. 13). God is love not because he loves us, but he loves us because he is Love in and of himself. God is *Agape,* a pure gratuitous gift of self in himself, before he bestows any gift upon us. His holiness is sublime, his glory rises infinitely beyond our conceptions, for it consists precisely in his being Triune in love.

If God is love, his sanctity is rooted in the love that is poured out in three distinct and correlative personal modes. The Father's mode is fontal giving, the origin who generates the Son. The Father generates by virtue of the fact that he is Love, which substantially gives itself without reserve. "If the Christian doctrine on the Trinity is taken seriously," writes Balthasar, "it seems that the divine Persons, Father, Son, and Spirit, if one wishes to hold firmly to the unity of God, may not be anything but pure love and self-renunciation *(Selbstlosigkeit).* This is so from all eternity, such that the person of the Father becomes the supreme mystery: 'the First Person does not generate in the sense of adding the act of generating a Son to his already complete person, rather the Father *is* the action of generating, of giving himself and pouring himself out . . . ; pure actuality.'"[9] The Father is an

9. H. U. von Balthasar, *Homo Creatus est: Saggi teologici,* vol. 5 (Brescia: Morcelliana, 1991), p. 109; with a citation from J. Ratzinger, *Dogma e predicazione* (Brescia: Queriniana, 1974), p. 178.

absolute gift of self whose divine substance is possessed by him precisely by virtue of the fact that it is given away and received by the consubstantial Son. This corresponding gift is confirmed by the Holy Spirit, who proceeds from their mutual consubstantial Love. "The authority of love that offers itself," writes Ferdinand Ulrich, "originally exists in Love itself: God in his very being is a shared life; the Trinitarian persons exist as relation, a reciprocal gift to one another. The absolute authority of the Father is therefore not based on his relation to the world he created and redeemed; . . . the authority of the Father is already rooted within the Trinity itself."[10]

The Father is Love based on the fact that he is Gift-Source, the original and inscrutable Mystery. The Son is Love by virtue of the fact that he is the "yes" to the Father, in infinite gratitude and absolute readiness to love as the Father loves. The Holy Spirit is Love as fruit of that eternal accord, personal exuberant fruit, infinite and shared joy.[11] The Spirit is called Holy precisely because he confirms divine sanctity, personally crowning the Trinity of Love. When the Church sings *Sanctus, Sanctus, Sanctus,* in the sacred liturgy, she unites and distinguishes God's sanctity with respect to the three Persons. God is Holy as Father, Son, and Holy Spirit. The sublime quality of God, his immense glory, his sanctity is Love. God the Father is the infinite source of Love, the supreme mystery from whom love flows and to whom it returns in the unity of the Trinity.

From this archetype of Trinitarian Love proceeds all of created reality, but in a special way, man created in the image of God as man and woman.[12] God made man in his image, as man-woman, to be fecund with him and like him.[13] Man's vocation to love is inscribed in the very being of man and woman, as persons created for communion. Thus, John Paul II insists that the human body carries in itself, in its masculinity and femi-

---

10. F. Ulrich, "L'humble autorité du Père," *Communio* [French edition] 3 (January, 1976), p. 16.

11. "Reciprocity of absolute love, which should seemingly be eternally content, but whose intimate character is of such exuberance that — one could say — it 'suddenly' and precisely *as* exuberance produces something, that is still one thing; the proof of reciprocity in love is the outcome, in the same way that the human child is at once the proof of the love between the parents and the fruit of this love" (H. U. von Balthasar, *Lo Spirito della Verità, Teologica,* vol. 3 [Milan: Jaca, 1992], p. 130).

12. John Paul II, *Familiaris Consortio* 11; *Mulieris Dignitatem* 6-7.

13. Cf. R. Hinschberger, "Image et ressemblance dans la tradition sacerdotale," *RSR* 59 (1985), p 192.

ninity, the interior dimension of the gift:[14] "For this reason a man shall leave his father and mother and be joined to his wife, and the two shall become one flesh" (Gen. 2:24; Eph. 5:31). Thus, love is not only a moral task of the spouses super-added to the juridical reality of their marriage. Rather, as John Paul II affirms, "we must say that the essence and role of the family are in the final analysis specified by love" (FC 17). The conjugal union of man and woman, upon which the family is founded, is therefore born from the reciprocal love inscribed in their sexual difference.

The interior dimension of the personal-corporal gift is further enriched by the gift of the sacrament which inserts the natural man-woman union within the Christ-Church relationship. If the baptismal grace of sonship introduces the Christian into the intratrinitarian relation of the Son and the Father, matrimonial grace confers upon the couple a new participation in the communion between the divine Persons.[15] Sent by the Father, Christ the Bridegroom "encounters Christian spouses" and "abides with them" in daily life to bless, redeem, and sanctify their love. With the Son comes the Spirit of Love who assumes authentic conjugal love into God's love, to make it a privileged expression of the Father's fecundity within the covenant between Christ the Bridegroom and the Church his Bride.

Holiness under the Profile of Fecundity

The proposal that conjugal and family holiness is characterized by fecundity may rouse some surprise or perplexity, for one would expect instead that such holiness be characterized by the dimension of the communion of persons or the ecclesial dimension of mission. By contrast, we propose that the sanctity of fathers and mothers be integrated around the category of

---

14. John Paul II, *Theology of the Body*, pp. 75-77.

15. "Thus the spouses in the celebration of marriage, at the moment in which they give themselves to one another, *in Domino*, however, manifest *coram Ecclesia*: The reception of the abnegation of the Father who gives the Son; of the Son who giving himself to the Father and the Church gives us the Spirit; of the Spirit as Gift — the One Given — so that a perennial hymn of praise to the omnipotent and faithful love of God may sound forth from the family which the spouses create." A. Triacca, "'Celebrare' il matrimonio cristiano: Suo significato teologico-liturgico (Anamnesis-Methexis-epiclesis), *Ephemerides Liturgicae* 93 (1979), p. 454.

fecundity. It must be immediately pointed out that we do not claim to re-introduce the opinion that procreation is the primary end of marriage; nor did the Second Vatican Council wish to endorse this view; thus it awaited a more profound integration of interpersonal love in the theology of marriage.[16] In this sense, Balthasar proposes a rethinking of Christian marriage in light of the act of faith upon which it is founded: "The acts of faith of the two marriage partners meet in God and are accepted, formed and returned to them by God, in whom they find the foundation of their unity, the witness of their union and the pledge of their fidelity. It is God who, in the act of faith, gives the partners to one another in the basic Christian act of self-surrender. Together, they offer themselves to God and receive each other from him in a gift of grace, confidence and Christian expectation."[17] Thus the act of faith is the first fruit of sacramental marriage, an act that generates the "sacramental couple" in their openness to and participation in the fecundity of God.

The proposal of sanctity as fecundity proceeds, therefore, from the inner logic of the Trinitarian mystery. The Father is the original gift whose fruit is the Son. The Son is fecund together with the Father in spirating the Holy Spirit as the fruit of their reciprocal Love. By contrast, the Holy Spirit is not the origin of another Person, but seals the unity of the Father and the Son in himself, as Person-Gift. Trinitarian life is communion in fecundity. In an analogous way, conjugal and family relations lived in faith are fruitful in God, with God, and of God himself. The reciprocal gift of the man and woman in faith first and foremost generates the couple as such, which is already a "third" in respect to the two individuals who constitute it. This third is a gift of grace, the presence of the Holy Spirit in their midst who gives them a new unity, not only human, but Trinitarian. On the basis of this grace given by the Father, fathers and mothers can develop holy and fruitful relationships of love in the image of God.

From this perspective, it is possible to think of how fathers and mothers on earth are intimately connected to the mystery of the Father in heaven. This connection does not exist on account of a natural continuity between divine paternity and human parenthood. There lies an infinite

---

16. Cf. A. Mattheeuws, *Les "dons" du mariage: Recherche de théologie morale et sacramentelle* (Paris: Culture et Vérité, 1996), pp. 146ff.

17. H. U. von Balthasar, *The Christian States of Life* (San Francisco: Ignatius, 1983), p. 245.

distance between the Creator and the creature. In fact, human parent-hood has no basis in and of itself apart from the "gift" of the heavenly Father who creates man in his image in order to lavish upon him the mystery of his own fatherhood. "The Father in his authority wills that man be free, so he can bestow upon him all that he has to give, that is, essentially himself."[18] Man and woman are therefore called to open themselves up to the heavenly Father in order to receive the spiritual and physical gifts that only he can create. "I have gotten a man with the help of the Lord," exclaims Eve from the beginning (Gen. 4:1). But the greatest gift of the Father is his own Son, who elevates human fathers-mothers to the dignity of participants in the mystery of the divine fatherhood. When Christian parents receive a child from the Creator, they immediately think of baptizing him in the Church, which confers on him an intimate and direct relationship to the Father of Christ. Their fatherhood and motherhood therefore encompass a sacramental dimension in relation to the creature entrusted to their care.

This spiritual motherhood and fatherhood requires the couple to live a life of faith in loving obedience to the dead and risen Christ. In effect, the spiritual parenthood of Christian spouses flows from the paschal mystery of Christ, who reveals the glory of the Father. They must therefore place their love for God above every other love, including even that of their own parents, spouse, and children. In God's original plan that was fulfilled in Christ, spiritual parenthood is the origin and foundation of physical fruitfulness, which is a sacrament of the former. Unfortunately, original sin detached the transmission of human life from the communication of grace. Baptism and faith re-establish friendship with God, without nevertheless recovering the perfect unity of physical and spiritual fecundity. Therefore, Christian fathers and mothers cannot directly communicate the grace of adoptive sonship to their children with the gift of life. They must ask for it from Christ who left us Baptism as a sacrament of his sonship. The intimate union of fathers and mothers with the heavenly Father therefore passes through Christ, who unites their fatherhood and motherhood to the baptismal and eucharistic fecundity of his paschal sacrifice.

18. F. Ulrich, "L'humble autorité du Père," p. 17.

Growth as Persons in the Community of Life and Love

The Gift of the Holy Spirit, Source of Personhood

In light of the foregoing discussion regarding Trinitarian fecundity, we can now deepen our reflection on the growth of persons knowing that "the primordial model of the family is to be sought in God himself, in the Trinitarian mystery of his life. The divine 'We' is the eternal pattern of the human 'we,' especially of that 'we' formed by the man and the woman created in the divine image and likeness."[19] We have already reflected on the personal properties of Love in God. The divine We eternally lives by the mutual donation of the divine Persons, which manifests itself as love: gratuitous, reciprocal, fecund, and united. "The family is in fact a community of persons whose proper way of existing and living together is communion: *communio personarum*" (LF 7).

The Holy Spirit, Gift of gifts, seal of divine unity, ultimate source of communion and personhood, pours out into human hearts the eternal life of Love. "The Holy Spirit who is poured out in the sacramental celebration offers Christian couples the gift of a new communion of love that is the living and real image of that unique unity which makes of the Church the indivisible Mystical Body of the Lord Jesus" (FC 19). This gift of the Holy Spirit comes with his own personal characteristic which consists in being the seal of Love,[20] the most profound intimacy of the Father and Son, and at the same time a distinct Person, absolutely personal in his mode of loving.

The spouses reflect this mystery by the fact that they are indissolubly joined by the conjugal bond, thus becoming a temple of the Trinity. Life circulates between them like energy which runs through invisible lines of electrical waves. From this the conjugal dialogue is strengthened by an invisible, but very concrete "third," who animates their communion from within. That third is not extraneous to their love; rather he is its most intimate and hidden source who always keeps the hope of love alive. The ir-

19. John Paul II, *Letter to Families* 6.

20. Cf. Chapter 5 of this book, "The Holy Spirit, Seal of the Conjugal Covenant"; for the original Italian publication see M. Ouellet, "Lo Spirito Santo, sigillo dell'alleanza coniugale," R. Bonetti, ed., *Il matrimonio in Cristo è matrimonio nello Spirito* (Rome: Città Nuova, 1998), pp. 73-96.

ruption of the Holy Spirit in conjugal life marks, therefore, the beginning of a movement of Trinitarian love towards the depths of God the Father.

The Metamorphoses of an Unconditional Covenant

The Christian couple is brought to birth by the sacrament of Christ the Bridegroom and his Bride the Church, like a child who needs to learn how to walk and grow before reaching the great adventure of fatherhood and motherhood. Therefore, the Holy Spirit concentrates the initial grace of marriage on the communion of the I and the thou. Each discovers himself beyond his or her own self, and precisely in the other with whom he or she from now on forms a new unity. "Wishing to be one, Adam and Eve find that they are now three."[21] They are no longer two, but have already become a community in which the presence of God dwells. Christ abides with them, affirms *Gaudium et Spes*. The couple consecrated to Christ is therefore inserted in a new way in the life of the Son, precisely according to the modality of his spousal love for the Church, seeking to fulfill in him and with him the entire will of the Father for their love and life.

Thus a moment of filial growth in the life of the spouses emerges, comparable to the beginning of Jesus' public life when he was baptized, and then sent into the solitude of the desert to meditate on the mission he had received. In the same way, the newly married couple needs intimacy and space precisely to learn how to live together, to share everything, to dialogue often with one another in order to understand more deeply the other's mode of being, to accept the other as he is, and not only as he is dreamed of being. The first metamorphosis of the couple then marks the passage from being in love to really loving the person. Being in love always carries an element of illusion and the projection of one's own I. It is not exempt from a hidden egoism that emerges from the circumstances. By contrast, love accepts the other as she is, and not as the ideal person he would like her to be.[22] The Holy Spirit supports this passage from being in love to love itself, thus sustaining the mutual gift and fidelity of the spouses when their expectations may be different and sometimes disappointing. The

---

21. C. Massabki, *Le Christ rencontre de deux amours* (Paris, 1958), p. 105.

22. Cf. X. Lacroix, *Les mirages de l'amour* (Paris: Cerf, 1998), esp. Chapter 6, "De l'amour à l'alliance."

Spirit effects the passage from love of self in the other to love of the other for his own sake. He carries this growth forward maintaining the new couple in obedience to Jesus, who sought his way in the midst of temptations and provocations from the evil one.

A second metamorphosis of the conjugal covenant is described in *Familiaris Consortio* as follows: "conjugal love reaches that fullness to which it is interiorly ordained, conjugal charity, which is the proper and specific way in which the spouses participate in and are called to live the very charity of Christ who gave himself on the Cross" (13). The more the sanctifying Spirit takes possession of conjugal love, the more he progressively conforms it to its archetype: Christ's spousal love for the Church. He therefore moves the spouses to more fully welcome the divine-human love upon which their unity rests. Little by little the charity of Christ becomes the "form" of their love, with its characteristics of pure gratuity, proven fidelity, and perpetuity. The Holy Spirit teaches each of them to love the other person "for his own sake," but ever more in Christ and through Christ. This passage from love to theological charity presupposes a life of prayer, radical obedience to Christ, renunciation of self, patient listening to the other, and a readiness to begin again after difficult moments.

A third metamorphosis of love flows from the gift of children. The sincere gift of the spouses interiorly leads to their transcendence of self in service to the human and divine life of their children. While the spouses totally and respectfully give themselves to one another, "they become cooperators with God. . . . Thus the couple, while giving themselves to one another, give not just themselves but also the reality of children, who are a living reflection of their love, a permanent sign of conjugal unity and a living and inseparable synthesis of their being a father and a mother" (FC 14). This spiritual and physical fecundity in love entails the exigency of responsible fatherhood and motherhood, namely, the task of educating their children.[23] The arrival of children therefore introduces a new sacramental dynamic into the exchange of love between parents. Their love becomes paternal and maternal in the image of the heavenly Father, whose goodness they must represent to their children. This new dimension of love leads to a deeper discovery of the mystery of the Father and the mission entrusted to their love.[24] Christian fathers and mothers therefore receive

23. Cf. A. Mattheeuws, *Les "dons" du mariage*, pp. 520ff.
24. "'Honor your father and your mother,' because for you they are in a certain sense

from the Holy Sprit a new awareness of the "mission to guard, reveal and communicate love, and this is a living reflection of and a real sharing in God's love for humanity" (FC 17).

Fatherhood and Motherhood as an Experience of Spiritual Growth

By following the path the Holy Spirit offers them, believing parents experience a certain participation in divine paternity, through the experience of spiritual fatherhood and motherhood rooted in their faith in Christ, as well as that of physical parenthood brought about by the blessing of procreation. Christian spouses, consecrated to God in faith, are called to integrate their physical parenthood ever more deeply into their spiritual fatherhood and motherhood. Through sharing their daily lives with one another and educating their children, in such a way as to live their faith concretely, they not only share human values of the nation and culture with their children, but above all the treasure of faith. Thus they present their baby for Baptism, because the child of a sacramental marriage has an intrinsic right to it. The child was given to the couple by the Father in order to be given by them to his Son in faith. Since their children belong to Christ, parents learn to see Christ in them and to serve in such a way that he may grow in them. While they grow in the love of Christ, who is present in their children, fathers and mothers thus become ever more transparent to the Love of the Father for his Son.

The growth of children and their difficulties in life in turn directly affect the spiritual growth of fathers and mothers. The couple's commitment to family unity creates an environment for the human growth of their children, and in a particular way for their religious experience. In fact, the experience of a united family leads to an increase in joy and a sense of gratitude which is offered up to the Father in eucharistic thanksgiving. Children's lives, their development, and choices often lead their fathers

---

representatives of the Lord; they are the ones who gave you life, who introduced you to human existence in a particular family line, nation and culture. After God, they are your first benefactors. While God alone is good, indeed the Good itself, parents participate in this supreme goodness in a unique way. And so, honor your parents! *There is a certain analogy* here *with the worship owed to God*" (John Paul II, *Letter to Families* 15).

and mothers back to the Father, in prayers of praise, petition, and thanksgiving for the unexpectable and incalculable gift of his fruitfulness.

Through the course of family life lived in faith, the concerns of the parents become ever more essential. While they avoid interfering in a direct manner with the decisions of their adult children, prayer, sacrifice, and when possible, respectful dialogue intensify in order to sustain the weak, encourage the weary-hearted, and aid those who have fallen into the errors of the present age. Thus fathers and mothers reach a deeper level of interiority, where they are more united in the Spirit who extends the fruits of their communion not only to their children, but to the Christian community, in fact, to the whole Church. Their fatherhood and motherhood thus arrives at a greater spiritual maturity in service to Christ and the Church.

Very often in certain cases today, their growth is accompanied by the sign of the Cross, of disappointment, of unwarranted tragedies. How many parents must impose upon themselves a discipline of silence, of respect for the other's freedom, accepting the humiliation of their children who contradict the values transmitted in the family. It is here where the mystery of the Cross directly enters into play, the *kenosis* of the Son who emptied himself in utter abandonment, in order to allow himself to sense in his pierced heart the wounded love of the Father. In his image, fathers and mothers sense more painfully the problems of their sinful children; but even while intimately participating in their dramas, they allow them to remain free to make their own decisions and to suffer the consequences of their sins. The presence of Mary at the foot of the Cross then becomes the pillar of support and model of every spiritual motherhood and fatherhood in the domestic Church. Her "yes" to the Incarnation of the Word became a "yes" to the death of her divine Son. The fruit of this new "yes" was a new son, the beloved disciple (Jn. 19:26), who represents all of humanity. In the shadow of the Cross, Christian fathers and mothers therefore learn about the Cross's fruitfulness, which consecrated virgins have chosen for love of the Kingdom of heaven.

The Holy Family, Model of Readiness to Receive the Fecundity of the Heavenly Father

The holiness of fathers and mothers is not confined to the restricted circle of the family where divine grace purifies, sanctifies, and makes their love fecund. Union with the heavenly Father in obedience to Christ, Bridegroom of the Church, leads the couple and the family to transcend the limits of their home in order to radiate the light of the gospel in the Church and society. The spouses' availability for this extension of their fruitfulness receives powerful assistance from the intercession and contemplation of their unique model and archetype, the Holy Family.

The Holy Family as Model

More than a model, the Holy Family is the *original* domestic Church, as John Paul II maintains in his apostolic exhortation *Redemptoris Custos*.[25] In the first place, Mary and Joseph lived a real marriage, open to family and fulfilled according to the law of Moses. St. Augustine was the defender of the authentically human marriage of Mary and Joseph, which although lived in virginity, lacked none of the requisites for a true marriage: "In these parents of Christ all the goods of marriage were realized: offspring [*proles*], faithfulness [*fides*] and the bond [*sacramentum*]. We know there to be offspring, for there is the Lord Jesus himself; fidelity in that there was no adultery; and the bond because there was no divorce."[26]

Mary and Joseph expressed their "yes" to God in faith, handing themselves over totally to God in service to his will. Their mutual consent was blessed by God beyond every expectation. In the case of Mary, the initial "yes" to marriage was elevated to the highest degree by the grace of the Annunciation which defined her maternal mission in relation to the Son of God. Joseph's "yes" to marriage was marked by the "yes" of Mary, to whom he had to adapt his projects and responsibilities. Both consented before God to the mystery of their matrimonial vocation, but Joseph had to do so in dependence upon Mary, accepting God's plan for her and their family. Joseph therefore consented to the grace of the virginal relationship. Having to renounce his physical fecundity, he received a reinforcement of his paternal figure in order to fulfill the position of Jesus' putative father.[27]

It is relatively easy to imagine the personal enrichment of Mary and

---

25. John Paul II, *Redemptoris Custos* 7.

26. Augustine, *De nuptiis et concupiscentia* I.13.11 in PL 44.421.

27. Adrienne von Speyr, *Handmaid of the Lord,* trans. E. A. Nelson (San Francisco: Ignatius, 1985), p. 54.

Joseph, who were united to each other not only by bonds of human affection and obedience to the law of Moses, but above all by the gift of the incarnate Word. God chose them in advance to give them his Only Begotten Son, made flesh, so that they could give him to the world. In their daily family life, Mary and Joseph were taken up into the divine-human relationship that Jesus had with his heavenly Father. "Jesus, the God-man, united in himself forever, through the mystery of the Incarnation, the divine Trinity with that earthly trinity."[28] In the simplest experiences of their life of work, prayer, and conversation, Mary and Joseph were united to the Word of God made man; they contributed to educating him through the grace of a virginal fatherhood and motherhood.

Sacramental Fatherhood and Motherhood

The Holy Family did not live their predilection as a privilege, but rather as a mission of service for the salvation of the world. It is necessary to emphasize at this point, in the wake of John Paul II, the sacramental dimension of the relationships between the members of the Holy Family. The gift God made of himself to humanity in Jesus Christ passed through the authentic maternal mediation of Mary and, in a different way, the paternal mediation of Joseph. Since the maternal mediation is evident, we shall now focus on Joseph's paternity. "Inserted directly in the mystery of the Incarnation, the Family of Nazareth has its own special mystery. And in this mystery, as in the Incarnation, one finds a true fatherhood: the human form of the family of the Son of God, a true human family, formed by the divine mystery. In this family, Joseph is the father: his fatherhood is not one that derives from begetting offspring; but neither is it an 'apparent' or merely 'substitute' fatherhood. Rather, it is one that fully shares in authentic human fatherhood and the mission of a father in the family."[29]

The Pope sees this truth as a consequence of the hypostatic union: assuming the humanity of Jesus, the Word of God also assumes his constitutive relationships; hence the relationship with his mother and also, even if

---

28. T. Stramare, "Formulazione di una teologia attuale della Santa Famiglia," in *La Sacra Famiglia nei Primi XVI secoli della Chiesa: Atti del I Congresso sulla Sacra Famiglia* (Barcelona, 1993), p. 537.

29. John Paul II, *Redemptoris Custos* 21.

in a lesser degree, the relationship with his putative father. Thus, "Joseph's human fatherhood was also 'taken up' in the mystery of Christ's Incarnation. On the basis of this principle, the words which Mary spoke to the twelve-year-old Jesus in the Temple take on their full significance: '*Your father and I . . .* have been looking for you.'"[30] At this point we must take note of Joseph's individual relationship with the heavenly Father, who chose him to give a paternal face to the human growth of his incarnate Son. "Joseph is the man with whom God the Father, in a certain way, shared his own fatherhood."[31] Between the Father in heaven and the one on earth there is a sort of "covenant in paternity, in which Joseph took a greater part than Abraham."[32] Joseph's intimate relationship with the heavenly Father may be understood as a "model" or "role," but John Paul II in his previously cited homily takes up the language of "covenant" and "participation."

The heavenly Father gave the child Jesus to the Holy Family of Nazareth as one of the stages in his gift to the Church and to all of humanity. He continues to give this child to Christian families, above all through the sacrament of baptism, which generates his Son in the members of his Body. Jesus therefore lives in them and asks to grow with the help of the father and mother of the family, until he reaches the stature of being the perfect man. What Joseph and Mary lived is prolonged, therefore, in the family, the domestic Church. The daily relationships between parents and their children contain a "great mystery," the mystery of a spiritual fatherhood and motherhood in relation to the children they receive from the Father, who are brothers and sisters of the Only Begotten Son. In each of them, the heavenly Father sees his own Son and asks that they give a human face, hence, sacramental, to his love for the Son living in them. On the other hand, the children perceive in the fully human love of their father and mother, the beating heart of the eternal Father. Thus, they are awakened to the mystery of the Son who grows in them, and they learn to recognize the "gift of God" in the sacramental heart of their father and mother.

---

30. John Paul II, *Redemptoris Custos* 21.
31. John Paul II, Homily of October 9, 1994.
32. John Paul II, Homily of March 19, 1984.

The Mystery of Christian Fecundity

Fathers and mothers, may you be perfect as your heavenly Father is perfect! We considered the sanctity of Christian marriage as an authentic participation in the fecundity of God himself in Christ. This participation is not received by two individuals, but by virtue of the consecration of their conjugal bond, it is received by a new community, by an *"I-thou"* which has become a *"subjective-objective we."* This *"we of love"* is from this point onwards founded on faith, that is, grace. Adrienne von Speyr explains that "all of this occurs simply and solely as a result of the first Yes they said to one another in God, and in which they mutually abandon and leave each other to God. And the mystery of the natural as of the supernatural fruitfulness of Christian marriage is grounded in that mutual yes, given in God."[33] According to von Speyr, the specificity of marital fruitfulness is rooted in the sanctification of conjugal love, which generates a total openness in faith and without reserve to the fruitfulness that God wishes to share with the couple. "The grace of marriage is, of course, primarily the sanctification of the life of married people, for it bestows what the one possesses on the other, and makes it fruitful for him. The faith and love and sacrifice of one sanctifies both."[34] The sanctification that flows from the initial yes of the couple includes the yes to children, not as a result of chance of their interpersonal love, but as a gift of grace, for their love was consecrated to God in faith. Love and its fruit, spiritual and/or corporal, are therefore gifts of God to be received with grateful joy.

"The mutual love of husband and wife," continues Adrienne von Speyr, "is on the one hand so wide that God alone can fill it, and on the other side so much the gift of grace that it bears with it the promise of fruitfulness, a promise which in fact remains entirely with God and is not in the hands of the parents."[35] Accordingly, the logic of the gift demands an attitude of openness and availability on the part of the couple, which does not "calculate" children. To calculate children, to exclude them *a priori* (contraception) or to think of them as a right (artificial insemination), makes no sense to Christian spouses who live in grace: "Children are an

---

33. Adrienne von Speyr, *The Word: A Meditation on the Prologue to St. John's Gospel* (New York: David McKay, 1953), p. 99.

34. A. von Speyr, *The Word*, p. 99.

35. A. von Speyr, *The Word*, p. 100.

expression of freedom of fruitfulness and are therefore a symbol of the Holy Spirit."[36] The fulfillment of the promise of fecundity included in their love is therefore left to God and to the freedom of his grace: "Every Christian marriage is blessed by God and is fruitful in him, whether through the blessing of children, or the blessing of sacrifice. If God chooses the second alternative, the spiritual fruitfulness of marriage is increased and widened out invisibly so that it flows into the whole community."[37] In this case, the fruitfulness of the spouses approaches, by way of sacrifice, the supernatural fruitfulness of virgins.

The act of faith that consecrates conjugal love to Christ receives, therefore, a participation in the fecundity of the sacrifice of the Cross, source and model of every fruitfulness, direct form of the fecundity of virgins, and indirect form of the fecundity of the married couple. Balthasar writes: "*This gift of self in life and death is not unlike the ineradicable, eternal vow that is immanent in all love;* it is an act of such finality that it resembles a true 'loss of [one's] own soul' (Mt. 16:25). Only because the soul has sacrificed the right to dispose of its life as it wills can the right so to dispose of the body also be sacrificed: 'The wife has not authority over her body, but the husband; the husband likewise has not authority over his body, but the wife' (I Cor. 7:4)."[38] Through this greatest possible gift the spouses likewise become "cooperators with God for giving life to a new human person" (FC 14). The child is not simply the result of their "natural" love, but the fruit of their dedication to God in faith, which God blesses with the gift of a child or with the gift of supernatural fruitfulness.

Familiaris Consortio strongly affirms that "marriage and virginity or celibacy are two ways of expressing and living the one mystery of the covenant of God with His people" (FC 16). "Either one is, in its own proper form, an actuation of the most profound truth of man, of his being 'created in the image of God'" (FC 11). Fathers and mothers perfect their likeness to God the Father in cultivating filial openness towards him and, thus, the availability to welcome every form of fruitfulness that he would like to share with them. As they grow in their relationships of love together with their children and within the unity of the Church, "they increasingly fur-

---

36. A. von Speyr, *The Word*, p. 100.

37. A. von Speyr, *The Word*, p. 101.

38. H. U. von Balthasar, *The Christian State of Life*, trans. Sister Mary Frances McCarthy (San Francisco: Ignatius, 1983), p. 245.

ther their own perfection and their mutual sanctification, and together they render glory to God" (GS 48).

Conclusion

Concluding this discussion of Trinitarian sanctity for Christian spouses, we can synthesize the characteristic features of conjugal and family spirituality in the following terms: the path to holiness for fathers and mothers of families is a journey of filial and spousal love founded on faith and sustained by the Holy Spirit, seal and source of their love. With burning gratitude for their love, the spouses follow Christ the Bridegroom and the Church his Bride, who are united to one another in the obedience of the Cross. Participating in Christ's spousal love for the Church, they live a mystery of fecundity marked by their spiritual and corporal availability to the incommensurable fruitfulness of the heavenly Father; but before all else, every day they fall to their knees "before the Father, from whom every fatherhood, in heaven or on earth, takes its name" (Eph. 3:14).

In addition, it can also be observed that the sanctity of fathers and mothers is a gift of grace that pervades their relationships, making them sacramental based on the model of the Holy Family, well beyond the awareness they may have of it. The most important thing to married couples on their way to sanctity is the consciousness, nourished by prayer, of the "mystery" of their life, and not so much an emphasis on their rights and duties. In the daily relationships of love in the family, the interlacing Trinitarian relations of fatherhood, sonship, and fruitful unity, which constitute Trinitarian holiness, shine forth. The incarnate Word, shaped by the Holy Spirit through the hands of Mary and Joseph, brought forth this mystery in our midst and made possible the sacramental encounter between the Trinity in heaven and that on earth, the family, icon of the Most High.

All families are blessed by this sacramental mystery, including those who, due to the need for evangelization, have yet to know the secret hidden in their relationship and the transcendent destiny of their life. Even religious families founded on virginal consecration give witness to it in a diverse, but complementary way: the fruitfulness of their sacrifice and the fraternal communion of their relationships make already visible the eschatological fulfillment of human love in the Glory of Trinitarian Love. "By virtue of this witness, virginity or celibacy keeps alive in the Church a consciousness of the mystery of marriage and defends it from any reduction and impoverishment" (FC 16).

"Why should the 'fatherly' love of Joseph not have had an influence upon the 'filial' love of Jesus? And vice versa, why should the 'filial' love of Jesus not have had an influence upon the 'fatherly' love of Joseph, thus leading to a further deepening of their unique relationship? Those souls most sensitive to the impulses of divine love have rightly seen in Joseph a brilliant example of the interior life. Furthermore, in Joseph, the apparent tension between the active and the contemplative life finds an ideal harmony that is only possible for those who possess the perfection of charity."[39]

39. John Paul II, *Redemptoris Custos* 26.

CHAPTER VII

Christian Marriage, Sin, and Conversion

The meaning of sin in conjugal and family life should be measured beginning from the "goods" that the institution has received in God's plan. Among these, St. Augustine identifies three of primary importance, and they have been retained as common doctrine until this day: procreation *(proles)*, faithfulness *(fides)* and sacrament *(sacramentum)*.[1] Of these three, moral theology has reflected at length on the first two, while the third, despite being supernatural in order, has been too strictly limited to the juridical indissolubility of the matrimonial contract. To a large extent, the importance of this good, which is a gift from Christ, still remains to be discovered. Clearly, a theology considering sin cannot ignore it.

If sin essentially consists of an act which breaks the personal relationship with God, the sin of Christian spouses violates the covenant relationship with God who has blessed them and established them in unity. Just as original sin is measured from the starting point of the gift of original justice, the sin of Christian spouses is measured from the starting point of the gift of the sacrament. Here we should develop the direction Saint Thomas Aquinas takes in the *Summa Theologica* in affirming the superiority of the sacrament over the two other marriage goods.[2] This perspective invites a

---

1. Augustine, *De bono conjug.* 32, Patrologia Latina 40, p. 394; cf. P. Adnès, *Le mariage* (Paris: Desclée, 1963), pp. 55-58; Lorenzo Dattrino, *Il matrimonio secondo Agostino* (Milan: Ed. Ares, 1995).

2. *Suppl.*, q. 49, a. 3.: "Now inseparability, which pertains to the sacrament, is placed in

reflection on the theological and spiritual implications of sacramental marriage in so far as it indissolubly ties the Christian couple to the nuptial mystery of Christ and the Church.

The goal of our study is to deepen the understanding of this relationship and to bring to light the way in which the reality of sin in the life of a couple flows, primarily, from refusal of the sacrament. This point has hardly been developed at all by moral theology or by spirituality, both of which concentrate above all on the couple's relationship to moral law or to the general laws of the spiritual life.[3] Here, we will consider things from a dogmatic viewpoint, beginning with the vocation to love that flows from the grace of the sacrament of marriage; then we will see how sin acts against the good or the "gift"[4] of the sacrament; and finally we will conclude with the conversion of the spouses to the "gift" of marriage's sacramental fecundity.

The Vocation of Christian Spouses to Sacramental Love

In the Beginning Was the Gift

The Dogmatic Constitution *Lumen Gentium* clearly affirmed the vocation of spouses to holiness in marriage: "Finally, in virtue of the sacrament of Matrimony by which they signify and share in (cf. Eph. 5:32) the mystery of the unity and fruitful love between Christ and the Church, Christian married couples help one another to attain holiness in their married life and in accepting and educating their children. Hence by reason of their state of life and of their position they have their own gifts among the People of God."[5]

---

the definition of marriage (Q. 44, A. 3), while offspring and faith are not. Therefore among the other goods sacrament is the most essential to matrimony"; furthermore, "*offspring* and *faith* pertain to matrimony as directed to an office of human nature, whereas *sacrament* pertains to it as instituted by God."

3. Cf. Pierre Gervais, "Péché — Pécheur, II. Réflexion théologique et spirituelle," *Dictionnaire de Spiritualité,* vol. XII, pp. 815-53.

4. Cf. Alain Mattheeuws, *Les "dons du marriage": Recherche de théologie morale et sacramentelle* (Brussels: Culture et Vérité, 1996).

5. *Lumen Gentium* 11. A note is added referring to 1 Cor. 7:7 to underline that the spouses' charism is to be found in conjugal chastity as distinguished from continency: "Unusquisque proprium donum (idion charisma) habet ex Deo: alius quidem sic, alius vero sic." Cf. Augustine, *De Dono Persever.* 14.37, PL 45, p. 1015: "Non tantum continentia Dei donum est, sed coniugatorum etiam castitas."

The specific gift of Christian spouses lies in the "community of life and love" that is built upon the couple's covenant, that is to say, on their irrevocable personal consent (GS 48). By this solemn act of faith, the spouses mutually give themselves and receive one another and enter together into a new relationship with the Creator and Redeemer God, the Author and the ultimate guarantee of their covenant. The spouses' vocation to love is therefore rooted in this sacramental gift which takes up and transforms their natural love into a sacramental love. Vatican II teaches that "authentic married love is caught up into divine love" by the grace of the sacramental consecration that penetrates their life of faith, hope and charity so that they sanctify each other and together give glory to God.[6]

The spouses' vocation to sacramental love does not spring simply from a restoration of the grace lost at the origin; or from the remedy for concupiscence that the nuptial blessing brings. Nor is their vocation exhausted in a generous procreative cooperation in service of life. This vocation incorporates the spouses into the mission of Christ and the Church because their community of life and love participates in the nuptial mystery that unites Christ and the Church. This participation began on the day when they exchanged their love "in the Lord," receiving one another from him, and consecrating themselves together to him, for the service of his glory. From the day of their matrimonial consecration, Christian spouses are put, and put themselves, at the service of Christ, the Bridegroom of the Church, original sacrament of Trinitarian Love.

God's plan for sacramental marriage and the family, consequently, embraces the whole spectrum of tension that spans from the original creation to the definitive fulfillment brought by Christ. The Book of Genesis teaches that in the beginning man was made man and woman in God's image, and that the man shall leave his father and mother to join himself to his wife, and the two shall be one flesh (1:27, 2:24). This plan was disrupted by the sin of the first couple, but was not destroyed. The author of Genesis 3, with the story of the Fall and its consequences, allows us to catch a glimpse of the victory of the woman's offspring over the serpent's. This offspring is Jesus, who allows himself to abolish divorce because he himself offers both the remedy to "hardness of heart" and the grace of an absolute faithfulness to the new Covenant, which he establishes in his own Person. Starting from this sacramental gift, marriage and conjugal love are pro-

6. *Gaudium et Spes* 48.2.

moted to the dignity of a truly supernatural vocation that transcends the functions and duties of the order of creation, while at the same time fulfilling them.

The Gift of the Sacrament and the Ecclesial Mission of Spouses

The broadening and deepening of the supernatural mission of spouses are well demonstrated in the apostolic exhortation *Familiaris Consortio,* which underlines the gift of the Holy Spirit as the rule of spousal communion: "the Holy Spirit who is poured out in the sacramental celebration offers Christian couples the gift of a new communion of love that is the living and real image of that unique unity which makes of the Church the indivisible Mystical Body of the Lord Jesus." This new communion is not imposed from without on a human relationship that might be more or less fragile; it embraces the very impulse of the spouses towards one another, while respecting and promoting all of this momentum's dynamism: "The gift of the Spirit is a commandment of life for Christian spouses and at the same time a stimulating impulse so that every day they may progress towards an ever richer union with each other on all levels — of the body, of the character, of the heart, of the intelligence and will, of the soul — revealing in this way to the Church and to the world the new communion of love, given by the grace of Christ."[7]

Here it is useful to dwell upon the particular form of this gift of the Holy Spirit, which enriches the conjugal communion in such a singular way. Theological reflection distinguishes between two distinct but closely associated dimensions of the particular gift of the spouses. One objective dimension consists essentially in posing the divine seal on the conjugal bond.[8] Constituted by the exchange of vows, the conjugal bond, bound together by the Holy Spirit, sets a divine seal on the spouses' act of total and irreversible gift. It constitutes the first dimension of the sacrament, which allows the couple to represent and reproduce the mystery of nuptial union of Christ and the Church, even in their carnal union. Although the conjugal bond is constituted by the spouses' subjective act, once concluded and

---

7. John Paul II, *Familiaris Consortio* 19.

8. Cf. Louis Ligier, *Il Matrimonio: Questioni teologiche e pastorali* (Rome: Città Nuova, 1988), p. 114.

consummated in the flesh, it no longer depends on the spouses' subjective fluctuations; it is sealed by God, because the gift of the Holy Spirit has objectively rendered the spouses participants in the indissoluble relationship of Christ and the Church. This is the reason for the absolute indissolubility of sacramental marriage *ratum et consumatum,* which even the Roman Pontiff cannot dissolve.[9]

If the conjugal bond is the first effect of the sacrament *(res et sacramentum),* the gift of new communion in the Holy Spirit also brings with it a subjective dimension that touches the spouses' community of daily life and love from within. The Council of Trent already affirmed that the grace of the sacrament perfected natural love from within, confirmed its indissolubility and sanctified the spouses.[10] The description of its grace was thereafter made explicit in terms of healing, elevating and perfecting the spouses' love with a view to accomplishing their specific mission. Therefore, this broader and more widespread effect of grace embraces the spouses' whole life and renders them able to form a true community of persons, that is to say, to "guard, reveal and communicate love, and this is a living reflection of and a real sharing in God's love for humanity and the love of Christ the Lord for the Church His bride."[11]

The Horizon of Serving God in the Communio Personarum

As we have underlined elsewhere, the Holy Spirit is the great craftsman of this sanctification of conjugal love.[12] He transmits to the spouses something of his own way of being communion of Persons. Having taken possession of their love by the seal of the conjugal bond, he becomes the interior Master of their love, he teaches them to savor the joy of communion in a deeper and purer way; he invites them to love one another with his own love, which effaces itself, gently and sincerely, to leave to the other the pri-

9. Code of Canon Law, 1141.

10. "Gratia vero, quae naturalem illum amorem perficeret, et indissolubilem unitatem confirmaret, coniugesque sanctificaret, ipse Christus, venerabilium sacramentorum institutor atque perfector, sua nobis passione promeruit," DS 1799.

11. John Paul II, *Familiaris Consortio* 17.

12. Marc Ouellet, "Lo Spirito Santo, sigillo dell'alleanza coniugale," R. Bonetti, ed., *Il matrimonio in Cristo è matrimonio nello Spirito* (Rome: Città Nuova, 1998), pp. 73-96. The English translation of this essay is included as Chapter 5 of this book.

macy of gift or of welcome. In difficult times he patiently achieves the conversion of their hearts through the suffering of humiliation and reconciliation after sin; in all circumstances, he teaches prayer as the starting point of life, for the growth and the holiness of those persons called to sacramental love.

This description of the sacramental grace of marriage allows us to catch a glimpse of the fact that the spouses' mission goes far beyond the natural order of procreation and education of children. A certain classic representation of this grace tended to describe it exclusively in function of nature, emphasizing the perfection of nature and its ends as all there is to say about sacramental marriage. However, Vatican II underlined more the personal dimension of the sacrament and of conjugal love. It expressed sacramental grace in terms of an encounter with Christ and a consecration in the Holy Spirit: ". . . so our Savior, the spouse of the Church, now encounters Christian spouses through the sacrament of marriage. He abides with them. . . ."[13]

This more Christocentric and personalistic vision of this grace brings about a change in perspective which allows a deeper understanding of the spouses' relationship with God. Since the event of their sacramental marriage, Christian spouses are incorporated into the mission of the Holy Spirit, who not only perfects their natural love, but introduces them into the eschatological love that unites Christ and the Church: "Conjugal love reaches that fullness to which it is interiorly ordained: conjugal charity, which is the proper and specific way in which the spouses participate in and are called to live the very charity of Christ who gave Himself on the Cross."[14] Consequently, conjugal love is assumed and entered into by Christ's love, who incorporates it within, and in the service of, his own spousal gift for the Church. A perspective such as this underlines the personal character of this grace, the dramatic interplay of the divine Persons who come to the spouses' encounter, who bless them with their Presence, and who commit them to serving and giving glory to God through dwelling in the temple of their divine Communion.

---

13. *Gaudium et Spes* 48.2; cf. G. Baldanza, *La grazia del sacramento del matrimonio* (Rome: Edizioni Liturgiche, 1993), pp. 161-303.

14. John Paul II, *Familiaris Consortio* 13.

The Sin against the Sacrament of Marriage

"'So they are no longer two, but one. What therefore God has joined together let no man put asunder." They said to him, "Why then did Moses command one to give a certificate of divorce, and to put her away?" He said to them, "For your hardness of heart Moses allowed you to divorce your wives, but from the beginning it was not so." (Mt. 19:6-8)

When Christ denounces the "hardheartedness" of the sons of Israel and restores the marriage wanted in the beginning by the Creator, he does more in affirming the indissolubility of the conjugal bond than to exclude divorce; he poses the foundations for the elevation of marriage to the dignity of "a real symbol of that new and eternal covenant sanctioned in the blood of Christ. The Spirit which the Lord pours forth gives a new heart, and renders man and woman capable of loving one another as Christ has loved us."[15] Refusal of this gift constitutes the sin of Christian spouses, to the point of determining the quality of all their ethical choices. It is necessary to grasp the nature and extent of this in the light of the biblical conception of sin.

The First Couple's Sin, Archetype of Refusal of the Covenant

For the Bible, as Lyonnet explains, what happened at the beginning of history proposes a meaning for this history itself. Through the description of the first couple's sin, clearly presented as a prototype of all others, the Bible particularly means to reveal the true nature of sin.[16] This appears first of all as a conscious and voluntary violation of a precept given by God and accompanied by a punishment: "of the tree of the knowledge of good and evil you are not to eat, for on the day you eat of it you shall most surely die" (Gen. 2:17). However, the sinful character of the external act is seen above all in the interior attitude which is at its origin: "before provoking the act, the sin corrupted the spirit. As Christ reminds us, sin is 'within, in man's heart' (Mk. 7:21)."[17]

---

15. John Paul II, *Familiaris Consortio* 13.

16. Stanislas Lyonnet, "Péché-Pécheur," *Dictionnaire de Spiritualité*, vol. XII.1 (Paris: Beauchesne, 1984), pp. 790-815 (here 791); Cf. G. Quell, *Peccato*, GLNT 1 (Brescia, 1965), pp. 755-69.

17. Lyonnet, "Péché-Pécheur," p. 791.

The origin of the sin committed by the woman and then by the man, at the instigation of the Tempter, is "greed" for a privilege considered as being divine: they wanted to be "like gods who know good and evil" (Gen. 3:5), that is, according to the most common interpretation, "to make themselves judges of good and evil" (Gen. 3:22), or at least to "purport to conquer what they could only receive."[18] Von Balthasar comments, taking his inspiration from George Bernanos, that "the sin of Eve in paradise and of all her guilty children: (is) curiosity, or, expressed in a more theological way, knowledge without love . . . the forced anticipation of the vision God wants to bestow through grace but into which impatient man bites as he bit into the forbidden apple."[19] This greed, which for Saint Paul sums up all sins (Rom. 7:7-11), disregards the primacy of the Covenant relationship offered freely by God. "Sin means refusing Yahweh as Lord of the Covenant, and it has its clearest form in idolatry, the first sin forbidden by the Decalogue, of which the prophets often accused the people and which is sometimes considered to be the origin of all sins (Ex. 20:3, Amos 2:4ff., Wis. 14:22-31, Rom. 1:18-32)."[20]

In likening greed to idolatry, the Bible reveals, in fact, the lack of "faith" that corrupts man's relationship to God: "Doubting at the same time in His love and in His truth, man stops 'believing' in God, that is, in the biblical sense we find throughout the Old Testament, of 'trusting' him, of 'becoming steadfast in him.'"[21] Unfaithfulness to the covenant, which constitutes the essence of sin, is the people of Israel's lack of faith: "evil arises precisely at the point where this God seems insufficient to Israel, which therefore turns away from him to look for other gods. Evil *is* this very act of turning away."[22] This is illustrated by the episode of the golden calf at the foot of Mount Sinai, which is erected at the very moment when the covenant is concluded. From this point, the Yahwist retrospectively interprets the whole of historical man: "Adam, placed in the state of original grace, at once renounces obedience, in order to create for himself a rela-

18. Lyonnet, "Péché-Pécheur," p. 791; cf. Jerusalem Bible on Gen. 3:22.

19. H. U. von Balthasar, *Bernanos: An Ecclesial Existence* (San Francisco: Ignatius, 1996), p. 139.

20. Piet Schoonenberg, "Peccato e Colpa," *Sacramentum Mundi*, vol. IV, p. 221.

21. Lyonnet, "Péché-Pécheur," p. 791; also J. Pedersen, "The Breaking of the Covenant is the Quintessence of Sin," cited by G. Quell, *Peccato*, p. 744.

22. Hans Urs von Balthasar, *Glory of the Lord*, vol. VI: *Theology: The Old Covenant* (Edinburgh: T&T Clark, 1990), p. 216.

tionship to God after his own liking in 'eating and drinking and playing,' outside the grace and space given him by God."[23]

The first human couple's disobedience therefore appears as an act of unfaithfulness and ingratitude which provokes divine disapproval, there where a relationship of election had existed. From this comes the symbolism of God the Bridegroom, betrayed and abandoned by his unfaithful bride, which is so central to the prophets. Moreover, the offense need not be directly against him; to provoke the anger of the jealous God it is enough that it touch those whom God loves. David, an adulterer and a murderer, learned this from Nathan, who denounced his sin: by striking down Uriah the Hittite, David "disregarded" not only the word of Yahweh but "Yahweh himself"; he "sinned against Yahweh" (2 Sam. 12:13). God forgave David's fault but the child died as a sign of divine reprobation. In fact, sin separates man from God and expels him from the paradise of familiarity with him (Gen. 3:8-24); it deprives man of the divine love that made the man and woman "one flesh" (Gen. 2:24). It is not surprising, therefore, that the man himself breaks this unity by placing on the woman the responsibility for his own disobedience: "It was the woman you put with me; she gave me the fruit, and I ate it" (Gen. 3:12).

With Saint Paul, theological reflection on original sin was forced to deepen its understanding of the solidarity of all human beings in Adam, in the light of the solidarity of salvation "in Christ." The apostle began this reflection in chapter 5 of the letter to the Romans: "as by one man's disobedience many were made sinners, so by one man's obedience many will be made righteous" (v. 19). In this light, Saint Thomas clarifies on the essence of the first sin: it is a fault of disobedience by pride, which has mortally corrupted nature itself in diverting it from its ultimate end by a vain self-love. This is why, according to him, original sin, transmitted to all the descendants of Adam, essentially consists of "the absence of original justice"; this was lost because Adam and Eve turned away from God *(aversio a Deo)* in wildly coveting the created good that God had made available to them *(conversio ad creaturas)*.[24] Christ paid the ransom of Adam's sin through the merits of his redeeming obedience, which poured forth divine mercy on

---

23. Balthasar, *Glory of the Lord,* VI, p. 217.

24. Thomas Aquinas, *ST* Ia-IIae, qu. 82, art. 3; IIa-IIae, qu. 163-164; De Malo, qu. 4, art. 2; cf. R. Bernard, *"Le Péché originel": Notes doctrinales thomistes* (Desclée: Ed. de la Revue des Jeunes, 1995), pp. 340ff.

all of humankind and, by the gift of sanctifying grace, re-established the Covenant relationship on a level well beyond original justice.

Another important aspect of the first couple's sin is the loss of the "mediation of grace for others."[25] God's original plan included, with the gift of life, the transmission of the free gift of original justice. This is what John Paul II calls the "primordial sacrament."[26] The loss of this grace provoked the undoing of humanity's unity: Origen was able to say *"Ubi peccata, ibi multitudo,"*[27] describing original sin as separation and division, while God wanted everything to contribute to the unity of humankind. The first couple was only able to keep the commandment of procreation, but a procreation which was now deprived of the gift of original justice offered by God. From that point onwards, as the Fathers of the Church would say, they participate in giving God's "image" to their children but no longer in giving "likeness" with God. Christ would re-establish the sacramental mediation of grace in the life of the couple, but without restoring at the same time the privilege of original justice. The children of Christian spouses are born with the same want as all the other descendants of Adam. It is by faith and by baptism, thus through a personal action by Christ, that they receive the grace of divine filiation. This passage through the sacrament brings out the eminently personal character of grace. Furthermore, it is appropriate that God's personal commitment in Christ invites in reply a personal act of faith which is expressed in the action of the Church's action of bringing its children to baptism.

This rapid overview of the origins of sin can be concluded in affirming that sin shows itself above all as an absence of "fear of God" according to the fullest sense of this concept in the Bible, an absence which affects God and offends him in his love. Therefore, sin is first of all an "act against

25. Cf. Luis Ladaria, *Antropologia teologica* (Rome: PUG, 1983), pp. 245-46: "El pecado no es solo un alejamiento personal de Dios, sino también una ruptura de la mediaciòn de gracia para los demàs" (p. 246).

26. John Paul II, *The Theology of the Body* (Boston: Pauline, 1997), pp. 327ff.: "[I]t (marriage) should serve not only to prolong the work of creation. That is, of procreation. It should also serve to extend to further generations of men the same sacrament of creation, that is, the supernatural fruits of man's eternal election on the part of the Father in the eternal Son — those fruits which man was endowed with by God in the very act of creation" (p. 336).

27. Origen, *Homily 9 on Ezekiel*, n. 1 : *Ubi peccata sunt, ibi multitudo, ibi schismata, ibi haereses, ibi dissensiones. Ubi autem virtus, ibi singularitas, ibi unio, ex quo omnium credentium erat cor unum et anima una."*

God" (Ps. 51:5-6), which David recognizes in the psalm *Miserere;* it is "the breakdown of a personal relationship between man and God and not simply a violation of a moral or social order; a breakdown which destroys communion with God and, consequently, surrenders man to himself, abandoned to his own strength."[28] Furthermore, it is not enough that man asks to be healed, but as the New Testament says it is necessary that he "be reconciled to God" (2 Cor. 5:20). This means that he must renounce all "self-sufficiency" and, like Job, experience a "broken heart," recognize his inability to love, and suffer from it. Then God can make things new, "create a new heart."

Jesus' Reply to the Hardness of Heart That Destroys the Conjugal Relationship

Jesus' reply to the wretchedness of the sinner essentially concerns the restoration of his relationship with God and with his neighbor, because, as Saint Maximus writes, "the devil, man's tempter from the beginning, had separated him in his will from God, had separated men from each other. . . ."[29] By his life, death, and resurrection, Jesus eradicates the sinner's separation from God, in paying the price of the purification of heart that divine friendship, the unity of the couple and the unity of humankind all require. Jesus is the unique mediator of the New Covenant. His teaching, actions, and sacrifice throw new light on sin and on the mystery of iniquity that has bloodied human history. Here we shall first of all set out some of the more general aspects, before presenting Jesus' reply to the hardness of heart that had justified the Israelites' practice of repudiation.

Sin and Forgiveness in Jesus' Mission   St. Luke, in chapter 15 of his Gospel, perfectly expresses what Jesus meant by sin: "sin is to leave the father's house, it is to live without God and far from God, be it in the joys or in the trials of this world."[30] It is important to note here that sin is not only an act but also a state and condition of living without relationship to God. In go-

---

28. S. Lyonnet, "Péché-Pécheur," p. 802.
29. Maximus the Confessor, *Epist.* 2 (PG 91, 396-7); cited in H. de Lubac, *Catholicism* (San Francisco: Ignatius, 1988), p. 35.
30. W. Grundmann, "Peccato," *GLNT,* vol. I (Brescia: Paideia, 1965), p. 820.

ing far from the father's house, the sinner turns away from God's presence and doubly alienates himself by living a dissolute life. He loses familiarity with the Father, which immediately leads to the clouding of his filial identity. "The sinner is he who contests God's absolute authority over life, in refusing him complete love and obedience (cf. Rom. 12:1 ff., 1 Cor 1:19ff.)."[31]

The goal of Jesus' preaching was to place the sinner in front of the full reality of God and to make perfect communion with him possible. Announcing the forgiveness and mercy of the Father was aimed at this goal which concerned all mankind, that is to say not only the "sinners" but also the "righteous"; the righteous needed to be purified of their own justice and their self-centered and overly self-assured devotion. Christ's message was of such novelty that it provoked astonishment and even outrage. The deep reason for this outrage was that he confronted his listeners not only with the challenge of a moral conversion but also with the challenge of an unconditional adherence to his own Person. This adherence, called "faith," allowed the disciples to participate not only in a new wisdom, but also in the coming of God's Kingdom in history.

Grundmann writes that "the forgiveness proclaimed and practiced by Jesus is not something particularly self-evident, but always an extraordinary event; it constitutes a triumph over sin and then, consequently, the sudden emergence of the Kingdom of God; it is, therefore, an eschatological event. This is particularly clear at the Last Supper."[32] Effectively, Jesus reveals that he is conscious of giving up his life for the salvation of the multitude, and declares explicitly that he will not drink wine until he drinks the new wine in the Kingdom of God, in the company of the saints (Lk. 22:18). Origen comments that he "will drink it again in the future when all things shall have been made subject to him, when all have been saved and when with the abolition of the death of sin it will no longer be necessary for him to offer sacrifice for sin."[33] "The decisive element in the New Testament message is to be found in its eschatological vision of history: Christ, in winning the victory over death, has inaugurated a new world; sin (the reality which, in each person, shapes the present world) signifies rebellion against God; the meaning of redemption lies in the forgiveness of sins." "All of this characterizes the New Testament and distin-

31. K. H. Rengstorff, *"Peccatore,"* in *GLNT,* vol. I, p. 903.
32. W. Grundmann, "Peccato," p. 823.
33. Origen, *Homily 7 on Leviticus,* n. 2 (text cited by H. de Lubac, *Catholicism,* p. 399).

guishes it from Hellenism and Judaism; understanding this means understanding the Christ-Event."[34]

The characteristic features of sin that we have observed in the Old Testament are present in the New Testament, but radical and even more personal. Indifference to God (Rom. 1:21) is not merely perceived as an offense against divine majesty, but as an active hostility and an open resistance by man who wants to live for himself and be master of himself. St. Paul lambasts the sin of the Jews as self-trust, finding one's own justification in the fact of being able to observe the law. This is the sin of self-justification, "the will to link salvation to oneself, to one's own performance or honor, rather than receive it as a gift from God."[35] In Paul, the sinner rejects neither precept of man nor one of God, but rejects "God himself who gives . . . his Holy Spirit" (1 Thess. 4:8-9; Rom. 8:4).[36]

In St. John the same eschatological tension accompanies the choice and the division of those who are for or against Jesus. "The word 'sin' no longer designates, as is the case in the synoptic catechesis, a sinful act, but rather the mysterious reality that engenders it: a powerful hostility to God and to his Kingdom."[37] Sin is certainly "violation of the law" (1 Jn. 3:4), refusal of the word of truth (Jn. 15:21-22, 16:9), but it is above all "hate towards God" (Jn. 9:41, 8:44, 5:16). Jesus is he who "takes away the sin of the world" (Jn. 1:29); he triumphs over it by the word of truth and by way of his sacrifice which atones for sin and frees from its slavery (Jn. 8:34), in baptizing in the Holy Spirit (Jn. 1:33) and in giving his Trinitarian love (Jn. 13:34). In the Johannine letters the characteristic feature of the Antichrist is that he denies the incarnation of Trinitarian love; this is apostasy, mystery of iniquity, the supreme sign of sin within the Church (1 Jn. 2:18-25, 4:2-3, 5:10-12).

Thus, the whole New Testament turns on Jesus' mission, which is essentially to win the victory over sin in the flesh, so as to reconcile the world with God and make man free from sin and alive for God. The letter to the Hebrews presents him as the merciful High Priest who atones for sin (Heb. 5:1), he who is "without sin" (4:15) and "separated from sinners" (7:26) but who "offered himself in an eternal spirit" (9:26-28) for the forgiveness of

---

34. W. Grundmann, "Peccato," p. 862.
35. H. Schlier, *Linee fondamentali di una teologia paolina* (Queriniana, 1985), p. 65.
36. S. Lyonnet, "Péché-Pécheur," p. 812.
37. S. Lyonnet, "Péché-Pécheur," p. 808.

sins. Saint Paul underlines the importance of his death that atones "once and for all" (Rom. 6:10; 1 Cor. 15:3; Gal. 1:4); he became sin (2 Cor. 5:21) for us, propitiary victim by his own blood (Rom. 3:25); in this way God wanted to show his justice in raising him from among the dead and in making of him our justification through faith (1 Cor. 15:17).

"You Shall Not Commit Adultery"   When Jesus speaks to the pharisees in order to re-establish purity in marriage according to God's original plan, he encounters opposition from them, but also incomprehension from his disciples. Faced with the absolute faithfulness which it requires, they no longer see what advantage there is in getting married (Mt. 19:10). Jesus replies that "It is not everyone who can accept what I have said, but only those to whom it is granted" (v. 11) and refers them to the gift of grace that makes possible the choice of voluntary continence for the Kingdom: "There are eunuchs who have made themselves that way for the sake of the kingdom of heaven." This verse is typically interpreted in relation to consecrated virginity, but it can also be applied, and even more so, in the immediate context, to a man who repudiates his wife for misconduct (*porneia* v. 9) and who does not enter into a new union, in order to avoid committing adultery, imposing upon himself the sacrifice of voluntary continence for the Kingdom of Heaven.[38]

On the subject of the prohibition of adultery, Jesus goes much further still in situating the purity required by the ethos of the Kingdom in the realm of the heart and of desire: "But I say this to you: if a man looks at a woman lustfully, he has already committed adultery with her in his heart" (Mt. 5:28). Pope John Paul II meditated at length on the meaning of this sin of "adultery in one's heart" which follows from the threefold concupiscence of the flesh, and which can even be committed by a man with regard to his own wife.[39] Fallen from original innocence, man lost the nuptial

---

38. "Because divorce, as Jesus understands it, does not break the conjugal bond, a husband who divorces his wife for misconduct must oblige himself to live voluntarily like a eunuch, only in this way can he be admitted to the Kingdom of Heaven" (Dom Jacques Dupont, *Mariage et divorce dans l'Evangile* [Brussels: Desclée de Brouwer, 1959], p. 220).

39. John Paul II, "Blessed Are the Pure of Heart," in *The Theology of the Body,* second cycle of catechesis on human love, pp. 103-77; particularly pp. 138-70, 156. The Pope frequently uses the term *ethos* to designate the concrete condition of value perception from where follows the conscience of having to act according to a certain recognized (ethical) norm. Cf. the note to the Italian edition of these catecheses, *Uomo e Donna Io creò* (Rome: Libreria

meaning of the body, made for the communion of persons *(communio personarum)*. He perverted the body's language of gift by lowering it to the level of the self-centered desire for possession of the other in order to satisfy a sexual need. In this way the other is reduced to the state of being an object for the satisfaction of a disordered bodily desire. Jesus condemned this carnal concupiscence, which is rooted in the heart and endangers the communion of persons willed by God from the beginning as a fruit of the mutual gift of the man and the woman in what constitutes their masculinity and femininity. Consequently, he restores the interior principle of purity of heart.[40]

In addition to this, Jesus guarantees the grace of fidelity and purity of heart in marriage through the total commitment of his own Person. The giving of his own life, out of love, for the coming of the Kingdom, is about to be accomplished in Jerusalem. This gift will bring the forgiveness of sin, not only with the healing of hardness of heart but also with the gift of a new heart in his own likeness. This redemption of heart will restore divine love within the "one flesh" of Christian spouses, who will henceforth be able to give testimony to one another and to the Church of a faithfulness that the world does not know. This faithfulness is given to the couple by the sacrament, and it establishes, in the same moment, the sacramental ethos which governs the ethical requirements of Christian marriage. Christ's gift is, moreover, accompanied by the gift of virginity for the Kingdom of God: another absolute novelty arising from Christ's nuptiality which clearly indicates, along with the indissolubility of marriage, the eschatological character of Jesus' mission in human history.

The Sin against Marriage in the Light of the Sacramental Ethos[41] When St. Paul addresses Christian spouses at the end of his letter to the Ephe-

---

Editrice Vaticana, 1995), p. 116: "This term does not precisely signify ethics as a philosophical science — and even less so the concrete behavior of the person. 'Ethos' is simultaneously a perception of value, from which flows the knowledge-conscience of a duty (to recognize the perceived value), and the act of the person, that can be conformed-unconformed to the recognized value" (our translation).

40. John Paul II, *The Theology of the Body*, pp. 194ff.

41. "In the context of Christian churches and precisely in the ecclesial tradition of the orthodox east, . . . ethos is not an objective measure by which to evaluate character and behavior, but it is a dynamic response to personal freedom for truth and for the authentic existence of man," Christos Yannaras, *La libertà dell'ethos* (Bologna: EDB, 1984), p. 9 (our translation).

sians, he roots the specific spousal ethos in the new life in Christ: "Therefore be imitators of God, as beloved children. And walk in love, as Christ loved us and gave himself up for us, a fragrant offering and sacrifice to God" (Eph. 5:1); "Do all you can to preserve the unity of the Spirit by the peace that binds you together" (4:3); "[do not go on] grieving the Holy Spirit of God who has marked you with his seal. . . . Be friends with one another, and kind, forgiving each other as readily as God forgave you in Christ" (4:30-32). What is striking in Paul's parenetic address is the constant reference to the divine Persons who become, in a certain way, the environment where those who have been regenerated in baptism develop. Saint Maximus summarizes this perfectly in saying: "put on the New Man entirely, he who is created by the Spirit in the image of God."[42] Christian moral action, although specified because of the end and the object proper to human acts,[43] nevertheless proceeds directly from adherence to Christ and from the unity of the Holy Spirit. This is why Saint Cyril of Alexandria constantly affirmed that "his straying children can only find the way to the Father if they are gathered together in one Body, the new Man whose head is our Redeemer."[44]

Having put on the New Man through baptism, the Christian rediscovers in Christ true moral knowledge, and in the light of this can practice all of the virtues. This practice does not obey a self-sufficient moral ideal, but proceeds from a "spiritual transformation of judgment" (Eph. 4:23) that allows a "discerning of what is pleasing to God" (5:10). In other terms, Christian ethics is radically theological, even when it concerns the most daily of human relationships, like those concerning domestic moral life: "Be subject to one another out of reverence for Christ" (5:21). Saint Paul places the spouses in front of Christ, who is not only the "model" but before all else the "Lord" of their union. This lordship cannot be reduced to a relationship of authority; it is equivalent to a partnership or rather a true covenant which allows Christian spouses to dwell, so to speak, within the relationship between Christ and the Church. They are a sign of it, a reproduction of it, a real symbol containing the mystery of Christ's nuptial love for the Church, as we have mentioned earlier.

---

42. Maximus the Confessor, *Capitula theologica et oeconomica*, cent. 2, c. 27 (PG 90, 1137).

43. Thomas Aquinas, ST I-II, 1,1,2,3; I-II, 18,6.

44. Henri de Lubac, *Catholicism*, p. 47.

This is why those who are married "in the Lord" should break with impure, idolatrous and sterile pagan behavior in order to adopt the way that Christ, Spouse of the Church, acts; he who loved the Church and gave himself up for her, "that he might sanctify her, having cleansed her by the washing of water with the word" (Eph. 5:26). "In the same way, husbands must love their wives as they love their own bodies" (28). And women should be suject to their husbands as to the Lord (22). It is the relationship of Christ to the Church that justifies and determines the relationship of the man and the woman. Christ's spousal love becomes the "norm" of conjugal existence precisely because it becomes its "form."[45] Without compromising the equal dignity of the persons, Christ's spousal love shapes the relationship between the spouses according to the asymmetrical reciprocity of Christ and the Church. This "great mystery" shines through, precisely, in the union of hearts and bodies that renders conjugal love a bearer of eternity.[46]

In this perspective, the sin of Christian spouses contradicts their vocation to sacramental love. The deep essence of their sin is, today as always, the refusal of the covenant with God. That is, obliviousness to, or disdain for, the theological dimension of their own union, the loss of the sense of Christ's presence in the heart of their relationship, and indifference towards the Holy Spirit as an intimate partner in their love. Clearly, one form of this sin against the sacrament is the refusal to receive it, when two baptized persons decide to unite their lives without getting married, or when they decide to contract a purely civil marriage. Thus, their act objectively constitutes an offense against Christ who is no longer recognized as the Lord of their love; he even finds himself excluded from their union by an act of disobedience against the Church, which has the responsibility, in his name, of determining the sacrament's canonical form.

If the Church passes severe judgment on the purely civil marriage of her children, this is because her Bridegroom and Lord feels sorrowfully the unfaithfulness — granted, an unfaithfulness mixed with great ignorance and unawareness — of those who have been chosen to be a sacramental sign to the world of his divine and human love. Christ espouses each soul in baptism, and fortifies and enhances it by the gift of confirmation. In the

---

45. H. U. von Balthasar, *New Elucidations* (San Francisco: Ignatius, 1986), p. 215.

46. "You also promise each other eternity . . . ," R. M. Rilke, *Les élégies de Duino* (Seuil, 1972), p. 351.

sacrament of marriage he wants to espouse each couple. Evdokimov writes: "By the sacrament, *each couple espouses Christ.* This is why in loving one another the spouses love Christ."[47] Denying him this love through refusal of this Covenant with him, which is the fruit of his paschal sacrifice, means to strike him in the depths of his being and to not allow him to heal, succor, and sanctify conjugal love through the gift of his own love. It is to deny him Lordship in a domain which is his.

Refusal of the sacrament can be expressed in many ways within a normally ratified and consummated Christian marriage. As well as the case of adultery, on which we commented earlier, we must mention spouses who neglect or completely cease to have recourse to the sacrament of reconciliation and the Eucharist; their act is not in direct opposition to the sacrament of marriage but it does lead, sooner or later, to their isolation from the ecclesial community and to a reduction in the sacramental quality of their own community of life and love.[48] Cut off from the Eucharist, which should be their union's center of gravity, they no longer benefit from its transforming and sanctifying energy, and retreat progressively towards the purely human horizon of their union, to the great detriment of the family and the Church.[49] Thanks to many "sacramental affinities,"[50] the Eucharist and reconciliation are indispensable gifts containing the great mystery of which marriage is the sacrament; they constantly revive and nourish the spouses' faithfulness to their own consecration, and do the same for the fruitfulness of matrimonial grace. In maintaining a living personal relationship to Christ, they guarantee the ecclesial quality of conjugal and

47. Paul Evdokimov, "Ecclesia domestica," *L'Anneau d'Or* 107 (1962) p. 358. Also *Le mariage, sacrement de l'amour* (Paris, 1944).

48. "The grace of the Eucharist brings purification, refinement, newness of life. It causes you to desire, for the person you love, infinitely more than what the most loving spouses who are ignorant of the promise of Christ could wish for each other, I mean the love and the joy of God, holiness. . . . Between a husband and wife who have this eucharistic vision of the body, one surmises without difficulty that their sexual relations themselves will be transformed. It is no longer a 'body for death' but a body for holiness that they give to one another to express their love as children of God." H. Caffarel, "Mariage et Eucharistie," *L'Anneau d'Or* 117-18 (1964), pp. 254-55 (our translation).

49. "Living the sacrificial ethos of the Eucharist 'mystically' irrigates and transfigures (i.e. changes the ontological presuppositions, rather than being content to merely improve them) the economy, politics, profession, the family and the structures of communal life." C. Yannaras, *La libertà dell'ethos,* p. 227 (our translation).

50. Cf. Mattheeuws, *Les "dons" du mariage,* pp. 431ff.

family relationships. Omitting these sacramental encounters, therefore, directly affects the spouses' relationship to God and to the family, as it does the sacramental fecundity of their marriage.

Here it is important to underline that the sins mentioned earlier are faults against the theological life which, thanks to baptism and marriage, should penetrate all of a couple's relationships in the family and society. Indeed, the sacramental nature of marriage depends on the theological act that is its foundation and that makes of Christ, Spouse of the Church, not only the supreme legislator of their conjugal community, but also an intimate partner of their covenant. Therefore, Christ finds himself personally involved in all of their human, moral and spiritual choices. In these choices they either obey his Spirit of unity, faithfulness and fecundity, or remove him from their home, thus offending the communion of grace with their Trinitarian Guest.

The Christian spouses' moral and theological action thus roots itself in the ethos of ecclesial communion, which feeds itself at the font of Eucharistic and Trinitarian communion. In this theological perspective, sin represents not only an objective shortcoming regarding natural and gospel ethics but, above all, a lack of reverence toward the Trinitarian Guest who dwells in the *ecclesia domestica*.[51] It signifies running away from the divine presence; it leads the spouses to desert their mission as mediators of the gift of Love and of Life. The spouses' sin, consequently, affects the priestly depths of their being, ordered towards divine service; because "spouses commit their couple in Christ's Act of saving the world."[52] "They are therefore the permanent reminder to the Church of what happened on the Cross. . . . Of this salvific event . . . memorial, actuation and prophecy."[53] If they shirk the

51. Cf. Evdokimov, "Ecclesia domestica," p. 356: "God created Adam and Eve so that there would be the greatest love between them, which would reflect the mystery of divine unity. The first of the Christian dogmas structures conjugal being in this way, and makes of it a little triad, icon of the Trinitarian mystery."

52. Mattheeuws, *Les "dons" du mariage*, p. 445: "Each receives the other from God and, in Christ the Priest, offers the other to God, 'gives' him or her in sacrifice. 'To love you, for me, is to give you to Christ. Not to keep you for myself, but offer you to God,'" p. 446; cf. H. Caffarel, "Mariage et Eucharistie," pp. 250-51.

53. *Familiaris Consortio* 55: "The Christian family too is part of this priestly people which is the Church . . . is continuously vivified by the Lord Jesus and called and engaged by Him in a dialogue with God through the sacraments, through the offering of one's life, and through prayer. . . . In this way the Christian family is called to be sanctified and to sanctify the ecclesial community and the world."

responsibility of their conjugal priesthood, they deprive the Church, of which they are an integral unit, of a concrete source of apostolic and missionary dynamism. In short, the wretchedness of the sin against the sacrament of marriage is measured with reference to the sublime nature of the sacramental and ecclesial vocation of spouses and of the Christian family.

Conversion to the Sacramental Fecundity of Marriage

God calls human persons to enter into communion with him. These persons are all sinners, "sold as a slave to sin" (Rom. 7:14), who have voluntarily accepted the yoke of sinful passions. Conversion to God's call first requires a conversion from them, then, an attitude of repentance throughout their lives. The Bible distinguishes between the interior aspect of repentance and the exterior acts it requires. The Greek Bible, for example "uses conjointly the verb *epistrephein,* which indicates a change in practice, and the verb *metanoien,* which aims at interior conversion."[54] *Metanoia* is repentance, penance. Jesus' call to conversion (Mk. 6:12) covers these two aspects, but with the inclusion of "a positive act of faith in Christ: the Jews will turn back *(epistrephein)* towards the Lord (Acts 3:19, 9:35)."[55] The act of conversion sealed by baptism is accomplished once and for all and cannot be renewed; but the baptized tend to fall back into sin and so they need the sacrament and the virtue of penance as an extension of baptismal conversion.

For spouses, conversion takes on a double requirement, practical and spiritual, of choosing ethically in harmony with the will of Christ and in communion with his Spirit. It requires the unity, faithfulness and fecundity of the couple according to the specific ends of marriage; but today, following the line of the apostolic exhortation *Familiaris Consortio,* it must differentiate itself by the primacy of the sacrament, that is, by the positive spiritual impact of the couple and the family: "For this reason they not only receive the love of Christ and become a saved community, but they are also called upon to communicate Christ's love to their brethren, thus becoming

---

54. Jacques Guillet & Pierre Grelot, "Pénitence — Conversion," *Vocabulaire de théologie biblique* (Paris: Cerf, 1961), p. 788.

55. Guillet & Grelot, "Pénitence — Conversion," p. 796.

56. *Familiaris Consortio* 49.

a saving community."[56] This perspective takes up the orientation of Vatican II concerning the Christian family who, thanks to its participation in the covenant of love that unites Christ and the Church, "will show forth to all men Christ's living presence in the world and the authentic nature of the Church."[57] Consequently, the conversion of Christian spouses should go beyond the horizon of morality and even spirituality, to embrace the sacramental dimension in its apostolic and missionary properties.

This conversion of the couple to Christ's love, received and transmitted, supposes a concrete and persevering openness to the action of the Holy Spirit, without which there is no holiness, no communion and no Christian mission worthy of the name. "Everyone moved by the Spirit is a son of God" (Rom. 8:14). The sacramental and missionary fecundity of the couple and the family is a theological work of the Holy Spirit. It is not the fruit of voluntarism, moralism, or pastoral activism. This is why Saint Paul insists on docility to the Holy Spirit (Rom. 8) for living "in Christ" and therefore for reaching holiness, the first good of marriage. A great Russian saint, Seraphim of Sarov, saw the goal of Christian life, in all states of life, as acquiring the gifts of the Holy Spirit, "and this hope is not deceptive, because the love of God has been poured into our hearts by the Holy Spirit which has been given us" (Rom. 5:5). The Holy Spirit is the artist *par excellence* who configures Christian spouses to the love of Christ, Bridegroom of the Church. It is He who shares with them his own fecundity so that the family might become more and more the sacred sanctuary and resplendent icon of the Holy Trinity.

Experience of this communion in the Spirit includes a spiritual joy that is the characteristic of union with God and the source of the Christian couple's spiritual fecundity. Indeed there is a fruit of love, a joy, a *gaudium* which is proper to spouses, because spousal love has a very particular character: "the giving of one's person (to another)."[58] This reciprocal gift of persons generates joy not only because it is in God's image, but also because it contains, humbly and authentically, God's "Gift," the Holy Spirit. Now, the Holy Spirit, writes von Balthasar, is in himself "exuberance" and "excess of love."[59] This is why he inspires this kindness and delight that

---

57. *Gaudium et Spes* 48.4.

58. K. Wojtyla, *Love and Responsibility*, 2d ed. (San Francisco: Ignatius, 1993), p. 96.

59. "If, from the beginning in the Father, God is already the marvel of love, in being himself in the gift, this marvel is accomplished in the Holy Spirit who precisely as excess of

wells up within a couple and without which "we do not act, we do not undertake, we do not begin to live well."[60] Consequently, the joy of giving generates generosity in giving and an ever more radical commitment in Trinitarian love, because "the gift makes reference to the giver. A spouse is a royal gift who radiates the presence of the Giver of life."[61]

If the joy of giving is a source of sacramental radiation, its contrary renders the conjugal covenant sterile. Saint Thomas Aquinas defined the sin of sloth[62] as sadness and distaste for action *(taedium operandi)* that is opposed to the enthusiasm of love. This capital but subtle vice, well-known in the monastic tradition,[63] corresponds to what in conjugal life is generally referred to as the "demon of the sixth hour." It can be recognized by signs such as withdrawal, boredom, instability, craving for something new, avoidance of returning home, lack of openness to having children, etc. Sloth is a theological vice, a sin against the joy of loving that the Holy Spirit diffuses. It closes the couple in mediocrity and paralyses its action, prevents the gift of self that creates communion; it takes away from love the joy of union with God: its sweetest fruit and the source of its radiance. This vice must be defeated by prayer, penance and a conjugal asceticism that the Orthodox liturgy recalls symbolically. According to Saint John Chrysostom, the crown of betrothal recalls the crown of martyrdom and calls for conjugal asceticism. Perfect love is love crucified, which, according to Saint Francis of Assisi, is also perfect joy.

The spouses' struggle for spiritual fecundity in Christ must, therefore,

---

Love, in his being-always-more is the elusive and insurmountable summit of absolute love: *Deus semper major* not only for us, but in himself." H. U. von Balthasar, *Theologik III: Der Geist der Wahrheit* (Einsiedeln: Johannes Verlag, 1987), p. 146 (our translation)

60. Saint Augustine, *De spiritu et lettera* 3.5; PL 44, p. 203.

61. Mattheeuws, *Les "dons" du mariage*, p. 456.

62. Saint Thomas Aquinas, ST I-II, q. 26, a.2; II-II, q. 35, a.1; for a detailed analysis of sin in the spiritual tradition see P. Gervais, "Péché — Pécheur," pp. 826-46.

63. Cf. Evagrius Ponticus, *Traité pratique ou Le moine* 12, SC 171, pp. 521-27; John Cassian and Gregory the Great prolong the subtle analyses of Evagrius, to which Saint Thomas will offer a remarkable theological development. I draw his thought from Brother Jean-Charles Nault, OSB, who recently completed doctoral studies at the John Paul II Institute for Studies on Marriage and Family. His thesis, written on the theme of sloth in the writings of Saint Thomas Aquinas, is published as *La saveur de Dieu: L'acédie dans le dynamisme de l'agir* (Rome: Lateran University Press, 2002). For reference in English, Timothy Driscoll, *The 'Ad Monachos' of Evagrius Ponticus: Its Structure and a Select Commentary* (Rome: Ed. Abbazìa San Paolo, 1991).

stand the test of time, patience and realism in faithfulness. Jean-Claude Sagne writes that "to love someone is to give him time," give without limits because the infinite value of the person transcends the limits of time. "To make an unlimited promise to someone is to give him life."[64] This gift without limit does not come from sentiment alone, even the noblest and deepest sentiment; it emanates from a commitment of will and it builds on unconditional faithfulness. In short, love must become a "covenant" founded on faith in the resurrection. Xavier Lacroix writes that "the notion of covenant implies the *idea of death* in four different ways: (1) a commitment until death; (2) in making a covenant one must die to a former life; (3) breaking it implies dying to a significant part of oneself; (4) a covenant consists in fighting together against death and the forces of death. To the finality of death, the covenant counterposes another finality, that of commitment beyond the point of no return."[65] This lasting radicality in love is an image of divine love victorious over death in Jesus Christ. Throughout its development, it supposes and requires faith, faith that trusts in God, in all and above all else. "Love is strong as death," the Song of Songs tells us (8:6). "The magnificent words of Saint Gregory of Nyssa respond to each weakening in our effort: 'Divine power is capable of inventing hope where there is no more hope, and a path through impossibility.'"[66]

The conjugal covenant, together with consecrated virginity, bears witness to the absolute love which came into human history with Jesus Christ. Through the paschal structure of the sacrament his testimony takes on an eschatological dimension. Although the love of Christian spouses belongs first of all to the first creation, it already participates in the "nuptial mystery"[67] that fulfills conjugal love's promise within Christ's eschatological love for the Church. This is the reason for the spouses' submission to the primacy of Christ's love and to the ethical requirements of a faithful, lasting and fecund love.[68] Christ's eschatological love for the Church al-

---

64. Jean-Claude Sagne, *L'homme et la femme dans le champ de la parole* (DDB, 1995), p. 48.

65. X. Lacroix, *Les mirages de l'amour* (Paris: Cerf, 1998), p. 216.

66. Evdokimov, "Ecclesia domestica," p. 362.

67. Angelo Scola, *Il mistero nuziale, 1. Uomo-donna* (Rome: PUL-Mursia, 1998).

68. "In the conjugal relationship, when both spouses offer themselves in a complete and reciprocal gift of self, they at the same time give themselves up to Christ, who in the same act gives himself to them as well. However, once again, they know that love for Christ should come before all else and that sometimes abstaining from sexual relations could be-

ready indwells the spouses' union and drives it on from within, by the power of the Holy Spirit, towards the eternal wedding feast of the Lamb. Thanks to the Christocentrism of Vatican II, we now see more clearly that "authentic married love is caught up into divine love,"[69] and that it becomes ever more the visible sacrament of this invisible love made palpable in the Eucharist. This is why Christian spouses, to avoid the threat of sterility, should never separate themselves from this inexhaustible source of sacramental fecundity that feeds their life of faith, hope and love; so that "together they render glory to God."[70]

Conclusion

Conversion to mission through the joy of communion; conversion to sacramental fecundity through union with God in marriage, authentic path to holiness. Such is, in a few words, the perspective we have sketched in reply to the question of sin in marriage and in conjugal life. Scripture teaches us that sin is a breaking away from the covenant: that is, the refusal of a personal relationship with God; in the concrete case of Christian marriage, sin first of all makes love sterile and then wretchedly destroys the spouses' community of life. This failure is all the more distressing and to be regretted because love, coming from the sacrament, should heal and perfect natural love to the point of making it a mediation of Christ's love for the Church and of divine love for the world. The wretchedness of sins against the sacrament can be measured against the greatness of the vocation to sacramental love, the greatness of a communion of love, the bearer of joy, whose spiritual fecundity opens out to the infiniteness of the Cross, and whose mission commits the family, today more than ever before, to the struggle waged by Christ and the Church against the mystery of iniquity. "More than ever, every Christian household is before all else an intermediary, a meeting point, between God's Temple and a civilization without God."[71]

---

come, when it is morally required and even when it is freely chosen (1 Cor 7:5), the sign of their unconditional love for the Lord." M. Séguin, *La contraception et l'Eglise. Bilan et prospective* (Montreal: Mediaspaul-Pauline, 1994), p. 216.

69. *Gaudium et Spes* 48.2.

70. *Gaudium et Spes* 48.2.

71. Evdokimov, "Ecclesia domestica," p. 361.

If the sacrament of conjugal love, in its "one flesh," does not remain after death, it is not because of the sin that affects it, nor is it due to any unworthiness of the flesh or of its perishability. Rather it is by virtue of the death and resurrection of Christ, who carries forward the triumphal march of the history of salvation towards ever more glorious fulfillments. In this work of transfiguration nothing of the human and conjugal reality is lost; everything is caught up, purified and glorified in the Holy Spirit. The domestic Church, composed of living stones cemented by love, will gain entry to the eschatological banquet where the Father of Heaven has prepared the very best for the wedding feast of his Son. The domestic Church will be carried off into glory along with the whole history of love that characterized its joys and its dramas, and it will eternally share in the infinite fecundity of the divine Persons, of which Christ gave a first pledge in this world through his resurrection from among the dead.

"When this perishable nature has put on imperishability, and when this mortal nature has put on immortality, then the words of scripture will come true: *Death is swallowed up in victory. Death, where is your victory? Death where is your sting?* Now the sting of death is sin, and sin gets its power from the Law. So let us thank God for giving us the victory through our Lord Jesus Christ" (1 Cor. 15:54-57).

CHAPTER VIII

The Sacrament of Marriage
and the Nuptial Mystery of Christ

Our research on the relation between the sacrament of matrimony and
Christ's nuptial mystery is guided by what John Paul II wrote in his apostolic exhortation *Familiaris Consortio:* "The Eucharist is the very source of
Christian marriage. The Eucharistic Sacrifice, in fact, represents Christ's
covenant of love with the Church, sealed with His blood on the Cross. In
this sacrifice of the New and Eternal Covenant, Christian spouses encounter the source from which their own marriage covenant flows, is interiorly
structured and continuously renewed."[1] Commenting on this passage in
his address to the *Foyers des Equipes de Notre Dame* on September 23, 1982,
the same Pontiff grasps the essence of the relation between the Eucharist
and marriage in the following choice expression: "Christian marriage is a
paschal mystery." In this discourse, the paschal mystery of marriage is described by the language of gift: "If you knew the gift of God," in fact, expresses the title of what constitutes the Magisterium's fullest statement on
the relation between the Eucharist and matrimony, inspired by the words
of Jesus spoken to the Samaritan woman at Jacob's well.[2]

Since the Second Vatican Council and in the wake of John Paul II, the

1. John Paul II, *Familiaris Consortio* 57. Cf. D. Tettamanzi, "L'eucaristia al centro della
famiglia," in *La Famiglia* 97 (1983): pp. 23-42.
2. John Paul II, "Se tu conoscessi il dono di Dio" ["If you knew the gift of God"],
Speech given to Foyers des Equipes de Notre Dame, September 23, 1982, in T. Barberi and
D. Tettamanzi, *Matrimonio e famiglia nel magistero della Chiesa* (Milan: Massimo, 1986), pp.
436-45, esp. n. 3, p. 440.

theology of marriage has been developed in terms of "gift," bringing into relief not only the anthropological gift of persons, namely, human love, but the "theological" gift of the sacrament that assumes the conjugal covenant within the nuptial mystery of Christ and the Church.[3] In the same vein, we shall seek to deepen our understanding of the foundation of the sacrament of marriage, based on the nuptial mystery of Christ. In addition, we shall particularly emphasize the dimensions of confession and communion, which mark the eucharistic union of Christ the Bridegroom and his Bride the Church since the paschal fulfillment of the mystery of the Cross.

Our point of departure is the gospel episode of the Samaritan woman, culturally close to us in terms of marriage, but also rich in meaning to illustrate the thirst of Christ for the faith and fidelity of his Bride the Church. The nuptial mystery of the crucified, dead, and risen Christ is therefore deepened in its organic relation to the sacrament of matrimony, through the nuptial gift of the Eucharist,[4] which places the sacramental couple at the center of the Church's communion and mission.

If You Knew the Gift of God

Just as in the Old Testament, the mystery of the covenant in the New Testament is expressed through nuptial symbolism in reference to Christ and the Church.[5] Christ is often described as the Bridegroom, and the Bridegroom *par excellence.* In the gospels, besides the eschatological parables of the Kingdom (Mt. 22:1-10; 25:1-12), John the Baptist designates Jesus as the Bridegroom (Jn. 3:29), and even Jesus attributes this title to himself (Mt. 9:15). The Pauline texts allude to it twice (II Cor. 11:2; Eph. 5:23-25), as does the book of Revelation (Rev. 19:7; 22:17-20). The first of Jesus' miracles, in the Johannine account, is realized during a wedding feast in Cana

---

3. John Paul II, *The Theology of the Body* (Boston: Pauline, 1997), pp. 304-75; cf. A. Mattheeuws, *Les "dons" du mariage* (Brussels: Culture et Vérité, 1996); A. Scola, *Il mistero nuziale: 1. Uomo-donna* (Rome: Pul-Mursia, 1998).

4. Cf. M. Ouellet, "Trinity and Eucharist: A Covenantal Mystery," *Communio* 27 (Summer 2000), pp. 262-83. For the original French text see, "L'Eucharistie, cadeau nuptial," *Communio* 25 (2000).

5. Cf. L. A. Schökel, *I nomi dell'amore: Simboli matrimoniali nella Bibbia* (Casale Monferrato: Piemme, 1997).

in which reference is made to the paschal hour, to the fulfillment of the Son's spousal love for the world and the actualization of his wedding to which the Baptist had made reference (Jn. 2:1-11; 13:1; 3:27-30).[6] "Although the title of Christ-Bridegroom is ordinarily overlooked by christology, its whole significance must be brought to light for us," wrote Gustave Martelet more than twenty years ago, opening the road for deepening the "christology of marriage [which] should begin with this title of Bridegroom and the mystery it recalls."[7] A spousal ecclesiology to which the New Testament alludes in two fundamental passages: 2 Cor. 11:2 and Eph. 5:25-27, must correspond to this spousal christology. We shall speak of this in a subsequent section.

The Symbol of the Samaritan Woman and Her Five Husbands

"If you knew the gift of God, and who it is that is saying to you, 'give me a drink,' you would have asked him and he would have given you living water" (Jn. 4:10). Who is this man who comes to encounter the woman at Jacob's well and speaks of the gift of God? In the first instance we observe that Jesus inserts himself within a tradition, for the encounter at the well is a theme of patriarchal literature;[8] the earthly itinerary of the people of the exodus is marked by water that symbolizes the life God gives, a symbol referring primarily to messianic times.[9] In fact, the conversation with the Samaritan woman concerns the Messiah whom the Jews and the Samaritans await. Therefore, the evangelist places the theme of the messianic encounter between Jesus and the woman in the evangelical context where water becomes the symbol of the Spirit (Jn. 1:33; 7:37-39) and where Jesus appears as the Bridegroom who baptizes in the Spirit. In effect, Jesus' identity stands out since the first sign at Cana in Galilee (Jn. 2:1-12), where he is mysteriously revealed as the Bridegroom present at this wedding.[10] Shortly thereafter, in response to his disciples, John the Baptist

---

6. C. Rocchetta, *Il sacramento della coppia* (Bologna: EDB, 1996), p. 172.

7. G. Martelet, "Sedici tesi cristologiche sul sacramento del matrimonio," *Il Regno-Documenti* (1978), p. 390, thesis n. 4.

8. Gen. 24:10ff., 29:1ff.; Ex. 2:15ff.

9. Is. 12:3; 55:1; Jer. 2:13; Ez. 47:1ff.; Rev. 7:16, 22:17.

10. Cf. I. de la Potterie, "Les mystères des noces," *Marie dans le mystère de l'Alliance* (Paris: Desclée, 1988), pp. 183-231.

testifies to this: "He who has the bride is the bridegroom; the friend of the bridegroom, who stands and hears him, rejoices greatly at the bridegroom's voice" (Jn. 3:29). Luis Alonso Schökel comments: "The Messiah comes as a bridegroom to renew his marriage with the bride; John is the bridegroom's friend, not his rival."[11]

Hence, the episode with the Samaritan woman is placed precisely within this messianic and spousal context. Jesus appears as the point of arrival of God's long journey through history, from his first covenant with Abraham, or better still, with Adam and Eve, to the exodus through the sea and the desert, to the search for his unfaithful bride, to the point of the ardent words of the prophets which truly reveal the nuptial interpretation of his covenant. "For your Maker is your husband" (Is. 54:5). Corresponding to this theme of the divine Bridegroom is that of the unfaithful bride who plays the prostitute with her various lovers by means of her idolatrous practices and the vanity of her alliance with foreigners. The Samaritan with the five husbands symbolizes the infidelity of the pagan nations, neighboring the people of the covenant, but remaining attached to their gods.

The Encounter with the Thirsting Jesus, Source of Living Water

Jesus is the divine, thirsting Bridegroom who asks for a drink so that he may in turn give the living water of the Spirit.[12] Hearing Jesus' words arouses in the woman's heart the desire for this water, which she understands initially in a very limited and interested way. Hence, Jesus initiates the penitential sequence of the encounter: "Jesus said to her, 'Go call your husband, and come here.' The woman answered him, 'I have no husband.' Jesus said to her, 'You are right [. . .] for you have had five husbands, and he whom you now have is not your husband; this you said truly'" (Jn. 4:16-18). The woman, amazed, finds the entire truth of her

---

11. L. A. Schökel, *I nomi dell'amore*, p. 133: "The ancient tradition continued to elaborate upon the image of the Messiah as bridegroom."

12. "I invite the reader to place the text of Hosea 2:4-25 next to that of John 4:4-42 — as if it were a reflection in a mirror — , so that one can see how each deepens the meaning of the other in a reciprocal fashion" (L. A. Schökel, *I nomi dell'amore*, p. 185); Cf. R. Vignolo, *I personaggi del Quarto Vangelo: Figure della fede in San Giovanni* (Milan: Glossa, 1995), pp. 129-75.

life laid out before her. In admitting that she had no husband, she confessed to only half the truth, remaining silent about her relationships with the other lovers. Jesus makes the integral confession which brings to light the infidelity of Yahweh's bride symbolized by this Samaritan woman.[13]

This penitential dimension of the encounter must not be overlooked because it serves as the criterion for the conversion of the Samaritans. Many in fact believed in him because of the words of the woman who declared: "He told me all that I ever did" (v. 39). Therefore, Jesus' confession in the Samaritan woman's place prophesies and anticipates in some way his confession of all the sins of humanity on the Cross.[14] The truth of the New Covenant between the divine Bridegroom and the redeemed Bride is thus based on the truth of the sin confessed and the grace conceded. It will not be established upon falsehood, deceit, or half measures. Jesus performs this penitential sequence with the Samaritan woman because it is "for such [that] the Father seeks to worship him" (v. 23) who adore in Spirit and Truth, that is, who assume the confession of sin and grace as a condition of true adoration in Spirit and Truth.

The Greatly Desired Paschal Supper

The gift of God revealed in this dialogue culminates, in fact, in Jesus' confession of his messianic identity: "I who speak to you am he" (v. 26). Having requested the whole truth with regard to sin, Jesus tells the whole truth about his identity. Thus the woman can "know the Lord" in the nuptial sense of the text of Hosea: "I will betroth you to me forever. . . . I will betroth you to me in faithfulness; and you shall know the Lord" (Hos. 2:19-20). In this context, the reference to food also refers to Hosea 2:21-23, where the fecundity of the soil is presented as a gift of the Bridegroom thanks to his reconciliation with the Bride. "My food is to do the will of him who sent me, and to accomplish his work" (Jn. 4:34). Now, the gift of the Bride-

13. The Jews explained the origin of the Samaritans by the forced immigration of five pagan populations who remained faithful in part to their gods, whom the five husbands in v. 18 symbolize (cf. the annotation to Jn. 4:9 in the Jerusalem Bible).

14. The idea that Jesus confesses the sins of all on the Cross and receives absolution of their sins for them on Easter is one of the central intuitions of A. von Speyr, *Confession*, trans. D. W. Stott (San Francisco: Ignatius, 1985).

groom and his fruitfulness are the effect of his passion. Thus, his thirst refers to the thirst of the Crucified One,[15] and his food to the eucharistic fulfillment of the will of the Father. At the last supper, Jesus accomplishes the act of total and substantial self-giving as the bread broken and blood poured out for the salvation of all. This gesture brings together all the figures of the first covenant: the paschal lamb, the expiatory scapegoat, the suffering servant, the blood of the covenant, the manna in the desert; all these figures converge in the Person and action of Jesus who concludes the first covenant and institutes "his rite" of the New Covenant: "Take this, all of you, and eat of it; this is my body which is given up for you; do this in memory of me."[16]

The institution of the Eucharist is the heart of the nuptial mystery of Christ, because it identifies the giver with the gift in the encounter between the Bridegroom and the Bride. "In fact, the Eucharist makes the Covenant accessible to us, both the gift and He who is given at the same time," writes John Paul II. As "the sacrament par excellence of the Covenant, it is a mystery of communion, of unity, with regard to each person; 'Who eats my flesh and drinks my blood abides in me and I in him' (Jn. 6:56)."[17] Jesus' encounter with the Samaritan woman thus reveals the abiding thirst of God the Bridegroom, which culminates in the Eucharist of his only begotten Son. This is the man who ardently desires both to drink and to offer a drink from the cup of the messianic wine in the Kingdom of heaven (Lk. 22:17-18); but this will not be accomplished without having first drunk of the bitter cup of God's wrath on the Cross (Lk. 22:42), the whole truth of the justice and mercy of God. In his eucharistic gift, Christ the faithful and humble Bridegroom therefore gives himself to the extreme of love, to the point in which the giver is identified with the gift, that is, to the point of the gift of himself.

This gift of love, which is connected to the desire for the Bride's response of faith, radically redeems the Bride with respect to her freedom. Christ's nuptial love bears within itself the response that the Bride in turn

---

15. "Various authors, both ancient and modern, note how Jesus is humiliated to the point of needing and asking in order to be able to then give. The same thing will occur on the cross: he will cry out with thirst and from his side will flow water" (L. Alonso-Schökel, *I nomi dell'amore*, p. 187).

16. Cf. G. Mazzanti, *I sacramenti simbolo e teologia, 2. Eucaristia, Battesimo e Confermazione* (Bologna: EDB, 1998), 21-62.

17. John Paul II, "Se tu conoscessi" 2, p. 438.

is called to give to the divine Bridegroom. This response initially consists in taking and eating, in taking and drinking, which Jesus orders his disciples to do during the last supper. Christ, offered in sacrifice, wishes to be eaten and drunk: "This makes the mouth that consumes him an essential part of the sacrifice of the Lord. He does not act in the Cenacle as a soloist before an auditorium that listens to him, as an actor on stage before onlookers in theater seats. He always acts in such a way that he draws those who belong to him into his act."[18] Thus while we are nourished by his body and blood, he unites us to his sacrifice, and we are transformed and assimilated into the unity of his body. "Because there is one bread, we who are many are one body, for we all partake of the one bread" (1 Cor. 10:17). "When you received the fire of the Holy Spirit," comments St. Augustine, "it is as though you were baked. Be what you can see, and receive what you are. That's what the apostle said about the bread."[19]

Eucharistic communion is not unilateral. While he nourishes us with his body and blood, we become one with him, one body and one flesh in a nuptial union. In fact, we become responsible for his hunger and thirst for communion with everyone: "For I was hungry and you gave me food, I was thirsty and you gave me drink" (Mt. 25:35). Called together by his hunger and thirst which break down the barriers between rite and life, between his eucharistic body and his ecclesial body, we are therefore stretched outward in his love towards the fullness of his entire body in the Kingdom of heaven: "My food is to do the will of him who sent me, and to accomplish his work" (Jn. 4:34).

The Nuptial Mystery of Christ Is Eucharistic

The path followed thus far viewed the Eucharist as the point of convergence of the nuptial covenant between God and his people. The Eucharist is the constitutive event of the Church's identity, since it brings together the people of God, united around Christ's body given up and blood poured out. In this nuptial banquet, the scattered children of God are

18. H. U. von Balthasar, *Explorations in Theology*, vol. III, *Creator Spirit*, trans. Brian McNeil, C.R.V. (San Francisco: Ignatius, 1993), p. 34.

19. Augustine, "Sermon 272," in *The Works of St. Augustine: Sermons*, III/7, trans. Edmund Hill, O.P., ed. J. E. Rotelle, O.S.A. (New Rochelle, N.Y.: New City, 1993), p. 300.

gathered together at the wedding feast in proper attire in order that they, nourished by Christ's presence and inebriated by the new wine of the Spirit, may rejoice in the mystery of Trinitarian communion, in God who is all in all.

This eucharistic and eschatological perspective must now be grounded in the nuptial mystery of Christ, as it is the source and fulfillment of the mystery-sacrament of marriage. Because marriage is the oldest sacrament, originating with creation itself, we are compelled to relate the first sacrament of Adam-Eve to the second Adam, Christ-Church. In so doing we see how God's plan for man and woman is accomplished in the crucified Man, who has fallen into death's sleep; from his side arises the Woman, fit for Trinitarian communion in the one eucharistic flesh. The eucharistic nature of Christ's nuptial mystery makes the gift of the body of Christ stand out as a sacrificial offering, which is consumed in the fire of the Holy Spirit, in order to become the guarantee and nourishment of the spousal love of the married couple "in Christ."

The "Sleep" of the New Adam

God established the covenant with Moses and his people because he had in sight the new and definitive covenant with humanity in Jesus Christ, his only begotten Son made man. This Covenant willed by God is, in the first instance, rooted in the Person of the incarnate Word, whose two natures, divine and human, are joined "without confusion or separation," according to the formula of Chalcedon. Nonetheless, the union of the two natures is not a static fact, but rather the dramatic event *par excellence,* the understanding of which Hans Urs von Balthasar deepens in his Trinitarian christology by use of the dual term mission-obedience.[20] The theologian from Basel develops a conception of how the mystery of the covenant is fulfilled precisely in Jesus' extreme obedience, which comes at the end of the long sequence of obedience of the Old Testament prophets.[21] The Word descended to dwell in our midst following this succession of

20. Cf. H. U. von Balthasar, *Theo-Drama,* vol. III, *The Dramatis Personae: The Person in Christ,* trans. Graham Harrison (San Francisco: Ignatius Press, 1992), pp. 149-259.

21. Cf. H. U. von Balthasar, *The Glory of the Lord,* vol. VI, *Theology: The Old Covenant,* trans. Brian McNeil, C.R.V., and Erasmo Leiva-Merikakis (San Francisco: Ignatius, 1991), pp. 225-98.

growing obedience that led to the radical commitment of God and man in Jesus Christ. This mutual commitment is so total and irreversible as to confer on the history of this man the eschatological importance of the fulfillment of universal history. In effect, the passion, death and resurrection of Christ actualizes the historical-eschatological wedding that Revelation describes as the Wedding of the Lamb. The archetypal obedience of Christ, insists Balthasar, opens the dramatic space for an authentic play of freedom between God and man, in ultimately nuptial terms. The obedience-mission of Jesus Christ is therefore the concrete extension of the hypostatic union, precisely his "incarnation" and "historical-salvific" manifestation.

Now, in the Incarnation, the human and divine are joined together, giving life to the highest and most paradoxical form of nuptiality: "He set out to come to us," affirmed St. Augustine, "when first he entered the Virgin's womb. There a human creature, mortal flesh, was wedded to him."[22] Hence Augustine also defines the incarnate Word as "the sacrament of divinity and humanity, the sacrament appearing in the flesh."[23] Nevertheless one must not lose sight of the fact that the event of the covenant in Jesus Christ is fulfilled as an event between *God* and *man,* that is, involving all the dimensions of the analogy of being. The distance and distinction between the created and the uncreated are not abolished, but rather confirmed in the unity of the being of the incarnate Word. Still there exists between the two partners, divine and human, an authentic bilateral covenant, fruit of the unilateral grace of God. Balthasar explains this in the following terms: "As the Word of God made man, Jesus incarnates in human form the *fides Dei,* that is, God's pact with humanity, his absolute fidelity to the covenant. However, precisely because Jesus is both — the ecstasy of divine love (Dionysius the Areopagite) and the substantial covenant between God and man — he can, as the perfect man, respond to God with filial obedience and with an otherwise perfect faith, thus also becoming 'the incarnate covenant of humanity with God.' Christ does not travel these two paths as alternative forms, but contemporaneously, in

22. Augustine, *The Confessions,* trans. Maria Boulding, O.S.B., ed. J. E. Rotelle (Hyde Park, N.Y.: New City, 1997), 4.12.19.

23. Augustine, *De natura et gratia* 2.2. St. Augustine influenced the specification of the term "sacrament," emphasizing that the sacraments are sacred signs; that they bear within them the likeness of and actually confer that which they signify. He therefore contributed to the working out of the scholastic definition of sacrament: *signum efficax gratiae.*

symphonic harmony." For Jesus Christ remains "the identity (hypostatic) of these two paths, and therefore the substantial covenant, the ontological bond between God and the world."[24]

It is important to note that among the most significant moments of Christ's nuptial mystery there is not only the active moment of his self-giving, but also the passive moment of his being given. When Christ entrusts his sacrifice to his disciples at the last supper, his attitude of delivering himself up under the species of consecrated bread and wine indeed expresses his extreme act of obedience to the Father on the Cross. Hence, Jesus not only gives himself up, but allows himself to be given up. Therefore, his eucharistic offering already contains the substance of the sacrifice of the Cross in which Jesus is reduced to the total passivity of One who is "processed" in order to be transformed into the food and drink of eternal life.[25] It is here where the significance of Christ's sleep emerges, that is, his death and burial among the dead, which are essential for accomplishing the eucharistization of his body and blood. While he lies in total passivity and availability, as a matter of the pure power of love, the heavenly Father together with the Creator Spirit who rejoices over him, works out the new creation, making flow from his open side and his body drained of all its blood, the body of the Bride the Church. The new and eternal covenant between Christ the Bridegroom and his Bride the Church is born precisely through the death of the New Adam who in the power of the Holy Spirit sets free the universal eucharistic fruitfulness of his donation.

The resurrection of Christ is therefore the glorification of his obedience to the point of death, which makes possible the transfiguration of his glorified body into the eucharistic body. The crucified Christ, having assumed *the flesh of sinners,* in fact, having resolved its internal contradiction within the obedience of love, now rises in victory over the power of death. Hence, the power of Trinitarian love revealed in his broken body and his

---

24. G. Marchesi, *La cristologia trinitaria di Hans Urs von Balthasar* (Brescia: Queriniana, 1997), 251; referring to the celebrated essay of Hans Urs von Balthasar, "Fides Christi," in *Explorations in Theology,* vol. II, *Spouse of the Word* (San Francisco: Ignatius, 1991), pp. 43-79.

25. "There is always something 'sacrificial' about food. Now, Christ 'treats' himself like food and detaches it from himself, 'allowing himself to be handled,' through the events which will follow, by the evil which is precipitated upon him and, more profoundly, by the Father who gives him up and delivers him over, and by the Holy Spirit who accompanies him" G. Mazzanti, *Sacraments, symbol and theology,* p. 285.

blood poured out culminates in the glorification of his sacrifice. Now, this glorification is the work of the Holy Spirit, who in this way crowns the nuptial mystery of Christ. In effect, in Jesus' resurrection from the dead, the Spirit of Truth seals in Christ's flesh the absolute reciprocity of love, which he seals between the Father and the Son in eternity. This act of glorification transforms Christ's flesh into living flesh that becomes, therefore, the principle of the life of the Spirit in the Church.

From this perspective, the Crucified One is not only glorified beyond death, but in death and with death, making it the supreme proof of the victory of Trinitarian love and the privileged instrument for the communication of eternal life. In fact, in being raised from the dead through the power of the Spirit, Christ takes death upon himself as his trophy, which is exhibited in his eucharistic body and blood. Every time you celebrate the Eucharist, says St. Paul, "you proclaim the Lord's death until he comes" (1 Cor. 11:26). However, this paradoxical permanency of the body and death of the Lord is a mystery of communion in the Spirit, who glorifies all the earthly events of Christ, including his death for us all (Jn. 16:14-15). Hence, this death contains our death to sin and our life in the Spirit. It is thus a source of eternal life that is not only received by the Church, but which constitutes the Church as the Body and Bride of Christ. Christ's nuptial mystery is therefore eucharistic, based on the fact that it identifies the giver with the gift of Trinitarian life through the sacramental virtue of the Holy Spirit in the Church.[26]

In this paschal light, the gift of the Holy Spirit appears as the fulfillment of the nuptial covenant between Christ and the Church. Just as the child born of his parents "confirms" their unity of love in his flesh, so the gift of the Holy Spirit "confirms" the nuptial mystery of Christ and the Church, being the root, bond, and fruitful energy that shapes their relationship with the very unity of the Trinity. In a word, Christ's resurrection, about to give birth to Pentecost, allows the intratrinitarian fruitfulness of the divine Persons to eucharistically flow into Christ the Bridegroom's gift for his Bride the Church.

---

26. The intimate connection between the Word and the Spirit in effecting the eucharistic mystery is expressed in this way by Nicola Cabasilas: "If the Paraclete is invisibly present, by the fact that he is devoid of a human form, the Savior chose, by means of divine and holy eucharistic gifts, to be seen and touched, having assumed our nature forever. Hence one is the Priest, the other the virtue of priesthood." N. Cabasilas, *Commento della divina Liturgia*, trans. A. G. Nocilli (Padua: Messaggero, 1984), p. 163.

The Bride Emanating from His Side

At this point, the episode of the lance piercing Christ's side in John 19:34, quite sober, yet extremely rich in symbolism, unites us to the patristic tradition, which is considerably close to the mysterious-sacramental sense of this gospel: "But when they came to Jesus and saw that he was already dead, they did not break his legs. But one of the soldiers pierced his side with a spear, and at once there came out blood and water" (vv. 33-34). The surprising solemnity within which the evangelist situates his testimony emphasizes the importance of this sign that is confirmed by two Old Testament citations: Exodus 12:46: "you shall not break a bone of it" and Zechariah 12:10: "when they look on him whom they have pierced, they shall mourn for him." Two complementary facts confirm this sign. "The first is the immediacy with which the water of life, the water promised in John 7:38, flows from his side when the Messiah receives the strike of grace; the second is the fact that the water and blood flow forth together: blood which is life given and sacrificed for love; and water which is life communicated."[27] Indeed the thrust of the lance that opens the side of the dead Christ allows the water and blood of the new creation to flow forth, namely, the baptismal water of rebirth in the Spirit and the eucharistic blood of life in the Spirit.

Based on these facts, a conception was developed and handed down throughout history that contemplates the Church, born from the side of the dead Christ, as Eve taken from the side of Adam who had fallen asleep. Tertullian writes that, "For as Adam was a figure of Christ, the sleep of Adam prefigures the death of Christ, who, dying, would have undergone a type of dormition; and so from the wound of his side the Church, true Mother of the living, takes form."[28] Commenting on Psalm 127(128), Augustine briefly states: "His wife is the Church; his Church, his wife, we ourselves are. . . . When her spouse slept, Eve was created: When Christ died

---

27. L. A. Schökel, *I nomi dell'amore*, p. 247. Saint Faustina Kowalska, canonized on April 30, 2000, explains this with the words she heard spoken by Jesus, the icon of the merciful Christ from whose heart flow white and red rays: "These rays signify water and blood. It is the water which justifies souls, the blood which is the life of the soul. They flow from my heart, opened on the cross. These rays protect the soul from the wrath of my Father. Blessed is he who lives in their shade: Justice will not strike him." M. Winowska, *L'icône du Christ miséricordieux* (Paris: Editions Saint-Paul, 1973), p. 278.

28. Tertullian, *De Anima*, 43: CSEL 20/I, 372, pp. 2-5.

the Church was created; she was born of her husband's side, whence a rib had been withdrawn; and the Church was born of the side of her Spouse, when his side was transfixed with a lance, and the sacraments flowed forth."[29] St. Ephrem for his part contemplates the mystery as follows: "Blessed are you Church, a king asks you to be his wife, with his sufferings you are made glorious. Your salvation flows in the moment in which he dies; having been drained of all his lifeblood: the cross was his nuptial chamber. On the day of his bitter death he generates you into a sweet life, he carries you off, blessed wife, to the throne of his heavenly kingdom."[30] One last testimony highlights the simultaneity of the birth and wedding of the Church: "O great sacrament of marriage! O great mystery of this Bridegroom and this Bride! [. . .] The Bride is born from the Bridegroom, and as she is born, she is immediately joined to him. Thus the moment the Bride is wedded is the moment the Bridegroom dies. The moment the Bridegroom is joined to her is the same moment he is separated from mortal things. When he is raised above the heavens, then she is fruitful in every land."[31] According to a long-standing tradition, therefore, the nuptial mystery of the Church flows from the pierced heart of Christ who fulfills beyond every measure the nuptial mystery of Adam and Eve present in every human couple.

In the wake of this tradition, John Paul II rereads the relationship between Eve and the Church in light of Christ's merciful and spousal love: "That gift of himself to the Father by obedience unto death (cf. Phil. 2:8) is contemporaneously, according to Ephesians, a 'giving himself up for the Church.' In this expression, redeeming love is transformed, I would say, into spousal love. Giving himself up for the Church, through the same redeeming act, Christ is united once and for all with her, as a bridegroom with his bride, as a husband with his wife. Christ gives himself through all that which is once and for all contained in his 'giving himself up' for the Church."[32] The Bride, the Church, thus flows from the gift of the Bridegroom, who through the bath of water (Baptism) makes her appear before him as a holy and immaculate bride (Eph. 5:26). The mission-obedience of the incarnate Word flows into the "yes" of the Church who welcomes the

---

29. Augustine, *Expositions on the Psalms*, 127.11.
30. Ephrem, *Hymn on the Church and Virginity*, 27.3, Lamy, col. 583-86.
31. Quodvultdeus di Cartagine, *De Symbolo*, I.6.10.11, CCSL 60, p. 321.
32. John Paul II, *Theology of the Body*, p. 314.

fidelity and fruitfulness of the divine-human Bridegroom. The New Adam, perfectly obedient, makes emanate forth from his "yes" to the Father, the "yes" of the Church, the New Eve. She becomes the Bride due to the sacrificial and nuptial gift of the Body of the Bridegroom. Therefore, this body given up (eucharistic) not only contains within itself all the fruitfulness of the divine Bridegroom, but all the faithfulness of the created Bride, and is the principle of her fecundity.

From this perspective, within the ecclesiological-nuptial context, the figure of Mary performs an essential role in the Church's participation in Christ's nuptial mystery. By virtue of the privilege of the immaculate conception, the Virgin receives at the foot of the Cross the gift of universal spiritual motherhood, which is founded on the *fiat* she gave to the passion and death of her Son. Due to this grace of pre-redemption, Mary, as the New Eve, welcomes and accompanies the sacrificial gift of the New Adam, being associated, *in actu primo redemptionis,* in the sacrificial offering of the Son and his universal fruitfulness.[33] While all the other members of the Church must be passively confessed and purified, she is already totally available and subject to Christ who finds in her the immaculate bride, the "helpmate," and the feminine "complement" of his divine-human fecundity. This privilege of immaculate Mary ensures that the Church is found not only on the side of sinners to be purified, but also, *by pure grace,* on the side of the redeeming love of the Bridegroom who purifies her. Hence, the Church is involved not only passively and instrumentally in the Trinitarian gift of grace to the world, but nuptially, that is, in the perfect correspondence of feminine love.[34]

Deepening this perspective helps to overcome the difficulty of contemporary ecclesiology regarding the relationship between Christ the Savior and the universality of the Kingdom of God, beyond the visible confines of the Church. Without any reservation the Second Vatican Council affirms the universality of redemption brought about by Christ: "for since Christ died for all, and since all men are in fact called to one and the same destiny, which is divine, we must hold that the Holy Spirit offers to all the

---

33. H. U. von Balthasar, *Explorations in Theology,* vol. III, *Creator Spirit,* trans. Brian McNeil, C.R.V. (San Francisco: Ignatius, 1993), pp. 224ff.

34. "For all that has been said contained a hidden presupposition all the time: . . . the perfect *fiat* of the *Ecclesia,* the perfectly loving agreement with the sacrifice of the Bridegroom. . . . This is why the dogma of the Immaculate Conception of Mary is a strict postulate of ecclesiology." Balthasar, *Explorations in Theology* III, p. 239.

possibility of being made partners, in a way known to God, in the paschal mystery."[35] The question of the sacramentality of the Church in relation to the Kingdom is one of the more pressing issues of theology at the present time. The tendency today is to distinguish the Church from the Kingdom in such a way as to reduce her sacramentality to a mere external sign of a universally communicated salvation, which lies outside of her mediation. A look at the nuptial mystery of the Marian Church permits us to overcome this insufficient view and to understand the Church as the universal sacrament of salvation, in the strong sense of the term, as a real participation in the universal sacramentality of Christ.[36] In principle, one must avoid separating the action of the Holy Spirit from the mystery of the Church, Body and Bride of Christ. The spousal fruitfulness of Christ does not transcend the Church in the sense that it would reach a universality to which the Church would remain extraneous. On the contrary, one must affirm that even in the dependence and total subordination of the servant of the Lord, the "nuptial mystery" of the Cross involves both, the Bridegroom and the Bride in the universal and sacramental gift of grace.

We conclude this section reaffirming the nuptial and sacramental meaning of Christ's obedience of love to the point of death — death on the Cross. The fact that this obedience culminates in the resurrection confers, in effect, a Trinitarian seal and a sacramental fruitfulness to the covenant accomplished in his body broken and blood poured out. The resurrection signifies indeed the irruption of the Holy Spirit in the body of Christ, as the fruit of the reciprocal Love between the Father and the Son in his glorified flesh. It is here that the deepest dimension of Christ's nuptial mystery emerges, that is, its grounding in the intratrinitarian nuptial mystery in whose image man was created in Christ.[37] Angelo Scola does not hesitate

---

35. *Gaudium et Spes* 22.

36. The Church is "the fundamental sacrament flowing from Christ's corporality, participating in Christ's universal mission and strength of salvation (in this sense the often misunderstood motto could be availed of, that is, the *extra ecclesiam nulla salus*); she is like him, a particular body with a universal mission and universal efficacy for the world." H. U. von Balthasar, *Epilogo*, p. 161. On this pressing theme cf. "'Tout récapituler dans le Christ': A propos d'un ouvrage de J. Dupuis," *Revue Thomiste* (October-December 1998), pp. 591-630, especially pp. 613-18.

37. "A fundamental bridal and covenantal relationship exists between God and the world as such (compare the covenant with Noah) which from all time has arisen from the Logos' mediation at the creation and from the Spirit's hovering over the abyss. This fundamental relationship makes man, in the reciprocity of husband and wife, an image and a like-

to integrate this Balthasarian perspective as the ultimate foundation of the "nuptial mystery."[38]

The resurrection therefore confirms the hypostatic union as a mystery of the covenant, that is, a mystery of dual unity fruitful in the Holy Spirit. The Risen One is the confirmed witness to Trinitarian Love fully given and received by the man Jesus for all. The wedding between the Trinity and humanity thus receives in this mystery its irreversible and indissoluble seal. Jesus Christ is the divine-human Bridegroom, abased and exalted, established in the full power of his Trinitarian fruitfulness through the Holy Spirit, who makes him rise from the dead (Rom, 1:4). His original sacramentality thus opens up into the gift of the Holy Spirit to the Church, principle and foundation of their common spousal fruitfulness for the salvation of the world.

The Nuptial Union in the One Eucharistic Flesh

This nuptial mystery reaches its maximum expression in the eucharistic celebration. "Just as the opened side of Christ, from which blood and water gushes forth, simultaneously marks the *act of the Bride's birth,* of a beauty similar to the Bridegroom, and the *pact of the spousal covenant* through which the Body and Blood of the Bridegroom himself is entrusted to the Bride-Church, so also the Bridegroom and Bride are to become 'one flesh' (cf. Mt. 19:6), that is, one Mystical Body."[39] Jesus Christ instituted the sacrament of the Eucharist precisely in order to guarantee throughout history the permanence of the mutual "knowledge" *("conoscenza")* and "recognition" *("re-conoscenza")* of the Bridegroom and Bride, as well as to ensure the simultaneous presence of the reciprocal gift and the vital communion

---

ness of God: of the God who, in his eternal trinitarian mystery, already possesses within himself a nuptial form." H. U. von Balthasar, *The Glory of the Lord,* vol. I, *Seeing the Form* (San Francisco: Ignatius, 1989), p. 577. This passage, by now already dated (the original German edition was published in 1961), may serve as an example of the many references on this matter, above all those in *Explorations in Theology* I and the latest in the *Teologica,* vol. 3, pp. 130-31.

38. A. Scola, *Il mistero nuziale,* pp. 104-111.

39. A. M. Triacca, "Il sangue di Cristo: Mistero di alleanza nella vita coniugale," *Il mistero del sangue di Cristo e l'esperienza cristiana,* ed. A. M. Triacca (Rome: Centro Studi Sanguis Christi, 1987), pp. 385-417, esp. 393.

of both through the gift of his body and blood in the New Covenant. The *eucharistic one flesh* sealed in the blood of the Cross and offered to all generations in the eucharistic celebration brings the nuptial mystery of Christ and the Church to its fulfillment. What had been instituted at the Last Supper in the presence of the apostles, and was accomplished once and for all on the Cross in the presence of the immaculate Bride, opens up into the eucharistic Pentecost where the Church, the Bride, receives the superabundance of Trinitarian fruitfulness.[40]

Viewed in this way, the fulfillment of the nuptial mystery of Christ appears genuinely eucharistic. In fact, the Eucharist sets free all the fecundity that is contained in Christ's unique sacrifice and shared with the immaculate bride. In the face-to-face encounter between Jesus and Mary at the Cross, the Holy Spirit seals the unity of the shared nuptial sacrifice and attests to its infinite fruitfulness in the "common" ecclesial posterity of the Bridegroom and Bride, even within the abyssal difference between the Creator and creature. The same face-to-face encounter between the Bridegroom and Bride is found in every Eucharist, where the Holy Spirit generates and sanctifies the children of God and the Church through the faith of Mary, which is shared by the faithful and the ministerial priesthood. Thus, the eucharistic gift of the Bridegroom is entrusted to and shared with the pilgrim Church in need of purification, in expectation of the day of full communion at the wedding of the Lamb.

This nuptial fecundity of the Eucharist obviously presupposes a constant purification of sins, which the crucified and risen body of the Lord concretely places at the disposition of the Bride, the Church. Adrienne von Speyr writes: "The first body [crucified] gathered the total confession into itself, but the second [resurrected] offers itself as pure forgiveness; . . . It perpetually offers absolution from within itself; indeed, it gives itself in ab-

---

40. "Thus it is evident that the self-outpouring in the death and Resurrection of God's incarnate Word into the Church is truly the pouring forth of the Trinitarian life externally. The virginal man Christ is wholly . . . the generative organ *(instrumentum conjunctum)* of the eternally generating Godhead and the central organ in that it belongs to him alone to make himself (in the Eucharist) a seed and, at the same time — beyond any analogy with the way in which man and the Creator cooperate — to pour out his Spirit into what is produced, through his joint spiration with God the Father." H. U. von Balthasar, *Explorations in Theology*, vol. II, *Spouse of the Word* (San Francisco: Ignatius, 1991), p. 190; cf. S. Mahoney, *The analogy between the Eucharist and marriage according to Hans Urs von Balthasar*, Dissertatio ad doctoratum (Rome: PUG, 1999).

solution just as it gives itself in the Eucharist."[41] In welcoming forgiveness and receiving communion, the Church, the Bride is renewed in the faith of the covenant. Holy Communion is therefore the nuptial moment *par excellence*, the moment of strengthened fidelity in the Spirit of the Lord. In it the thirst of God and the thirst of man for intimacy, unity, and fruitfulness meet. And in it is rooted the happiness and ecclesial vitality of the conjugal covenant interiorly shaped and continually vivified by this mystery.

The Mystery-Sacrament of Marriage

We begin the last part of this chapter with a preliminary observation about the methodology that has been employed thus far and will be further developed in the reflection on the sacrament of marriage. Instead of proceeding from below to above, that is, beginning with the lived experience of conjugal love and seeking its transcendent model in God, we began from above to below, namely, from the sacramental "gift" lavished upon the couple by Christ in the matrimonial celebration. This neither pretends to be the only valid method nor the best; it nonetheless offers a descending perspective that helps us to become aware of the "gift" of God, that is, the grace bestowed upon the couple as a call and a mission. Theology must integrate the two methodological perspectives in order to provide an adequate vision, namely, one that is not only anthropocentric, but a trinitarian theocentric vision of the mystery-sacrament of marriage.[42]

At the level of content, we furthermore propose that marriage is a sacrament not only based on the fact that it is received and celebrated *(in fieri)*, but above all as a state of life *(in facto esse)*; we therefore presuppose that the couple receives the sacrament, not in a fleeting fashion, but permanently, based on the charism of consecration proper to marriage.[43] In ultimately considering that the conjugal relationship between man and woman, being a sacrament, is called to be ever more immersed in the mystery of Christ the Bridegroom and the Church his Bride, we believe it is useful, in fact necessary, to call attention to the ecclesial-mysterious di-

41. A. von Speyr, *Confession*, trans. D. W. Stott (San Francisco: Ignatius, 1985), p. 58.

42. Carlo Rocchetta offers a rich description of this following the ascending methodology; cf. *Il sacramento della coppia*, pp. 7-131.

43. Cf. L. Ligier, *Il matrimonio: Questioni teologiche e pastorale* (Rome: Città Nuova, 1988), pp. 114ff.

mension of the sacrament of matrimony. This will be developed beginning from the gift of Trinitarian unity-fecundity and will then point towards the couple's eschatological witness, through the mission of the family, the domestic Church.

Gift of Trinitarian Unity-Fecundity

The apostolic exhortation *Familiaris consortio* summarizes the essential mission of the Christian family as follows: "*to guard, reveal and communicate love,* and this is a living reflection of and a real sharing in God's love for humanity and the love of Christ the Lord for the Church His bride" (FC 17). This mission relies on the gift of sacramental communion that is generously bestowed upon the couple in the celebration of Christian marriage. This sacramental communion is intrinsically and inseparably trinitarian and anthropological-ecclesial. Assuming that the anthropological dimension of matrimonial grace is well-known, that is, the fact that it "elevates, perfects and sanctifies conjugal love,"[44] we shall at this point focus on the sacramental grace of marriage as it grounds the ecclesiality of the couple and the family in the nuptial faith that unites Christ to the Church.

Familiaris consortio affirms that "the Holy Spirit who is poured out in the sacramental celebration offers Christian couples the gift of a new communion of love that is the living and real image of that unique unity which makes of the Church the indivisible Mystical Body of the Lord Jesus" (FC 19). This sublime gift bestowed on them allows them to "live in their married and family lives the very love of God for people and that of the Lord Jesus for the Church, His bride" (FC 56). This love given to the couple is Trinitarian love in whose image man was created as man-woman and called to conjugal and ecclesial communion (cf. FC 11).

The common life of the couple in marriage and their conjugal love are therefore pervaded by Trinitarian love itself, which effuses in them its unity and fruitfulness. The couple is constituted as the domestic Church, as a "dual unity" sealed by the Holy Spirit. Hence, the couple is not only an image of the Church, but an ecclesial "reality" marked by its universal properties: the couple is united by the Holy Spirit and therefore is in some way one, holy, catholic, and apostolic. The Holy Spirit makes the couple a

44. DS 1799.

new reality, Trinitarian, namely a "third" in relation to their individual persons.[45] The conjugal "we" is inserted within the ecclesial "we"; in fact, it becomes an authentic "subject" of the ecclesial "we." Therefore, the couple finds itself engaged in the Trinitarian drama of the total gift of self for the other and with the other in the unity of a common fecundity.

In this light, not only does the being of the couple participate in the gift of the divine Persons, but also its action as a couple, in all of its aspects. Thus John Paul II writes, "For Christian parents the mission to educate, a mission rooted, as we have said, in their participation in God's creating activity, has a new specific source in the sacrament of marriage, which consecrates them for the strictly Christian education of their children: that is to say, it calls upon them to share in the very authority and love of God the Father and Christ the Shepherd, and in the motherly love of the Church, and it enriches them with wisdom, counsel, fortitude and all the other gifts of the Holy Spirit in order to help the children in their growth as human beings and as Christians" (FC 38).

The significance of this participation is deepened by John Paul II precisely within the context of the relation between the conjugal covenant and the eucharistic mystery: "The Eucharist in fact makes the Covenant accessible to us, both the gift and He who gives himself at one and the same time. . . . It manifests the communion between the Father and the Son in the Spirit inserting the faithful within this communion, who thereby find themselves in communion with one another (1 Cor. 10:17)." The Pope continues: "It [the New Covenant] 'shapes' their love from within: they love one another not only as Christ loved, but already mysteriously, with the very love of Christ, for his Spirit is their gift inasmuch as they allow themselves to be 'shaped' by him (Gal. 5:25; Eph. 4:23)."[46] A little further on, in comparing the Spirit's action upon the eucharistic species to that upon the couple, he adds: "The Spirit can make conjugal love become the Lord's own love; if the spouses let themselves be transformed, they can love with 'the new heart' promised by the New Covenant (Jer. 31:31)."[47]

45. "A travers eux, c'est toujours lui (L'Esprit Saint) qui agit, fonde, scelle et transfigure le don et l'engagement des personnes. Sans l'Eglise, il reste le 'tiers' intérieur à leur donation mutuelle." A. Mattheeuws, *Les "dons" du mariage: Recherche de théologie morale et Sacramentelle* (Paris: Culture et Vérité, 1996) p. 430.
46. John Paul II, "Se tu conoscessi," p. 439.
47. John Paul II, "Se tu conoscessi," p. 439.

Letting themselves be transformed is not a voluntaristically attainable moral goal. It is a gift of grace, in fact a prodigy of faith, whose nature is and always remains essentially marian, that is to say, one of assent and consent. Faith welcomes the Word of God and lets itself be shaped by it as Mary did. It is an assent and consent that allows them to go beyond themselves in order to entrust themselves totally to God in the power of the Holy Spirit. Faith is an unconditional "yes" given to the Church through the absolute "yes" of Christ to the Father and the immaculate "yes" of Mary to the incarnate Word. The "yes" of Christ signifies his coming out of self, remaining outside of self for the other and in the other, in order to be one with the other in Love; in this same light, the "yes" of the couple reproduces and incarnates the nuptial gift of Christ and the Church. Thus, their initial and permanent love is assumed within the love of Christ for the Church, thereby being transfigured in the paschal *agape* of the Lord. "Christian marriage is a paschal mystery" writes the Pope, exhorting the couple to walk with Christ along the way of the Cross towards the full joy of Trinitarian communion. The gift of their nuptial faith in Christ is, therefore, the path on which human love is led, elevating it to the inexhaustible spring of Christ's fidelity to the Father and the Church.

Ecclesial-Conjugal Communion

The reception of the sacramental gift in faith constitutes the couple as the domestic Church, whose authentic human love "is caught up into divine love and is directed and enriched by the redemptive power of Christ and the salvific action of the Church" (GS 48d) to fulfill a specific ecclesial mission. If the conjugal "yes" of the man-woman is assumed within the eucharistic-nuptial "yes" of Christ-Church, we must examine the consequences of this. The orthodox tradition sees in the Eucharist the seal that guarantees the sacramentality of the conjugal covenant.[48] The Latin tradition, even while emphasizing the distinction between the sacraments, nonetheless affirms that the natural place for the celebration of marriage is precisely within the eucharistic celebration. From the Eucharist, in fact,

48. J. Meyendorff, "Il matrimonio e L'Eucaristia," *Russian Christian* 119 (1971), pp. 7 -27; B. Franck, "L'Eucharistie: véritable sceau du mariage?" *Revue de Droit Canonique* 31 (1981), pp. 168-88.

proceeds the initial and permanent gift of conjugal charity and the living participation of the Christian family in the Church's mission.

Assumed within the kenotic-paschal drama of Trinitarian Love, conjugal love is therefore inserted into the missionary dynamism of the Church, sacrament of salvation. Natural *eros* and the personal love of the spouses, blessed by God the Creator and sanctified by Christ the Redeemer, belong to the sacramental order of the Incarnation. By virtue of the sacramental epiclesis of marriage, the couple is blessed by the Gift of God himself, who comes to encounter them, remaining and abiding with them all the days of their life. This real presence, as long as it is respected and not profaned by sin, creates a sacred and holy atmosphere in the family; the spouses learn to live each day in the presence of Christ in their midst; their *communio personarum* marked by "mutual subjection"[49] is no longer only private and personal, but an ecclesial reality because it now belongs to the great sacrament of Christ the Bridegroom's Love for his Bride the Church.

The spouses love one another, therefore, not only in their own names, but in the name of Christ, for they have received a "new heart" from him, the Spirit of love who seals the unity of their covenant. Antonio Sicari writes that "Thinking about how human love is always expressed in the gift of self, and how such a gift may always need to be expressed in 'gifts' (in gestures and words), they [the spouses] will be able to reflect in wonder-filled contemplation on the Person (Christ) who — alone — succeeds in being the very gift himself."[50] That impossible dream for human beings is offered to the spouses as a grace when they receive communion in the body and blood of the Lord. Taken up into the mystery of eucharistic *kenosis,* the spouses therefore mysteriously transcend their limitations, reconciled and united beyond themselves in the one eucharistic flesh of Christ. By virtue of their being assumed into the mystery, they give and receive one another from Christ, and give one another Christ himself. Their marriage thus becomes in faith, according to the fitting expression of Fr. Caffarel, "a Eucharist lived in two."[51] Every sacramental communion of the spouses is a new pentecost that renews the inebriation of unity and com-

---

49. John Paul II, *Mulieris Dignitatem* 24.

50. A. Sicari, *Breve catechesi sul matrimonio* (Milan: Jaca, 1994), p. 49; the author adds a poem of Pedro Salinas: "Come vorrei essere la cosa che io ti do/e non solo colui che te la da [*How I would like to be what I give you/and not only he who gives it to you*]."

51. H. Caffarel, "Le mariage, route vers Dieu," *L'Anneau d'Or* 117-118 (1964), p. 265.

munication, the fruitfulness of mission, and the hope of the fulfillment of the Kingdom.

In this eucharistic light, the heart of the spouses' ecclesial mission consists in being one in Christ and letting themselves bear the fruitful communion of their relationship. Their mission primarily consists in being the dwelling place of God, the temple of the Trinity, that is, the domestic Church. Their relationship of mutual charity, lived in faith, becomes, therefore, fruitful not only in bearing such fruit as children or spiritual works, but fruitful in terms of "bearing" God himself (Jn. 6:37). The divine fecundity of faith, in effect, which the spouses received in Baptism, becomes therefore the divine fecundity of the couple in a sacramental marriage celebrated in the Lord. In fact, since "authentic married love is caught up into divine love" (GS 48), it is not primarily they who are fruitful, but God in them, the God of the Covenant who loves them and shares his Trinitarian fruitfulness with them. It is shared under the species of children desired and received, or under the species of the sacrificial forgoing of children when God, in his sovereign freedom, chooses to give them a spiritual (greater) fruitfulness in the Church. In either case, it is clear that the primordial mission of the conjugal and family community is the fecund communion of persons, which radiates the Presence of the Trinitarian communion, having become palpable and therefore credible to the world in the domestic Church.

All the other dimensions of the family's ecclesial mission proceed from this sacramental communion. The procreative, educative, and social task of the family, as well as its evangelizing and religious mission, flow from the gift of ecclesial communion which is drawn from the Trinitarian font of Love revealed in Christ. Therefore, the whole life of the couple and the family becomes, in Christ and in the Church, a *sacramentum Trinitatis* that lets the gift of divine unity and fecundity pass through the life of the world. Hence, *Familiaris Consortio* sustains that "they not only *receive* the love of Christ and become a *saved* community, but they are also called upon to *communicate* Christ's love to their brethren, thus becoming a *saving* community" (FC 49).

The fidelity of the spouses in all the dimensions of their mission requires none other than cultivating the awareness of the mystery, which does not occur without committing themselves to "love 'to the end,' in giving and forgiving."[52] Therefore, the sacrament of reconciliation becomes

52. John Paul II, "Se tu conoscessi," p. 439.

indispensable for the couple who longs to be holy; but there exists a real need to evangelize in the area of confession in order to escape from the modern moralistic mindset. It is necessary that Adrienne von Speyr's proposal of confession as the *sequela Christi* be understood.[53] The crucified Lord confessed the sins of all to the Father on the Cross, and thus received from the Father absolution for everyone on Easter day, by the power of the Holy Spirit who raised him from the dead. "Peace be with you," exclaims Jesus on Easter evening; "And when he had said this, he breathed on them, and said to them, 'Receive the Holy Spirit. If you forgive the sins of any, they are forgiven" (Jn. 20:22-23). In the truth of this gift, the Lord aspires to see in us the fruit of his confession in the truth of our communion. In this light, every sacramental confession is a response to his thirst and becomes a grateful reception of the gift of the Spirit. Therefore, what was accomplished by the Lord in his Paschal Mystery, is accomplished in the couple as a paschal event of reconciliation. Every confession is therefore a source of sanctity for the couple insofar as it reconstructs the unity and humility of a true communion in the Lord.

Eucharist Lived in Love for the Kingdom

The paschal dynamism of confession, united to the unifying power of communion, directly involves the domestic Church in the Church's eschatological tension towards the fullness of the Kingdom. In fact, Trinitarian communion rooted in the Eucharist and incarnated in marriage, contains within itself a kenotic and paschal figure extended towards the fulfillment of history, or better still, the fulfillment of the *cosmos* in the Glory of God. The eternal life of God is absolute Love, that is, absolute gift, absolute receiving-gratitude and absolute reciprocal fruitfulness. This threefold way of love is offered to the Church and nuptially shared with her in Christ's eucharistic kenosis. The eucharistic-nuptial kenosis of Christ introduces in effect, in historical time, an incommensurable divine gift that

---

53. "His cry of dereliction could equally well have been the cry of a sinner who can see no possible way of escape. He himself had sold everything to buy for the Father the pearl of redeemed man; and man must follow him by selling all to return to the Father" (A. von Speyr, *Confession: The Encounter with Christ in Penance*, trans. A. V. Littledale [New York: Herder & Herder, 1964]). (Here we have cited an earlier English publication of *Confession*, due to our preference of translation for this particular part.)

founds, molds, and polarizes the whole reality of the Church and the whole universe towards the paschal fulfillment of history in the Glory of the Risen One.

The proclamation of this paschal fulfillment passes through Christian marriage and family, a privileged way of the new evangelization. Under the appearance of humility, discretion, simplicity, silence, everyday life, in a word under the appearance of the ordinary life of the Home of Nazareth, the good news of shared Trinitarian Love reaches all the ends of the earth. Obviously, the family is not the only way of the Church, which is also concerned with promoting the consecrated life of the evangelical counsels as the singular testimony to the event of the Kingdom already "in act." "Marriage and virginity or celibacy are two ways of expressing and living the one mystery of the covenant of God with His People. When marriage is not esteemed, neither can consecrated virginity or celibacy exist; when human sexuality is not regarded as a great value given by the Creator, the renunciation of it for the sake of the Kingdom loses its meaning" (FC 16). The specific mission of the consecrated life is to remind everyone that the "gift *par excellence* of God is not a creature, although he is loved, but the Lord himself: 'For your Maker is your husband' (Is. 54:4). The true Bridegroom of the definitive wedding is Christ and the Bride is the Church (Mt. 22:1-14)."[54]

Christian marriage keeps its own mystery alive when it is illuminated by this radical testimony founded exclusively on the Cross of the Lord: "Christian marriage is more than a fleshly reality. 'Love is more than love' (Paul VI). Transfigured by the Spirit, love is made for eternity because 'love never ends' (1 Cor. 13:8). However, at the same time authentic conjugal love, while shaped by tenderness and fidelity, does not allow one to pause before the conjugal relationship in undue adoration: it leads them from the conjugal covenant to the Covenant, from the image to its origin. This is why it is viewed as inseparable from another sign of the Covenant, celibacy 'for the Kingdom' (Mt. 19:12)."[55] Paul Evdokimov writes, "If the monk transcends time, the Christian couple begins the transfiguration of time."[56] Far from causing them to disregard the time that passes, the Christian couple, rooted in the Eucharist, brings the experience of the

---

54. John Paul II, "Se tu conoscessi," pp. 442-43.
55. John Paul II, "Se tu conoscessi," pp. 442-43.
56. P. Evdokimov, "Ecclesia domestica," in *L'Anneau d'Or* 107 (1962), p. 362.

eternal into time, an experience that grows with the appeal to an ever greater love following in the footsteps of the crucified Christ.

The testimony of the Spirit in the eucharistic fecundity common to Christ the Bridegroom and his Bride the Church is therefore prolonged in sacramental marriage and in virginity for the sake of the Kingdom. This testimony is not an exclusive prerogative of virgins as the eschatological love of Christ on the Cross is poured out in the covenant between spouses. Christian married couples are engaged, therefore, as the first persons in the paschal struggle for the coming of the Kingdom. Their grounding in the Eucharist "explodes the frontiers" of the family to live "a communion in no way closed in on itself, but completely open to mission."[57] Therefore, the overall commitment of the Christian family through its unity, hospitality, social promotion of families, and participation in the evangelizing activity of the Church, belongs intrinsically to the eschatological dynamism of faith: this is due to the fact that the eucharistic and spousal love of Christ is the source, the nourishment, and already the foretaste of the reward for the domestic Church's missionary dynamism.

Conclusion

From our discussion, what ultimately stands out is the need for a radical rethinking of Christian marriage in terms of faith, that is, as a gift. This gift involves the couple's own paschal mystery, tending towards the sacramental realization of the Trinitarian communion of Christ the Bridegroom and his Bride the Church, ever more concrete in the sphere of the family. The *communio personarum* lived in the Christian family becomes, therefore, a sacramental prolongation of the Church's nuptial mystery, which flows from the eucharistic heart of Christ.

In this font where the sins of the Church the Bride are confessed, and where she is reconciled, nourished, and sanctified, Christian marriage obtains the faith that makes the spouses faithful and fruitful in Him, the one who has fulfilled all of God's promises with his "yes" of absolute love to the Father for the salvation of all. The solemn commitment of the couple as a sacramental couple in the Lord's paschal mystery thereby opens wide the doors of the family to the missionary being and action of the Church. In

57. John Paul II, "Se tu conoscessi," p. 441.

light of the Eucharist, there exists between the Church and the family a *perichoresis* of life, faith, love, and mission, a *perichoresis* that is the basis for the ecclesial spirituality of the Christian family and its relevance for the Kingdom of heaven.

For conjugal and family spirituality, it is no longer enough to give a moralistic exhortation about fidelity, nor an invitation to generous fecundity, much less to offer the ideal of a communion lived in everyday life. Couples married in the Lord and committed to the Church's mission want to understand better the mystery of their communion; they desire insight into God's interest in their relationship, the benefit he draws from their unity and their fecundity for his glory. In a word, the enrichment of conjugal and family spirituality played out in the Church points to a clarification of the theological and eschatological nature of Christian marriage.

Let us leave the last word for John Paul II, who best expresses the nuptial mystery of Christ in Christian marriage: "Very beloved brothers and sisters, you live in the heart of the sacrament of the Covenant, nourishing your marriage with the Eucharist and illuminating the Eucharist with your sacrament of marriage; it is not simply a worldly reality. Despite your limitations and weaknesses, your light humbly and at the same time boldly shines among men. . . . Seeing the way you live, may they catch a glimpse of the Lord's enthusiastic 'yes' to authentic love!"[58]

---

58. John Paul II, "Se tu conoscessi," p. 445.

CHAPTER IX

Christian Identity, Personal Ethics, and Family Ethics

The quest for a theological and philosophical re-foundation of ethics has undergone a considerable development in the past ten years, in response to the crisis of modern ethics and the tendency of secularized society to an ever more pervasive and dehumanizing "culture of death."[1] "In seeking the deepest roots of the struggle between the 'culture of life' and the 'culture of death,'" writes John Paul II, "we have to go to the heart of the tragedy being experienced by modern man: *the eclipse of the sense of God and of man.*"[2] The Pope's engagement in the area of ethics, notwithstanding all the currents to the contrary, arises from the dramatic ascertainment of the loss of the *humanum* pervasive in all cultures. The extreme liberalization of mores and the expansion of legislation contrary to the supreme value of the human person are telling signs of this loss of the sense of God and man.

1. We may recall at the magisterial level the encyclical *Humanae Vitae* of Paul VI (1968), followed by John Paul II's *Familiaris Consortio* (1981), *Veritatis Splendor* (1992), and *Evangelium Vitae* (1995), without overlooking *The Catechism of the Catholic Church* (1992). To grasp the importance and dramatic nature of the theological debate over the foundations of ethics, cf. Albert Chapelle, *Les fondements de l'éthique: La symbolique de l'action* (Brussels: Institut d'études théologiques, 1988); *John Paul II and Moral Theology*, ed. Charles E. Curran and Richard A. McCormick (New York: Paulist, 1998); S. Pinckaers, *The Sources of Christian Ethics*, trans. Sr. Mary Thomas Noble (Washington, D.C.: Catholic University of America Press, 1995); Wolfhart Pannenberg, *Ethics*, trans. Keith Crim (Philadelphia: Westminster, 1981); Martin Rhonheimer, *La prospettiva della morale: Fondamenti dell'etica* (Armando Ed., 1994).

2. John Paul II, *Evangelium Vitae* 21.

In this context, the growing disparity between culture and faith outlines ever more clearly the need for a new evangelization of cultures based on the sense of man that arises from the Trinitarian mystery. Thanks to the strong impetus of John Paul II, the path is being cleared for the idea that the way of the Church for the re-evangelization of the contemporary world is through the family; this hinges on the creation of man as man-woman in the image of God to be fulfilled in the domestic Church, as a mystery of communion and participation in the Trinitarian *communio personarum* in Christ. Therefore, the challenge posed to theology and philosophy by John Paul and by the modern situation is the reproposal of an *"adequate anthropology"* based on these foundations, one that is capable of grounding an ethical discourse that is not only Christian, but rational and universally valid as well.

In our times the place of the family and the value of conjugal ethics are strongly contested by the secularized culture. This controversy is conditioned by modern individualism, the fruit of rationalism, which has caused society to no longer view the human person as rooted in the mystery of grace. The crisis of modern ethics, or, better still, its failure, is a result of the separation of faith and reason which detached ethics, now purely rational, from the ethos of faith, thus depriving man of the source of his action.[3] This failure of modern ethics results from replacing the dialogical principle of Christian faith with a monological principle (pure reason: ethical autonomy). Removed therefore from the ethos of grace, modern ethics was condemned to propose a high moral "ideal" that is impossible to live since it fails to furnish the resources necessary to attain it. This inevitably resulted in the overall refusal symbolized by Nietzsche and the present-day fall into relativism.[4] Today, purely rational norms no longer hold. The absolute value of the human person and promotion of the common good of society can no longer be sustained. Legislation regarding abortion and euthanasia clearly demonstrates this.

3. For a critical analysis of modern ethics see C. Yannaras, *La libertà dell'ethos: Alle radici della crisi morale in Occidente* (Bologna, 1984); A. MacIntyre, *After Virtue: A Study in Moral Theory* (Notre Dame: University of Notre Dame Press, 1981); G. Abbà, *Saggio di filosofia morale* (Rome, 1989), pp. 79-189; R. Spaemann, *Happiness and Benevolence* (Notre Dame: University of Notre Dame Press, 2000).

4. On this subject see the warning of *Veritatis Splendor* concerning *"the risk of an alliance between democracy and ethical relativism,* which should remove any sure moral reference point from political and social life, and on a deeper level make the acknowledgement of truth impossible" (101).

The aim of these reflections is to recover the ethos of grace and the anthropological and ecclesiological presuppositions that support not only the structure of Christian family ethics, but also that of personal and social ethics in general, since they are rooted in the family. The family is the fundamental relational matrix that gives shape to man's inseparably personal and social identity. This fundamental matrix receives an unprecedented fulfillment from Christ, which adds not only new ethical content, but a sacramental dimension to ethics as well. Therefore, based on the sacramental gifts, the communion of persons in the Christian family is supported by a foundational reality where man is molded by the Trinitarian mystery that envelops and pervades every relation between soul and body, individual and society, and person and community.

The crisis of man, which now openly irrupts into the secularized culture, cannot be resolved without returning to the "beginning" of creation "in Christ," which reveals the being and action of man as man-woman in the image and likeness of God. Our point of departure will therefore be Christian, Trinitarian, and eucharistic identity, the foundation of personal and social ethics (I). We shall next develop the notion of the fulfillment of the human person in the ethos of familial and ecclesial communion, the source and paradigm of ethics (II). We shall conclude with the epochal mission of conjugal and family ethics in the present-day world (III). In this way we hope to show, at least by highlighting the main themes, the theological and anthropological foundation that illuminates the intrinsic relation between Christian identity, personal ethics, and social ethics.

Christian Identity the Foundation of Personal and Social Ethics

We shall begin with a preliminary observation. We are interested in setting forth the anthropo-theological foundation of the ethical order. This foundation involves an ontological and epistemological dimension that cannot be overlooked, but will not be developed within the confines of this work. Human action depends on an ultimate governing reality that is objective, but is perceived and interpreted in a more or less subjective way by individuals and by various traditions. Without getting into the distinctions between "foundations," "foundation," and "fundamentals," we limit ourselves here to affirming "reality considered in its wealth of being, prescinding from the subjective evaluations"; nonetheless, we continue to be aware of the complexity of the relation between "the epistemological-operative value of the foundation and the ontic-ontological depth of the foundations"[5] in accepting and extending the traditional axiom of the scholastics: "Action follows being."

Man Created in the Image of God: "The Unity of the Two"

The first step in our reflection is anthropological: *Who is man?* This question is posed to God: "What is man that thou art mindful of him, and the son of man that thou dost care for him?" (Ps. 8:4). The response of Sacred Scripture affirms the simultaneously personal and social identity of man: "God created man in his own image, in the image of God he created him; male and female he created them" (Gen. 1:27). The predominant tradition in the West, in the wake of St. Augustine and St. Thomas Aquinas and under the influence of the Greek heritage, confined the image of God in man to his purely spiritual dimension, overlooking the human being's body and sexuality. In our times we dramatically call to mind a new foundation for the value of the body and its sexuality based on the rediscovered biblical message, reinterpreted in its original linguistic and historical context. Without forcing the meaning of the biblical texts, John Paul II took up this challenge in very bold and prophetic terms: "God is love and in Himself He lives a mystery of personal loving communion. Creating the human race in His own image and continually keeping it in being, God inscribed in the humanity of man and woman the vocation, and thus the capacity and responsibility, of love and communion. Love is therefore the fundamental and innate vocation of every human being."[6]

---

5. Serio de Guidi, "Per una teologia morale fondamentale sistematica secondo la storia della salvezza," *Corso di Morale I, Vita nuova in Cristo,* ed. Tullio Goffi and Gianni Piana (Brescia: Quiriniana, 1989), p. 204: "The scholastics, distinguishing between knowledge with an ontological basis and knowledge as a logical fact, could still connect ontology with ethics, therefore the axiom 'action follows being' remains valid. It is not, however, in the sense of a foundation, that is, of a deduction of the norm from being, but from the perspective of the foundations of the entire moral fact in ontological anthropological being."

6. *Familiaris consortio* 11, with references to 1 Jn. 4:8 and *Gaudium et Spes* 12. Cf. Carlo Cafarra, "L'uomo immagine di Dio Amore," *La Familiaris Consortio* (Rome: Libreria Editrice Vaticana, 1982), pp. 89-93.

Man, created *for love* as man and woman, becomes himself in love inasmuch as he responds to *Love*. "The vocation to love is what essentially makes man the image of God."[7] The love between man and woman takes part in God's original plan for humanity and is inserted within the Covenant relationship between God and his creature. The biblical text adds immediately after the creation of man as male and female: "And God blessed them, and God said to them, 'Be fruitful and multiply, and fill the earth'" (Gen. 1:28). "Thus the couple, while giving themselves to one another, give not just themselves but also the reality of children, who are a living reflection of their love, a permanent sign of conjugal unity and a living and inseparable synthesis of their being a father and a mother."[8] The human couple's vocation to love is therefore primarily *realized* in marriage and family. The communion of persons in love is the source of happiness ("This at last is bone of my bones and flesh of my flesh!" [Gen. 2:23]) and of life ("I have gotten a man with the help of the Lord" [Gen. 4:1]).

Since the beginning of creation, God united the couple's love to the gift of life. "Even here," writes Ratzinger, "marriage reflects its prototype, the love of God for man in the covenant."[9] This sacramental dimension of marriage, already present at the creaturely level, will be fully illuminated in Christ, where the covenant between God and man reaches its fulfillment in the Church. John Paul II speaks of the dual unity as a "primordial sacrament" that had been lost, but was then redeemed and integrated into the sacramental order of redemption.[10] The family, founded on marriage, is therefore the first "community of life and love," which prefigures the nuptial mystery between Christ and the Church. In his unitary plan of salvation, God willed that he be reflected in the human family at both the creaturely and ecclesial levels. The original *communio personarum* of Adam-Eve as *imago Dei* refers, therefore, proleptically to the Trinitarian

7. Joseph Cardinal Ratzinger, "Matrimonio e Famiglia nel piano di Dio," *La Familiaris Consortio* (Rome: Libreria Editrice Vaticana, 1982), p. 78.

8. *Familiaris consortio* 14.

9. Ratzinger, "Matrimonio e Famiglia nel piano di Dio," p. 85.

10. Cf. John Paul II, *The Theology of the Body: Human Love in the Divine Plan* (Boston: Daughters of St. Paul, 1997), pp. 336-41: "Marriage as a primordial sacrament constitutes, on the one hand, the figure (the likeness, the analogy), according to which there is constructed the basic main structure of the new economy of salvation and of the sacramental order. This order draws its origin from the spousal gracing which the Church received from Christ, together with all the benefits of redemption" (339).

Communio Personarum present in the ecclesial family founded on faith in Christ. Therefore, the human and Christian family is the *fulcrum* where the identity of man as *imago Trinitatis* is brought to light.

At this point it is important to set forth some complementary points of John Paul II's thought that lead towards a more explicitly Trinitarian anthropology. He calls the original relationship of man and woman, the "unity of the two" willed by God from the "beginning" as a relationship of love, a "primordial sacrament." Affirming the value of every human person as the image of God, in accordance with the tradition, the Pope nonetheless emphasizes the *interpersonal* character of the image: "Being a person in the image and likeness of God thus also involves existing in a relationship, in relation to the other 'I.' This is a prelude to the definitive self-revelation of the Triune God: a living unity in the communion of the Father, Son and Holy Spirit." This more explicit perspective of *Mulieris Dignitatem* relates the primordial sacrament, "the unity of the two," to the call "to live in a communion of love, and in this way to mirror in the world the communion of love that is in God, through which the Three Persons love each other in the intimate mystery of the one divine life."[11]

John Paul's emphasis on the interpersonal character of the *imago Dei* incorporates within the ecclesial Magisterium a widespread awareness in contemporary thought concerning not only the substantial nature of the person, but also his relational nature.[12] The mutual implication of the subjects appears above all in the analysis of the dynamism of love and freedom. Balthasar addresses this when speaking about the foundation of the moral conscience: "Man, that is to say, extrabiblical man, is awakened to a theoretical/practical self-awareness thanks to a voluntary and loving challenge on the part of his fellow man."[13] The mother's smile directed towards her baby phenomenologically expresses this original ontological call. In it the call of God is in some way incarnated. The transcendental relation of man to the absolute Good rightly set forth by St.

---

11. *Mulieris Dignitatem* 7.

12. To name just a few of these contemporary thinkers: Martin Buber, Maurice Nédoncelle, Ferdinand Ulrich, Pedro Lain Entralgo, Gabriel Marcel, Klaus Hemmerle, Claude Bruaire; cf. R. Habachi, *Une philosophie ensoleillée: Essais sur la relation* (Paris: Cariscript, 1992); A. Mattheeuws, *Les "dons" du mariage: Recherche de théologie morale et sacramentelle* (Paris: Culture et Vérité, 1996), pp. 27-126.

13. Hans Urs von Balthasar, "Nine Propositions on Christian Ethics," *Principles of Christian Morality* (San Francisco: Ignatius, 1986), p. 96, no. 7.1.

Thomas Aquinas,[14] is mediated through a dialogical relationship with another human being. In this light, Balthasar maintains that the man-woman reciprocity can be considered "as a paradigm of that community dimension which characterizes man's entire nature."[15] And ultimately, this dialogical structure of human freedom reflects the infinite Freedom of the Trinitarian Archetype, which is not a solipsistic freedom, but one of communion. God is free by the fact that he gives himself and thus brings into being that which is "Other than Himself," with whom he shares his freedom. In this way, even on the creaturely plane, human freedom given by God and the solidarity of this freedom in love are two inseparable dimensions of the human person's being in the image of God.

The expression "unity of the two," theologically coined by John Paul II, encounters certain developments in contemporary exegesis and theology. To be sure, there has been a significant convergence towards a Trinitarian anthropology such that some authors are little by little integrating relationality, the man-woman asymmetrical reciprocity or complementarity, into a more profound doctrine of the *imago Dei*.[16] The challenges that henceforth arise from the new religious currents and the theoretical abolition of sexual difference demand an extension of the reflection in this direction so as to arrive at an adequate anthropological foundation, which may at the same time include an authentic philosophical anthropology accessible to everyone. But in order to remain within the confines of this chapter on Christian identity, we need for the moment to incorporate what has been said with the revelation of man's fulfillment in Christ.

The Identity of the Person "in Christ"

Man's response to the call inscribed in his freedom receives a further determination in the biblical sphere based on the revelation of the *telos* of creation: "In him all things were created" (Col. 1:16). "[H]e chose us in him before the foundation of the world, that we should be holy and blameless

14. Thomas Aquinas, *De Veritate*, 22.5.

15. H. U. von Balthasar, *Theo-Drama*, vol. II, *The Dramatis Personae: Man in God,* trans. Graham Harrison (San Francisco: Ignatius, 1976), p. 364.

16. Cf. A. Scola, *Il mistero nuziale* (Rome: PUL-Mursia, 1998), pp. 43-61, with bibliographical reference in the area of exegesis and dogmatic theology.

before him. He destined us in love to be his sons through Jesus Christ, according to the purpose of his will" (Eph. 1:4-5). The New Testament casts light on the very foundations of creation. What appears both inside and outside the biblical sphere as a fascinating, but unfulfilled promise of communion (the unity of the two broken by death), indeed, emerges in the New Testament as the realization of a definitive communion between the divine and the human founded on the gift of Christ. The relationship between man and woman refers back to its fulfillment in Christ and the Church. Therefore, erotic love, elevated by the Song of Songs to the level of a supreme anthropological symbol of the covenant relationship, is fulfilled in the suprasexual but authentically spousal *agapē* of the corporal-eucharistic encounter between Christ and the Church. What St. Paul calls *mystērion*, that is, the mystery hidden in God from all eternity, discloses itself in the nuptial mystery of Christ the Bridegroom who makes the Church, his Body and Bride, emerge from within himself.[17] This event, henceforth being sacramentally fulfilled in the Holy Spirit, constitutes the purpose and summit of God's new and eternal covenant with humanity "in Christ."

This nuptial mystery reveals the radical novelty of its anthropological meaning in light of the theological concept of the person developed by Hans Urs von Balthasar. The theologian from Basel sustains that man cannot be defined in his personal uniqueness either by his individual characteristics or his interpersonal relationships. To ground what theology designates as a "person" there must be nothing less than a Word which flows from the profound mystery of God and calls the "human subject" to let himself be generated as a child of God "in Christ." The concept of the person, which derives from the most intimate reality of man, originates therefore within the ambit of Christian revelation; despite its universal philosophical diffusion, it must be restored to its origin in order to account for the irreplaceable dignity of the human person.

"It is when God addresses a conscious subject, tells him who he is and what he means to the eternal God of truth and shows him the purpose of his existence — that is, imports a distinctive and divinely authorized mis-

---

17. Cf. Romano Penna, *Il "mysterion" paolino: Traiettoria e costituzione* (Brescia, 1978); For the lexical history of *mystērion*, cf. G. Bornkamm, "Mystērion," *Grande Lessico del Nuovo Testamento*, vol. 7 (Brescia, 1971), pp. 645-716. Cf. above all John Paul II, *The Theology of the Body*, esp. "Christ's Redemptive Love Has a Spousal Nature," pp. 321-24.

sion — that we can say of a conscious subject that he is a 'person.'"[18] Balthasar establishes a distinction between the "conscious subject" which corresponds to what classical theology calls a person and the "theological person" which corresponds to the same subject inasmuch as he is enriched with a supernatural mission that he receives from the Word of God: "'Person' is the 'new name' by which God addresses me (Rev. 2:17) and which comes from 'the beginning of God's creation' (Rev. 3:14); it always implies a task, namely, to be 'a pillar in the temple of my God' (Rev. 3:12)."[19]

Christ is the archetype of the event through which the divine Word personalizes a human subject. The man Jesus is assumed in the Person of the incarnate Word to the point that in his archetypal case, Person and Mission coincide. Christ is the One Sent by the Father to reconcile the world to God. In him there is an ontological identity between Person and Mission which is founded upon the *a priori* reality of the hypostatic union. By contrast, in all the other subjects the person-mission relation is *a posteriori* because it depends on the divine call and the subject's temporal response to the mission, which makes him become a "person in Christ." It follows that human persons find their theological identity "in Christ," in the progressive and dramatic identification with the Word-mission which defines their role in the body of Christ.

This radically Christocentric concept of person has a corresponding ecclesial dimension. Every participation in the universal mission of Christ simultaneously involves relation to the ecclesial community: "When a human being becomes a person, theologically, by being given a unique vocation and mission, he is simultaneously de-privatized, socialized, made into a locus and a bearer of community."[20] It follows that the person and the community depend on each other without confusion or separation. As an

18. H. U. von Balthasar, *Theo-Drama,* vol. III, *Dramatis Personae: The Person in Christ,* trans. Graham Harrison (San Francisco: Ignatius, 1992), p. 207.

19. H. U. von Balthasar, *Theo-Drama* III, p. 208; cf. M. Ouellet, "The foundations of Christian ethics according to Hans Urs von Balthasar," *Communio* 17 (Fall 1990), pp. 375-401.

20. H. U. von Balthasar, *Theo-Drama* III, p. 271. In the context of his dramatic mariology, Balthasar adds: "In this way, there is a mutual interpenetration of the diverse missions and the persons who identify themselves with them: this is what is meant by the *communio sanctorum.* Evidently it is not only the goods and values of their persons that become common property but the persons themselves. There is an analogy here with the way Christ (and, through him, the whole triune God) becomes the 'common property' of those who share his flesh and blood and his Holy Spirit," pp. 349-50.

integrated reality of freedom and grace, the person and the community coincide and mutually overlap. They are not constituted independently of each other, but together form the *"communio sanctorum,"* which is born from communion in Christ's eucharistic body. Balthasar develops a whole phenomenology of persons-missions which constitute ecclesial communion in the image and likeness of the Trinitarian circumincession.[21]

In affirming that the profound identity of the person is found "in Christ," Balthasar defines the person by his belonging to Christ, namely, by his being a member of the body of Christ, which is the Church. Furthermore, in basing the relation to Christ on the mission-charism to be accomplished in the Spirit, Balthasar simultaneously works out a radical integration of the person in the community. Thus we reach the point of speaking not only about an ecclesial dimension of the person, but the *ecclesiality* of the person. In the eucharistic context, the author arrives precisely at this expression: "The sacraments, primarily baptism into his death and Resurrection (Rom. 6:3-11) and the Eucharist, which is a sharing in the one body of Christ, making us into one Body (1 Cor. 10:16f.), not only give us personhood: they also fashion us into a community. Everyone who participates in the pneumatic body of Christ, shared out in the Church, not only becomes a member of the Church community: he actually acquires an intrinsically ecclesial quality."[22]

The advantage of this Christocentric and ecclesial understanding of the person is that it ties together, in a more intrinsic way, Christian identity, personal ethics, and social ethics. To be sure, from this perspective, Christian action spurred on and sustained by grace is not primarily aimed at the self-realization of the person, as in autonomous rational ethics, but at serving Christ and the Church in faith. Christian moral action expresses, in the first instance, the dynamism of the Holy Spirit effused in hearts, which pulsates and unites, or better still, "sends" the person to others in order to share the good of communion with Christ. This good, also

---

21. We cannot on this occasion expound upon his rich symbolic ecclesiology, which is worked out based on this theological concept of person; cf. H. U. von Balthasar, "Who Is the Church?" in *Explorations in Theology*, vol. II, *Spouse of the Word*, trans. A. V. Littledale (San Francisco: Ignatius, 1967), pp. 143-91; see also his *The Office of Peter and the Structure of the Church* (San Francisco: Ignatius, 1986), Part II.

22. H. U. von Balthasar, *Theo-Drama* III, p. 281: "Was so durch den kirchlich verteilten pneumatischen Leib Christi in jedem Partizipierenden entsteht, ist nicht nur Gliedsein an der Gemeinschaft Kirche, sondern Kirchlichkeit selbst," p. 258.

resulting from the natural dynamism of human acts, is the fruit of the gift of the person himself, animated by the Spirit of Christ; in belonging to the Trinitarian communion, he also becomes the possession of the Church and her mission. "For all who are led by the Spirit of God are sons of God . . . and if children, then heirs, heirs of God and fellow heirs with Christ, provided we suffer with him in order that we may also be glorified with him" (Rom. 8:14-17).

Trinitarian and Eucharistic Identity

This perspective obviously presupposes the grace of sonship given in Baptism and confirmed with the gift of the Holy Spirit in Confirmation. We are predestined to be sons in the Son, to the praise and glory of his grace. The specificity of the gift of the Spirit in Confirmation consists in confirming filial identity through the gift of witnessing, that is, for a mission. These gifts therefore constitute the Trinitarian identity of the Christian: from all eternity we were predestined and generated by the Father through his Son in the power of the Holy Spirit. Christian identity results from participation in the life of the Trinitarian Family. Through the action of the three divine Persons, we are fully inserted within the ecclesial communion, receiving the quality of members of the Body of Christ from the moment in which we participate in the eucharistic banquet of the children of God. All the other gifts of God, both natural and supernatural, converge towards the nuptial-eucharistic mystery celebrated in the Church in the name of all of humanity. So we say with C. Yannaras and the Eastern tradition: "The manifestation of the Trinitarian ethos, the image of the 'ethos' of God in the *being* of man, constitutes the *ethos* of the Church, the event of 'gathering together into one the scattered children of God' (Jn. 11:52), the reality of the Church. In other words, Christian ethics is a eucharistic event, an existential event of unity and communion."[23]

An ethical perspective based on the Trinitarian ethos communicated in the eucharistic event helps to free ethics from a certain prevailing philosophical approach that begins from below in order to construct the ethical order on the impulse of nature tending towards its fulfillment, an impulse not exempt from ambiguity. "Christian ethics must be modeled on Jesus

---

23. C. Yannaras, *La libertà dell'ethos* (Bologna: EDB, 1984), pp. 78-79.

Christ,"[24] affirms Balthasar emphatically. The Father gave the world the substantial gift of his Son to indicate the way of salvation for all men (Jn. 3:16; 11:52); This man Jesus brings the Holy Spirit with him, who makes a saving faith possible (Lk. 1:35). Certainly this Trinitarian gift contains the fulfillment of all the desires of the human heart, which signifies also the integration of natural ethics discovered by reason; but this gift moves man beyond his *cor inquietum* along the way of the *sequela Christi* and therefore of mission. The measure of ethics becomes not only rational, but christological, that is, Trinitarian.

Christ is "the concrete categorical imperative"[25] of Christian morality, not only the "universal" norm, but the "concrete and personal" norm of every ethical situation and of every Christian responsibility in the world. If this is true, if grace is the point of departure for Christian ethos, the concrete figure of Christ, as depicted in the Sermon on the Mount in Matthew 5:1-12, becomes the form of life of the Christian: "You must therefore be perfect, just as your heavenly Father is perfect" (Mt. 5:48). Its consequences come about not only at the formal level of an increased moral obligation, but also at the level of content.[26] The ethics of faith assumes the natural ethics of the virtues, but goes far beyond it due to the handing over of one's entire person to Christ, which creates a true friendship with Him. "No longer do I call you servants, . . . but I have called you friends. . . . You did not choose me, but I chose you and appointed you that you should go and bear fruit and that your fruit should abide" (Jn. 15:15-16). Friendship with Christ in faith bears within itself a more intimate and personal call that requires a going forth and bearing fruit in communion and mission: "This I command you, to love one another" (Jn. 15:17).

The "more" or "ever more," pertaining to the very content of this personal friendship with Christ, proceeds from the love of the crucified Redeemer, who assumed the sin of all men in order to offer in exchange for each one the grace of his obedience of love. This friendship is made even more concrete and fecund by the fruit of his sacrifice, namely by the gift of the Holy Spirit. The Spirit is diffused in the hearts of men as Person-Love,

24. H. U. von Balthasar, "Nine Propositions on Christian Ethics," *Principles of Christian Morality* (San Francisco: Ignatius, 1986), p. 79, no. 1.

25. Balthasar, "Nine Propositions on Christian Ethics," p. 79, no. 1.

26. "Faith also possesses a moral content. It gives rise to and calls for a consistent life commitment; it entails and brings to perfection the acceptance and observance of God's commandments" (*Veritatis Splendor* 89).

who abides and makes it possible for everyone to respond to the Father "in Christ."[27] At this point it would be opportune to introduce the very beautiful discourse of St. Thomas Aquinas on the Holy Spirit and his gifts as the *Lex Nova* that governs from within the hearts of the children of God.[28] "Human action is not born from autonomy, but from a friendship in which the Friend moves us."[29] The entire novelty of Christian ethics is therefore rooted in friendship with God, which the Holy Spirit, as the bond of Trinitarian love, fosters and personally seals. This absolute novelty not only consists in the fact that the friend of Christ can love his neighbor as Christ has loved him (Jn. 15:12), but in the unheard-of miracle that allows the friend of Christ to love God with the same Love with which the Father and the Son love one another: "I have made known to them your name, and I will continue to make it known, so that the love with which you loved me may be in them, and so that I may be in them" (Jn. 17:26).

In this light, Christian ethics is not founded so much upon man's natural impulse as on the call of grace, that is, the gift and pledge of the three divine Persons, who envelop human freedom and its longing for happiness, integrating and fulfilling it by participation in the beatitudes of Christ.[30] This approach effects a change in horizon from that of classical ethics, shifting the accent from the desire for beatitude more or less philosophically understood, to the embracing of the beatitudes Christ offers to satisfy the human desire for happiness. We shall return to this further on.

At this point it is worth recalling with *Familiaris Consortio* that "Christian revelation recognizes two specific ways of realizing the vocation of the human person, in its entirety, to love: marriage and virginity or celibacy."[31] The "unity of the two" upon which we have insisted for grasping the fundamental structure of the *humanum*, does not exclude, but rather requires the

27. Cf. M. Ouellet, "The foundations of Christian ethics according to Hans Urs von Balthasar," pp. 381-86.

28. Thomas Aquinas, *Super Ep. Ad Romanos,* c. VIII, lect. 1, n. 603: "Et haec quidem lex spiritus dicitur lex nova, quae vel est ipse Spiritus Sanctus, vel eam in cordibus nostris Spiritus Sanctus facit." *Ier.* XXXI, 33: "Dabo legem meam in visceribus eorum, et in corde eorum superscribam eam." Cf. *Summa Contra Gentiles,* 21-23; *S.Th.* I-II, q. 68, 69; II-II, q. 23-24.

29. José Noriega, "Lo Spirito Santo e l'azione umana," *Domanda sul bene e domanda su Dio* (Pul-Mursia, 1999), p. 246.

30. Cf. L. Melina, "Amore, desiderio e azione," in *Domanda sul bene e domanda su Dio* (Pul-Mursia, 1999), pp. 91-108.

31. *Familiaris Consortio* 11, 16.

fulfillment of Christian marriage in the mystery of Christian virginity. The example of the Holy Family, already celebrated by Saint Augustine, is a powerful illustration of this: "In these parents of Christ all the goods of marriage were realized: offspring [*proles*], faithfulness [*fides*] and the bond [*sacramentum*]. We know there to be offspring, for there is the Lord Jesus himself; fidelity by the fact that there was no adultery; and the bond because there was no divorce."[32] Inserted by vocation into the event of the incarnation of the Son of God, Mary and Joseph nevertheless live a true marriage according to the Old Law, but one which effects the transition to the Kingdom of God inaugurated in the Person and work of their Son. Thus, enveloped in the grace of the incarnate Word, they live their virginal and family relationships sustained by the presence of the Holy Spirit, who chose them to mold the holy humanity of the Redeemer. In their relationship the ethos of the total gift of self to the point of sacrifice, that is, the ethos of the beatitudes, finds its most transparent and fruitful source, both for the life of families and for communities founded on virginal consecration.

Christian Ethics, the Fulfillment
of the Human Person in Ecclesial Communion

The Ethos of the Gift and the Good of Communion

The Trinitarian and sacramental foundation of ecclesial ethos sustains all the dimensions of personal and social ethics. It illuminates the world of work, economy, and politics, as well as that of art and communication, but its light shines even brighter in the ambit of conjugal and family ethics, to which we shall limit our reflection. The reason for this Trinitarian reflection on the family is rooted in the sacramental dimension that flows from the assumption of the man-woman relationship "in Christ."[33] The fact that marriage is a sacrament of the nuptial mystery of Christ and Church signifies a privileged access to the Trinitarian unity that joins Christ the Bridegroom to his Bride the Church, from which derives not only the imperative of the imitation of a "model," but participation in a "communion." Between familial communion and Trinitarian communion there is an authentic analogy, to

---

32. Augustine, *De nuptiis et concupiscentia*, I.13.11; PL 44.421.

33. For a more in-depth study on this aspect cf. A. Scola, *Il mistero nuziale*, pp. 91-116; see also H. U. von Balthasar, *Teologica* III, pp. 130-31.

which the Holy Family attests precisely by virtue of the hypostatic union of the incarnate Word.[34] The ethos of the gift that flows from it does not, therefore, appear as a voluntarism of imitation, but rather as an intimate consent to being oneself, "with and for others" in God and with God. The result is a progressive personalization by means of the dynamic of love, which unites the person and society thanks to the fruitfulness of communion.

John Paul II repeatedly insisted on this ethical dynamic which results from the insertion of man-woman into the sphere of Trinitarian relations, where being Person and being Love coincide. Relying upon the conciliar text of *Gaudium et Spes* 24, the Pope develops the relationship between person, communion, and gift as the foundation of all Christian ethics including that of marriage and virginity. "Being a person means striving towards self-realization (the Council text speaks of self-discovery), which can only be achieved *'through a sincere gift of self.'* The model for this interpretation of the person is God himself as Trinity, as a communion of Persons. To say that man is created in the image and likeness of God means that man is called to exist 'for' others, to become a gift."[35]

Against this background, the sacramentality of marriage acquires an extraordinary importance that impacts upon the ethical consequences of marital life. Following St. Paul in his letter to the Ephesians 5:21-33, John Paul links the most ancient sacrament, based on Genesis 2:24, with the spousal union of Christ and the Church, the source and culmination of the entire sacramental order. Meditation on this supreme foundation of conjugal ethos clearly places anthropology and ethics in the light of redemption in Christ and its sacramental consequences. As a result, the pauline parenesis on marital and family relationships, "be subject to one another out of reverence for Christ" (Eph. 5:21), does not primarily rely on the analogous exemplary nature of the love of Christ and the Church, but on the sacramental realism of the couple's insertion "in Christ," by virtue of baptism and the Lord's eucharistic-spousal gift to his Bride, the Church.

Paul can insist upon mutual subjection out of reverence for Christ

---

34. Cf. P. Coda, "Familia y Trinidad," *Mistero trinitario y familia humana*, Semanas de Estudios trinitarios, Ed. Secretariado Trinitario (Salamanca, 1995), pp. 195-227, esp. 217ff.; see also Blanca Castilla y Cortazar, "La Trinidad como familia," *Annales theologici* 10 (1996): pp. 381-416.

35. *Mulieris Dignitatem* 7; see also the *Letter to Families* 6-13, especially 11: "Love causes man to find fulfillment through the sincere gift of self. To love means to give and to receive something which can be neither bought nor sold, but only given freely and mutually."

(Eph. 5:21) precisely because there is an authentic participation of the couple, married in the Lord, in his kenotic-paschal gift. The ethical imperative that follows this relies on the objective reality of sacramental grace and not only on the simple proposal of an ideal. The Second Vatican Council reaffirmed that the spouses, married in faith, receive a gift from the Lord that constitutes their charism among the people of God[36] and is the basis of their ecclesial mission in relation to society. It is this sacramental gift which justifies the categorical imperative of faithful and fecund love. Their vocation to love, with all its anthropological and ethical components, unfolds within the nuptial union of Christ and the Church, which imprints the Trinitarian likeness promised by God from the "beginning" upon their reality as a fecund couple. Such a vocation to love is not limited to the sanctification of a natural institution in line with the first creation; it promotes an authentic *sequela Christi* in the daily life of the couple and the family. In fact, the Trinitarian blessing of the couple, symbolically expressed in the liturgy of matrimony, places the Christian family at the center of the institutions of the Kingdom of God and opens to its faithful members the ethical sphere of the beatitudes.

The example of the Holy Family permits us once again to concretely grasp the overturning of the common sense of existence that results from the event of the Incarnation. Mary and Joseph illustrate the passage from the ethos of desire to the ethos of service or mission. Called by name to receive the gift of God himself, they are committed to give themselves to one another to the point of sacrificing their own aspirations, obeying the Word, and serving God's plan for their union. The natural desire for happiness is assumed, fulfilled, and surpassed in serving Christ and his Kingdom. An ethos of desire which is never satisfied is replaced by an ethos of the gift of self to the point of a disinterested sacrifice in response to the unheard-of Gift of the incarnate Word. The search for beatitude in God is converted into service to Christ through the vitality of the beatitudes. Thus at this point human action is not only perfected, but is elevated to the insuperable dignity of sacramental service to the Trinitarian *Communio Personarum.* One can then speak of an authentic existence in mission as Trinitarian glorification.[37]

---

36. *Lumen Gentium* 11, with reference to 1 Cor 7:7: "Each has his own special gift from God, one of one kind and one of another."

37. Cf. Marc Ouellet, *L'existence comme mission: L'anthropologie théologique de Hans Urs von Balthasar* (Rome: PUG, 1983), pp. 133-46.

The event of the Incarnation, therefore, radically changed the ultimate sense of human action, causing it to become a synergistic, nuptial, and eucharistic action, in which the divine initiative assumes and converts the creature's natural dynamism into a sacrament of the divine gift. In the man Jesus, for example, the human action of the incarnate Word, without losing any part of its intentional structure as human action, is infinitely raised to the *service* of divine action. Analogously, by virtue of their closeness and participation in the life of Jesus, the moral action of Mary and Joseph, far from being mortified by a renunciation of the natural impulse of the heart, is elevated above itself in service to the incarnate God. An ethics of infinitely fruitful consecrated virginity becomes possible, then, as a fulfillment of conjugal ethics already perfected by the sacrament of matrimony. From this perspective, the divine-human synergistic action, both virginal and conjugal, takes place under the sign of ecclesial fruitfulness.

The Personal and Ecclesial Fruitfulness of Conjugal Love

The integration of person and mission that we developed in the first section helps us to understand more deeply the meaning of *Familiaris Consortio*'s emphasis on love as the fundamental mission of the family. "Thus, with love as its point of departure and making constant reference to it, the recent Synod emphasized four general tasks for the family: (1) forming a community of persons; (2) serving life; (3) participating in the development of society; (4) sharing in the life and mission of the Church."[38] All of the family's particular tasks are in fact ascribable to love as a fundamental mission. Obviously this love does not only imply human sentiments, emotions, and the growth stages of interpersonal relationships between the spouses and their children. These subjective dimensions are taken up into the mystery of the covenant, namely, into the love of Christ and the Church. Their anthropological depth, not to be overlooked, is placed at the service of the *agapē* of Christ, thus reaching an authentically sacramental dimension.

Christ and the Church, therefore, find in the couple and the family a place of sacramental incarnation, a place of growth and of missionary ser-

---

38. *Familiaris Consortio* 17.

vice to the world, in expectation of the revelation of the children of God. To be sure, the love which is at stake in conjugal and family relationships is the supernatural love of Christ for the Church; this love is entrusted to the couple and the family to be lived, celebrated, served, and handed down to new generations. As *Familiaris Consortio* declares, "The Holy Spirit, who is poured forth in the celebration of the sacraments, is the living source and inexhaustible sustenance of the supernatural communion that gathers believers and links them with Christ and with each other in the unity of the Church of God."[39]

In this light, the first fruit of marriage is the initial act of faith and love that indissolubly unites two baptized persons. "The human act by which the partners mutually surrender themselves to each other" founds "the intimate community of life and conjugal love."[40] Such a community does not lose its inclusive sacramental character when the most precious gift of children is not given to crown the mutual donation of the spouses: "Every Christian marriage is blessed by God and is fruitful in him, whether through the blessing of children, or the blessing of sacrifice. If God chooses the second alternative the spiritual fruitfulness of marriage is increased and widened out invisibly so that it flows into the whole community."[41] Human love is in itself its own end and fruitfulness, by virtue of the fact that it is a communion of persons. If the mission of transmitting the gift of life to other creatures does not become concrete in the birth of children, the acceptance of this sacrifice opens the couple up to new possibilities for spiritual and apostolic fecundity in the Church and the world. Nevertheless, in the majority of cases, the fundamental mission of the spouses is the total and faithful gift of self in an openness to procreation and the Christian education of their children. In this way they grow as persons by giving themselves to one another "in the Lord" and in giving society and the Church new children destined for the worship of God.

The key to a deeper understanding of the sacramental fruitfulness of Christian marriage is precisely the ecclesiality of the person and the couple, which we have already mentioned. By virtue of the total gift of their persons, a gift sealed by the Holy Spirit and conferred in the sacramental

---

39. *Familiaris Consortio* 21.

40. *Gaudium et spes* 48.

41. A. von Speyr, *The Word: A Meditation on the Prologue to St. John's Gospel*, trans. Alexander Dru (New York: David McKay, 1953), p. 101.

celebration,[42] the couple is constituted as a domestic Church, enabled by the Holy Spirit and rooted in the unity of the Trinity. Their identity is not only that of a couple blessed and called to holiness according to a specific matrimonial modality; their identity is ecclesial in the sense that their relationship itself becomes a sacrament of the objective sacramental relationship between Christ the Bridegroom and his Bride the Church. The love between Christ and the Church is poured out in the man-woman relationship and flows into a common fruitfulness for the benefit of both. The Church's fecundity is continued in the family, while the spiritual and human fruitfulness of the family makes the Church grow both quantitatively and qualitatively.

The domestic Church's mission is not limited, therefore, to assuming a "meritorious" moral task which follows a solemn commitment. It consists above all in the dynamic and organic extension of a sacramental community inserted within the objective structure of the Church. Vatican II reaffirmed that the spouses have their own "charism" among the people of God. This objective charism is first and foremost the Christian conjugal bond, which consecrates the couple to be a "community of life and love."[43] This community in and of itself serves life and society, and undertakes an educative and evangelizing task, or better still, an ecclesial ministry which incarnates in various manners a fundamental service for the love of Christ and the Church.

Conjugal and Family Ethics as a Paradigm

At this point we must mention the dramatic dispute between the Church's Magisterium and public opinion over the issue of birth control. This dispute focuses on a very concrete point, the intrinsic bond between Christian identity, personal ethics, and social ethics. The importance of this dispute and its consequences confers upon Christian conjugal and family

42. Cf. Chapter 5 of this book, "The Holy Spirit, Seal of the Conjugal Covenant"; for the original Italian version see my essay *Lo Spirito Santo, sigillo dell'alleanza coniugale,* R. Bonetti, ed., *Il matrimonio in Cristo è matrimonio nello Spirito* (Rome: Città Nuovo, 1998), pp. 73-96.

43. On this subject cf. L. Ligier, *Il matrimonio: Questioni teologiche e pastorali* (Rome: Città Nuova, 1988), who develops, in the wake of H. Mühlen, the idea of the conjugal bond as "a charism of consecration," p. 114ff.

ethics a paradigmatic value in the face of the current mentality, which separates love from sex and from procreation.

The publication of the encyclical *Humanae Vitae* by Paul VI on July 25, 1968, marks a turning point in the relationship between the Church and the contemporary world. The enthusiasm aroused by the opening of the Second Vatican Council came to a sudden cool-down, to the point of provoking a crisis not yet completely resolved within the Church itself. Confirmation of the Church's traditional position rejecting artificial means of birth control marked a profound rupture between a great portion of the faithful and theologians on the one hand, and the official Magisterium on the other, which was accused of taking a step backwards and closing itself off from modernity. The encyclical's line of reasoning was not understood. Theologians, in their impassioned reactions, placed the "biologism" of *Humanae Vitae* and the "personalism" of *Gaudium et Spes* in opposition.[44] The debate that later evolved showed that what was at stake was essential and called into question not only one particular issue, but a fundamental anthropological vision.

The key point of the pontifical message was precisely the affirmation "that each and every marriage act *(quilibet matrimonii usus)* must remain open to the transmission of life."[45] This affirmation is based on an inseparable connection, willed by God, between the two meanings of the conjugal act: the unitive and the procreative. "By safeguarding both these essential aspects, the unitive and the procreative, the conjugal act preserves in its fullness the sense of true mutual love and its ordination towards man's most high calling to parenthood."[46] Proposing such a doctrine signified: (1) maintaining as primary the sacred meaning of the transmission of life as an act of cooperation with God; (2) maintaining the bond between true love and real openness to the gift of life; and (3) declaring as immoral contraceptive means that exclude an openness to life and therefore communion with God, since the spouses are "not to be the arbiters of the sources of human life, but rather the ministers of the plan established by the Creator."[47]

Reaffirmed on numerous occasions and fully re-founded upon the "ad-

44. Cf. Michel Séguin, *La contraception et L'Eglise: Bilan et prospective* (Montreal: Paulines, 1994).

45. Paul VI, *Humanae Vitae* 11.

46. Paul VI, *Humanae Vitae* 12.

47. Paul VI, *Humanae Vitae* 13; cf. Gustave Martelet, "Pour mieux comprendre l'encyclique *Humanae Vitae*," *NRTh* 90 (1968), pp. 897-917, 1009-1063.

equate" anthropology proposed by John Paul II,[48] this doctrine holds up against any confrontation with secularized anthropology, which separates love from life, sex from love, and the person from his body. The contraceptive mentality that, with the help of the mass media, has up until now won the assent of the majority, pushes the moral drift towards one bordering on dehumanization. Procreation becomes "reproduction" of an individual of a species; it can from now on be accomplished without either love or sex by means of the technique of artificial insemination or even, in the near future, with the more aberrant technique of cloning.[49] An anthropology without God, based on the divorce between freedom and truth, leaves man and his constitutive relationships at the mercy of the most bitter fruits of a nihilistic culture: boredom, despair, violence, teen suicide, divorce, and so on.

Maintaining the intimate connection between the person, love, sex, and life, the Church protects man from falling into ethical relativism and nihilism, which ever more pervade the ethos of secularized society. The decision to maintain the inseparable unity of the two meanings of the act of conjugal love, unitive and procreative, has stirred up an epochal crisis in the Church, but has at the same time provoked a more in-depth study of the anthropological and sacramental foundations of Catholic conjugal ethics: "According to the Pauline doctrine, the sexual relationship between two baptized spouses acquires a particular richness: it becomes not only the expression of the total and definitive gift that each makes of himself or herself to the other, but by the will of Christ, it becomes in some way the expression of the total and definitive gift of Christ to his Church, a concrete participation in Christ's love for the Church, an efficacious sign of the Lord's gift to the spouses: it becomes a sacrament. . . . Each of the spouses, giving his or her love and expressing it in his or her bodiliness, is a mediator of Christ's love for the other."[50]

---

48. Cf. *Familiaris Consortio* 32: "Thus the innate language that expresses the total reciprocal self-giving of husband and wife is overlaid, through contraception, by an objectively contradictory language, namely, by not giving oneself totally to the other. This leads not only to a positive refusal to be open to life but also to a falsification of the inner truth of conjugal love, which is called upon to give itself in personal totality." See also John Paul II's catechesis on human love in the divine plan: *The Theology of the Body,* "Reflections on *Humanae Vitae,*" pp. 386-423.

49. Cf. Angelo Scola, ed., *Quale vita? La bioetica in questione* (Mondadori, 1998).

50. M. Séguin, *La contraception et L'Eglise,* p. 157; cf. Edouard Hamel, S.J., "La sexualité illuminée par la Révélation," *Studia missionalia* 27 (1978): p. 324.

This sacramental perspective, perhaps too implicit in *Humanae Vitae*, more deeply confirms and justifies its position. The ethics of total gift receives its confirmation from the truth of the sacrament, which seals the interweaving of person and love, corporality and communion, in the conjugal act. Conjugal love makes ethically explicit the gift of self to Christ and the gift of Christ to the couple, which, celebrated and lived in faith, is and becomes a sacrament of Christ's love for the Church. Therefore, the couple's action is not only determined anthropologically by the objective good of communion in the total gift of self which respects the language of the body and openness to life; the couple's action is determined sacramentally by the relationship of love between Christ and the Church, which is internal to their love and therefore must mark its sacramental quality.[51] This action, to the extent that it is good and holy, is and becomes sacramental. It not only confers a higher degree of moral perfection upon the couple and the family, but serves in extending the kingdom of God through the objective action of Christ and the Church, which pervades the couple's holy and fruitful mutual donation.

From this perspective, one can better see how opportune it is for the Church to intervene in the intimate sphere of the spouses, to safeguard not only the good of *proles* and of love, but also the good of the sacrament, which, according to St. Thomas, surpasses the first two in excellence.[52] The good of the sacrament is not only indissolubility, but the spiritual fruitfulness which flows from the couple who are always open to the divine "Third" abiding within them. "He who abides in me, and I in him, he it is that bears much fruit" (Jn. 15:5). Despite the resistance of the hedonistic and nihilistic culture, the conjugal and family ethics promoted by the Church represents a *kairos* and a paradigm yet to be discovered. Precisely

51. H. U. von Balthasar, "A Word on *Humanae Vitae*," *Communio* 20 (Summer 1993), pp. 437-50.

52. This perspective takes up the Augustinian and Thomistic formulation of the supernatural good of the sacrament, which surpasses the goods of *fides* and *proles*: "As for excellence, the sacrament is the greatest among the goods (ends) of marriage, for it belongs to them by virtue of the fact that marriage itself is a sacrament of grace. By contrast, the other two goods (ends) belong to it by the fact that they are a natural duty *(naturae officium)*. Now the perfection of grace is more excellent than that of nature." Thomas Aquinas, *Suppl.*, q. 49, a. 3. The good of the sacrament is the "community of life and love" founded on the indissoluble conjugal bond that makes visible in the "sacrament of the couple" (C. Rocchetta) the union between Christ and the Church.

because it requires the grounding of conjugal life in prayer, sacrifice, and sacramental practice, it protects family life, making the man and woman capable of an authentic love in the image of God, who is Love. Couples and families who, with docility and readiness, take seriously the fidelity, indissoluble unity, and fruitfulness of love not only attain to a deeper and lasting happiness, but they surpass themselves, becoming caught up in the sacramental gift of Christ to the world."

The Epochal Mission of Christian Conjugal and Family Ethics

Family Communion, First Gift to Society

"The Creator of all made the married state the beginning and foundation of human society"; therefore, the family became "the primary vital cell of society."[53] This conviction must guide the efforts to offer society the gift of family communion with all its dimensions of unity, fidelity, and fecundity, and to promote with every possible means the fundamental value of the family for the harmonious and peaceful development of the human person and society. Thus, it is necessary to heed the Council's appeal to overcome "a merely individualistic morality" and to dare to intervene socially and politically for justice and love, promoting "public and private organizations devoted to bettering the conditions of life."[54] This appeal is more urgent than ever before, but somewhat difficult given the pressure of the modern means of social communication that openly oppose the Catholic Church's positions.

The gift the family makes of itself to society must be repaid, so to say, with the recognition and protection of its fundamental rights. Family communion, which offers "the first and irreplaceable school of social life," must be sustained by adequate family politics for the good of society itself, which is becoming ever more depersonalized and disfigured into a mass: "Faced with a society that is running the risk of becoming more and more depersonalized and standardized and therefore inhuman and dehumanizing, with the negative results of many forms of escapism — such as alco-

---

53. Vatican Council II, The Decree on the Apostolate of Lay People, *Apostolicam actuositatem,* 11; FC 42.

54. *Gaudium et Spes* 30; *Familiaris Consortio* 44.

holism, drugs and even terrorism — the family possesses and continues still to release formidable energies capable of taking man out of his anonymity, keeping him conscious of his personal dignity, enriching him with deep humanity and actively placing him, in his uniqueness and unrepeatablity, within the fabric of society."[55]

There is no doubt that conjugal and family virtues, deeply rooted in the ethos of sacramental forgiveness and eucharistic communion, can contribute in a very significant way to the recovery of the social fabric. The Fathers of the Church knew this, primarily St. Augustine, who considered the family as a *"seminarium civitatis,"* a place of sowing seeds for the City of God,[56] or, according to the formula of Gratian, a *"seminarium caritatis,"* that is, a place for sowing the seeds of love.[57] Therefore, what is essential for the witness of Christian spouses is not a social or political activism, but the very presence of the Christian family in the world and the peaceful and silent strength of its communion. What can better edify youth in need of help but the beauty of a united and open family who knows how to share its material and spiritual goods through hospitality. Thus St. John Chrysostom thought: "because all happiness is derived from our hospitality in the home, I want to seek this virtue before all else."[58] In this way, following the great tradition of the Fathers, the Christian family can serve God by radiating the light of love that issues forth from Christ, *Lumen Gentium,* who is present in the midst of those who are his own (Mt. 18:20).

The Domestic Church, Star of the New Evangelization

The Fathers of the Second Vatican Council overcame the predominantly juridical formulation of the doctrine on marriage by applying the comprehensive Christocentrism of Vatican II to the spouses' "community of life and love." Thus, they opened the way to the sacrament's permanent dimension, which is not exhausted in the celebration of matrimony, but accompanies the spouses and their family throughout their entire lives.

---

55. *Familiaris Consortio* 43.

56. Augustine, *The City of God,* 16.84: CCL 48, cf. 15-16.

57. Gratian, *Decretum* 1, C. 35.91; cited in Giuseppe Nardin, *Famiglia e società secondo i Padri della Chiesa* (Rome: Città Nuova, 1989), p. 57.

58. John Chrysostom, *Eulogy of Maximus,* VI, in the Italian translation *L'unità delle nozze,* trans. G. Di Nicola (Rome, 1984), 112-14.

Christ "abides with them," affirms *Gaudium et Spes* 48, thus opening for them a way of the *sequela* within their state of life. These openings are still not totally integrated in the life of couples and their pastoral care. Still very absent from family life and marriage preparation is the awareness of the sacramental dignity of the conjugal union grafted in the nuptial mystery of Christ and the Church. The moral demands of conjugal and family ethics, when not silenced, are still too often justified by an extrinsicist and legalistic perspective that fails to make the spouses see and desire their intimate sacramental participation in the spousal mystery of Christ and the Church. For example, the famous Pauline passage of Ephesians 5:21ff. is often explained in its parenetical dimension without grasping its profound sacramental richness.

"Husbands, love your wives, as Christ loved the Church and gave himself up for her, that he might sanctify her, having cleansed her by the washing of water with the word" (Eph. 5:25-26). Here we find the foundations of the sacramentality of the Church in general and of marriage in particular.[59] The spousal gift of Christ is not only offered as a model, but, as we shall see further on, it constitutes the ontological source of the Church's sacramental being: "that he might present the church to himself in splendor, without spot or wrinkle or any such thing, that she might be holy and without blemish" (v. 27). Conjugal ethics therefore sinks its roots into the ethos of the gift of Christ, which is lavished upon the spouses by virtue of what we may call the couple's baptism into the nuptial mystery of Christ, the Bridegroom of his Bride the Church.

The couple's ecclesial responsibility can be founded upon this sacramental basis. The awareness of being intimately involved in the mystery of the Church flows from the conviction of being a domestic Church, with all the characteristics of an ecclesial *reality:* communion, worship, proclamation of the Word, baptismal priesthood, and so forth. What for ease of expression *Familiaris Consortio* lists at the end of the tasks of the Christian family as "sharing in the life and mission of the Church" (17), embraces indeed the previously mentioned dimensions: forming a community of persons; serving life; and participating in the development of society. The ecclesial being of the Christian family is not limited to explicitly ecclesial activities, but includes personal and social tasks because baptism and matrimony consecrate the whole personal and social being of the married

59. Cf. John Paul II, *The Theology of the Body,* p. 322.

couple to Christ and the Church. As Rocchetta reaffirms: "it is precisely the human reality of the couple that is called to become a sacrament."[60] From this perspective the ethos of the gift, adequately determined by conjugal chastity, reveals its sacramental import. The total commitment of the spouses to fidelity in love, service of life, and the development of society ultimately expresses their sacramental participation in the mission of the Church.

At the beginning of our discussion we evoked theological principles that undergird the synergy and mutual interpenetration of divine and human action: the creation of man in the image and likeness of God; the "communional" nature of the person founded upon the original openness of man and woman; the gift of the sacraments of Christian initiation and marriage, which place the fecund conjugal relationship within and at the service of the spousal relationship between Christ and Church; the personal gift of the Holy Spirit, which envelops the mutual gift of the couple and the overall ethos of their relations in the incarnational, kenotic, and paschal gift of Christ. The Christian action of the couple relies on these theological principles, which confer a theological value and sacramental significance upon the emotions, gestures, and virtues of the family. The mystery of the Holy Family is the paradigmatic illustration of this. The gestures and virtues of Jesus, Mary, and Joseph are fully and simultaneously human and theological, and their significance transcends the limits of the house of Nazareth to reach the frontiers of salvation history.

The Christian Family, Protagonist of the Civilization of Love

Taking as our point of departure this sacramental Trinitarian archetype of Christian action, one could rethink the relationship between personal ethics and social ethics, demonstrating how Christian identity radiates trinitarian communion in all personal and social relations. The intrinsic correspondence between person and community, the theological nature of relationships, and the sacramental fruitfulness of obedience to Christ reveal the horizon of meaning not only of conjugal life, inseparably personal

---

60. C. Rocchetta, *Il sacramento della coppia* (Milan: EDB, 1996). The author develops the intuition of E. Schillebeeckx already expressed prior to Vatican II: *Il matrimonio è un sacramento* (Milan, 1963), pp. 23-24.

and social, but that of human action in general, which is called to be fulfilled in the *communio sanctorum*. The Trinitarian mystery which the sacramental ethos of the Christian family discloses, envelops in fact all human relations and leads man's dramatic history little by little toward the eschatological fulfillment of the kingdom of God. The reason for choosing the family as a paradigm was for the sole purpose of illustrating the intimate interweaving of person and community and the fruitfulness of action, which is rediscovered also in the Church's social doctrine.

Personal and ecclesial fecundity of Christian action, both at the level of the family and in the broader social arena, receive their confirmation from the sacramental value that is inherent to them. A family interiorly transformed, that is, indwelt and animated by the Spirit of Christ, diffuses the light of Trinitarian love in society. It reawakens the human values of respect for life and the person; protects the good of the common life of society and the family; defends the reasonableness of a stable and definitive commitment; and prophesies about the transcendent dimension of human existence. The light that radiates from the Christian couple's heroic fidelity and responsible but not calculated fecundity remains for society a point of reference and assistance in protecting a widespread consent to the reasonable values of unity, fidelity, and tolerance. To overlook the sacramental good of the Christian family would cause grave damage, not only to the common good of society, but to the Church herself, who must be a witness in the world to the truth about man and his relation to the living God.

Upon these foundations we can construct a renewed Christian militancy. However, such renewal would consist neither in restoring a Christianity now waning in its historical forms of realization, nor in proposing a utopian project for a society in the future as if to anticipate the Kingdom of God on earth. Rather, Christian engagement in the world consists in giving clear and decisive witness to the dignity of the human person and his original social relations. In light of a Trinitarian anthropology of the family which is the domestic Church, the social doctrine of the Church, still being developed, can open up a new field of dialogue with contemporary men who are aware of the social dimension of man, but still confused about his familial dimension. Without imposing one particular model of the family or a universally valid project of society, the social doctrine of the Church nevertheless furnishes at the level of the family and society some sure principles for guiding men towards the unconditional respect for the human person and the common good of society.

Seeing and encountering God-Love in the Trinitarian image and likeness of the domestic Church, contemporary man, unsettled by the loss of the sense of God and man, rediscovers a way of concrete, human, and daily access to the *"Sacramentum magnum"* of the Church through the witness of holy couples and families. From now on they are "the way of the Church," as they are the symbol of the civilization of love proposed to lost and despairing men of our time. The first prophetic cry of John Paul II remains forever current: "Man cannot live without love. He remains a being that is incomprehensible for himself, his life is senseless, if love is not revealed to him, if he does not encounter love, if he does not experience it and make it his own, if he does not participate intimately in it."[61] Amidst the joys and the difficulties, despite the contrary cultural winds, the Christian family, evangelized and evangelizing, becomes ever more essential for bringing to today's world the incarnate gospel of Love.

Conclusion

We have addressed the question of the relationship between personal ethics and social ethics theologically in the context of the Trinitarian, sacramental, and ecclesial specificity of Christian identity. The result is not only a formal increase in ethical obligation, but a specificity based on content, rooted in a personal friendship with Christ, which is inhabited, animated, and intimately sustained by the gift of the Holy Spirit. The paradigmatic case of conjugal and family ethics illustrates — in a negative way by its controversiality and in a positive way by its fruitfulness — the "ever more" of an exigency and service that is the mark of Christian ethics founded on grace. This specificity, based more on content and sustained by a Christological and ecclesial concept of person, opens the horizon of the sacramental fecundity of conjugal communion and, therefore, the ecclesial mission of the family. In this light, rooted in the eucharistic and Trinitarian ethos of the Church, personal ethics and social ethics appear as two correlative and inseparable dimensions. Both are fulfilled in the unity of person and love in the *communio sanctorum*.

Many important questions remain on the margin of our discussion, and should be addressed in order to more deeply justify our position. A

---

61. John Paul II, *Redemptor Hominis* 10.

whole philosophical discourse on an adequate anthropology, which should correspond to the mutual belonging of persons and communion, remains yet to be addressed. Trinitarian ontology, currently being developed, would help us to better understand the metaphysical and ethical horizon of the ultimate reality which is the person. In addition, we would need to take up again the traditional discourse about man as *desiderium naturale visionis* in order to integrate the ascending philosophical perspective of the desire for beatitude into the descending theological perspective of service to the beatitude of God, who communicates himself to man in the embrace of the beatitudes of Jesus Christ. The synergy between God's action and man's action would appear, then, as the mutual glorification of God and man lived and thought about in a Trinitarian way. Hence, the ethical dimension of Christian existence would be integrated not only into the communion of the Church, but into her mission.[62] "May they all be one, just as, Father, you are in me, and I am in you, so that they also may be in us, so that the world may believe it was you who sent me" (Jn. 17:21).

62. Cf. my article "Woe to Me if I Do Not Preach the Gospel!" *Communio* 21 (Winter 1994), pp. 800-817.

CHAPTER X

The Celebration of the Sacrament of Marriage in the Church's Mission

"Spouses are . . . the permanent reminder to the Church of what happened on the Cross; they are for one another and for their children witnesses to the salvation in which the sacrament makes them sharers."[1] The apostolic exhortation *Familiaris Consortio* presents the vocation of Christian spouses as a visible and permanent witness of what happened on the Cross, *for the sake of the Church*. The document thus highlights the primordial link between the sacrament of marriage, the mystery of the Church, and the Paschal mystery. In the same perspective, the *Catechism of the Catholic Church* reminds us, "In the Latin rite, the celebration of marriage between two Catholic faithful normally takes place during Holy Mass, because of the connection of all the sacraments with the Paschal mystery of Christ" (CCC 1621). While stressing the spouses as ministers of the sacrament of marriage, the Latin Church nevertheless attributes a central role to the priest, as minister of the Eucharist that frames the celebration of the sacrament.

Today, the tradition of the Latin Church faces a new pastoral situation, which calls for renewed reflection on the meaning and the concrete form of the celebration of marriage. The question at hand is not simply being able to identify the ministers of the sacrament, the specific nature of this

---

1. John Paul II, *Familiaris Consortio* 13.

This chapter was translated by Michelle K. Borras.

ministeriality, and what possible adaptations it allows for in various pastoral situations. The possibility of an extraordinary form of the celebration in exceptional circumstances is already admitted by both the Latin and Eastern codes of canon law.[2] The most basic question is that of knowing how to welcome the many candidates who have no contact with the sacramental practice of the Church, and for whom the faith has no personal resonance. Should they be refused the sacrament? Or obliged to make a long and serious preparation? Or should they be offered something other than the sacrament, in order to recognize and affirm the human and religious meaning of marriage?

These questions cannot be dealt with lightly, and I do not claim to resolve them here. But if what is needed is a modification of the Church's current practice, we are obliged to make a serious discernment founded on theology, and not merely on short-term pastoral reasons. We can no longer limit ourselves today to seeking out the minimum required for the sacramental validity of a marriage. A more global approach is needed. To this end, I would like to contribute a few elements, which aim at better situating marriage within the sacramentality of the Church and providing several criteria for choosing the best means to respond to the challenge of dechristianization. As the title of this chapter indicates, my proposal concerns the celebration of the sacrament of marriage within the mission of the Church.

Should we depend more on the ministeriality of the spouses and on the assistance of a qualified lay witness? Or is it better to stress the presence of the ordained minister and his relationship to the ministeriality of the spouses? What long-term impact would either of these solutions have on the future of evangelization? We will first identify and explore the context of the debate over the ministers of marriage and what is at stake in it (part I); then we will reflect on the ecclesial hermeneutic of sacramentality (part II), in order to conclude by situating the meaning of the sacramental celebration of marriage within the mission of the Church. This approach privileges the theological and ecumenical perspectives, within the framework of John Paul II's constant call for a "new evangelization," which made its first appearance in the apostolic exhortation *Familiaris Consortio*. We find this challenge raised again in *Novo Millennio Ineunte*,

---

2. *Code of Canon Law* (CIC), can. 1116; *Code of Canon Law for the Eastern Churches*, can. 832.

with its invitation to all Christians, pastors, and faithful, to "begin again from Christ."

At first glance, my proposal may not seem to fit the public that confronts us every day. It will seem, I imagine, over their heads, inapplicable to the almost illiterate Christian who surfaces on the occasion of a marriage. But several years of teaching at the John Paul II Institute have allowed me to see that couples really are interested in God's plan for marriage and the family, and they are hungry for a spiritual message we do not always dare to give them. Some weeks ago, I was especially touched by the witness of a couple from the north of Italy, members of a community of families founded by a diocesan priest, Fr. Pietro Margini, who consecrated his life to the spiritual formation of couples and families. The well-balanced and discreet activity of this priest managed to transform a milieu strongly marked by the anti-clericalism of the communist left into fertile ground for vocations of every kind. As I accompanied this couple, I was acutely aware that their experience, and the theology that nourished it, represented an eloquent confirmation of the ecclesial mission of the couple and the family that has been the central message of John Paul II's pontificate.[3] These contacts and periods of study reminded me of the decisive witness given by the Catholic Action movement, and especially by the movements of conjugal spirituality that flourished in France in the last century; these made possible the great turn of the Second Vatican Council toward the promotion of the universal call to holiness and the apostolate of the laity in the Church.[4] I want to pay homage to these many witnesses, both past and present, who have carried the flame of the gospel into the heart of society by means of the family.

3. For some years now, an intense activity of theological study and meetings of couples and families, involving a vast participation of family movements, has taken place in Italy on both the local and national levels, under the aegis of the Italian Bishops Conference. Numerous publications nourish and deepen this reflection, in collaboration with the John Paul II Institute for Studies on Marriage and the Family.

4. I mention in particular the work of Father Henri Caffarel, the founder of the *Equipes Notre-Dame* and *L'Anneau d'Or,* which greatly contributed to the development of conjugal and familial spirituality. Cf. Jean Allemand, *Henri Caffarel, un homme saisi par Dieu* (Paris: Equipes Notre-Dame, 1997). Two of the most beautiful Magisterial texts on conjugal spirituality were addressed to the Equipes Notre-Dame: Paul VI's "Le mariage dans le Seigneur, vocation de sainteté" (May 4, 1970), *Documentation Catholique* n. 1564 (1970), pp. 502-506; and John Paul II's "Si tu savais le don de Dieu," Speech to the Equipes Notre-Dame (September 23, 1982), *Documentation Catholique* n. 1838 (1982), pp. 905-908.

Sacramental Marriage and Ministeriality:
The Context and Implications of the Question

The celebration of the sacrament of marriage in the context of secularized societies presents three major challenges. The first of these is the pastoral challenge posed by sacramental celebration in places where the number of ordained clergy does not correspond to the need of the faithful. One looks spontaneously for alternatives in the face of a shortage of clergy. Since the priest is not the minister of the sacrament as such, his presence is therefore not essential; a layperson could serve as a qualified witness to the spouses' exchange of consent. In the Latin Church, these latter are traditionally considered the ministers of the sacrament (CCC 1623). What is at stake in such a pastoral decision? Would the ministeriality of the spouses be weakened or affirmed? What, moreover, would be the impact of such a practice on the sacramentality of the Church in general, and on that of the domestic church in particular? Wouldn't the absence of a priest and his blessing during the ceremony have a negative effect on the way we understand the sacrament of marriage and its organic link to the other sacraments? In short, can the extraordinary form of celebration, intended in the *Code* to cover very exceptional cases of the danger of death or the absence of a priest in a mission territory, be promoted as a long-term solution? What would be the ecumenical repercussions of such a decision?

The second challenge involves the candidates' preparation for sacramental marriage. It is already clear that the vast majority of candidates are interested above all in the social and anthropological signification of a rite of passage. Their lack of preparation, the result of little or no contact with the sacramental practice of the Church, makes the celebration difficult and even painful for priests. How can we initiate couples who have difficulty believing in the sacramental meaning of marriage, and at the same time respect the point where they find themselves in their spiritual path? Doesn't such a situation invite us to offer future spouses a prolonged catechumenate, if they wish to celebrate their marriage covenant in a Christian way? Is it still theologically justifiable to stand by the minimal demand of the simple intention to marry according to the rites of the Church? In the context of secularization, this intention is no longer necessarily Christian, because the Church no longer enjoys the spontaneous adhesion given to her by the faithful of past generations.

The third challenge is presented by a general disaffection for the practice of the sacraments. Deep down, it is not the marriage that is the problem; it is the whole sacramental system, which appears today to have lost any meaningful context. The cultural shift currently in progress has profoundly obscured the "salvific" meaning of sacramental symbols. Such a situation forces theology to rethink the meaning of the practice of the sacraments and the categories that express it.[5] From the Middle Ages on, the sacraments were clearly defined as holy signs producing grace. The action of the minister acting *in persona Christi* highlights the efficacy of the holy rite, *ex opere operato*. After Vatican II, the accent of sacramental theology, under the dominating influence of Karl Rahner, shifted toward the ministeriality of the Church. The sacraments were considered more as real symbols of the Church's faith, symbols which express the Church's self-consciousness and self-realization.

This new perspective rightly stresses the dimension of faith, which is essential to the sacramentality of the Church. However, it remains vague regarding the relationship between Christ and the sacraments, and how the ministeriality of the Church is articulated with respect to Christ's action in the sacraments. Are the sacraments first and foremost the place where the Church receives herself from Christ, or the place where the Church expresses her faith in Christ before the world? What part is played by Christ and the Church in the sacramental action, and marriage in particular? We cannot avoid addressing these questions under the pretext that the two dimensions are inseparable, because what is at stake is an adequate perception of the sacramental celebration as the "mystery of the Covenant." The hylomorphic categories inherited from the Middle Ages do not satisfactorily express this mystery. But we do not yet possess a unified, common theological vision which would give impetus and coherence to pastoral action. This is the great challenge of sacramental theology in transition toward a new synthesis, yet to be defined.[6] Various approaches have been developed from the new methods — phenomenological, symbolic, linguistic, personalist — but none of them has managed to win a large consensus. In the meantime, pastoral work stagnates, and we see the collapse not only of Christian practice but of man himself, grappling with the culture of death.

5. Cf. Louis-Marie Chauvet, *Les sacraments: Parole de Dieu au risque du corps* (Paris: Les Éditions ouvrières, 1993).

6. Cf. Giuseppe Colombo, *Teologia sacramentaria* (Milan: Glossa, 1997); Louis-Marie Chauvet, *Symbole et Sacrement* (Paris, 1987).

For the most serious challenge now facing the pastors of the entire Church is not that of nursing a threatened sector of pastoral work back to health. It is not only marriage and the family that are in crisis; the human being as such is imploding for the lack of a spiritual foundation, threatening the fundamental values of human life and of coexistence among peoples. We watch helplessly as the aberrations unfold: the growing violence, the attempts to snuff out life at its beginning and its end, added to postmodern relativism, ever more subtle and pervasive forms of manipulation, the war of the sexes, and legislation contradicting the values of the family, and so forth. We are watching a collapse that is not only moral but anthropological, the effect of the eclipse of God in secularized societies. Contemporary man no longer knows who he is; he no longer knows that he is, according to the Judeo-Christian tradition, the partner of God and the subject of his Word. Hence the absence of reference points for the defense of his dignity and the loss of access to his own spiritual identity. Hence, too, the temptation to lose himself in distractions, consumerism, and drugs. The human being of the "culture of death" looks more and more like a floating wreck.

For an Ecclesial Hermeneutic of the Sacramentality of Marriage

The anthropological implosion we have just mentioned directly affects the lives of couples and families, but it does not cancel out the good news of Christian marriage in secularized societies. *Familiaris Consortio,* the great charter of the mission of the family, bears witness to the Church's confidence in this institution, which is at the heart of God's plan in Christ. Pope John Paul II's frequently repeated conviction was that the future of evangelization passes through the family, the domestic Church (FC 65). By renewing the doctrine of man created in the image of God as man and woman, he exalts the vocation of Christian spouses to sacramental love in Christ. Thus he indicates the basis for a conjugal and familial spirituality which flows from the sacrament and reflects the Church's fruitfulness, directly implied in that of the spouses. Through this mutual belonging of the couple and the Church, the community of life and love of the Christian spouses enters wholly into the Church's mission and becomes a protagonist of the good news of salvation in the midst of a dechristianized world.

Pastoral work must serve this great cause, helping the family to be not only a "saved" community, because it has received the love of Christ, but a "saving" community, which transmits this love to society (cf. FC 49).[7]

In recent decades, the theology of marriage has striven to go beyond the juridical perspective inherited from the Scholastic tradition and to demonstrate the spouses' ministeriality, not only at the moment of the celebration of the sacrament, but in the "community of life and love" that is also part of the sacramental sign. This broadening of perspectives is a relatively recent achievement owing its existence to the influence of the encyclical *Casti Connubii,* which prompted theological and spiritual reflection on marriage as a permanent sacrament. The celebration of the marriage is an essential moment in the constitution of the sacrament, but it is the couple's whole life that realizes the sacrament, through the continuous exercise of a ministeriality that remains in continuity with the mutual communication of grace during the celebration.

This recognition of the larger ministeriality of the spouses rests on a more lively awareness of their baptismal priesthood, thanks to the Christological re-centering of the mystery of the Church in Vatican II. The dogmatic constitution *Lumen Gentium* speaks of the Church in Christ as "a sacrament or as a sign and instrument both of a very closely knit union with God and of the unity of the whole human race" (LG 1). The Council changed the classical view of sacramentality, which hinged on the seven sacraments, by restoring an understanding of the sacraments that begins with Christ and the Church-Sacrament. From this perspective, the seven sacraments appear more clearly as concretizations and actualizations of the relationship between Christ and the Church. This allows in turn for an understanding of the sacraments not only as salvific gestures made by Christ to individuals, but also as the gift of Christ the Bridegroom to his Church, and as the fruitful response of the Church-Bride to her divine Spouse. "The entire Christian life bears the mark of the spousal love of Christ and the Church. Already Baptism, the entry into the People of God, is a nuptial mystery; it is so to speak the nuptial bath (cf. Eph 5:26-27) which precedes the wedding feast, the Eucharist" (CCC 1617). The sacraments in general, and marriage in particular, are the effect of acts in which

---

7. John Paul II's thought, including his famous catecheses on human love, is presented and interpreted in Alain Mattheeuws' remarkable work, *Les "dons" du mariage: Recherche de théologie morale et sacramentelle* (Brussels: Culture et Verité, 1996).

the Bride and Bridegroom encounter and unite with one another, while the divine Bridegroom constitutes the Church-Bride through the Paschal-eucharistic gift of his Body. He brings her into being, nourishes her, purifies her, sanctifies her in the Holy Spirit, and draws her after him in mission (cf. Eph 5:21-33).

This ecclesial and nuptial perspective of sacramentality is rooted in a rediscovery of the Pauline *mystērion,* which, along with John's nuptial and eucharistic symbolism, founds New Testament sacramentality. This latter articulates all of the sacraments according to the nuptial mystery of Christ and the Church, while carefully noting the difference between the primordial action of Christ the Bridegroom and the receptive and subordinate action of the Church-Bride. Thanks to this new perspective, marriage finds itself at the heart of the sacramentality of the Church, in a strict relationship to the Eucharist, the mystery of the covenant *par excellence.* The sacramentality of the Church is expressed in the sacrament of the couple[8] in a privileged way; the two become one sacramental flesh, in the measure in which they are rooted in and nourished by the eucharistic "one flesh" of Christ and the Church, the source and summit of all sacramentality. For this reason, the "community of life and love" that is the couple is rightly called a domestic Church, *ecclesia domestica,* because it incarnates the nuptial relationship between Christ and the Church. The family is not only an image of this relationship but also its concrete realization, founded on the truth of the sacrament of marriage.

This ecclesial dimension of marriage can already be discerned in the way we distinguish the effects of marriage. *Familiaris Consortio* stresses that "the first and immediate effect of marriage *(res et sacramentum)* is not supernatural grace itself, but the Christian conjugal bond, a typically Christian communion of two persons because it represents the mystery of Christ's incarnation and the mystery of His covenant" (FC 13). The Christian conjugal bond, which binds the spouses indissolubly together, is not in the first place a juridical reality. It is a gift of the Holy Spirit that Christ grants to the spouses to bless and sanctify them, and to take up their mutual self-gift into his own gift of himself to the Church. The first effect of the sacrament is thus above all ecclesial. It constitutes the couple as a public sign of their radical belonging to the Church, and of the fact that their mutual gift in the Lord is taken up and blessed by him, enriched and trans-

---

8. Cf. Carlo Rochetta, *Il sacramento della coppia* (Rome: Edizioni Dehoniane, 1996).

formed in order to be placed at the disposition of the Church. Heribert Mühlen and Louis Ligier speak of this objective ecclesial bond as a "charism of consecration,"[9] which is the source of, though not identical with, the supernatural grace the couple receives. The grace of the conjugal union can be lost through a failure in the partners' dispositions, but the ecclesial bond remains indissoluble. It expresses the couple's belonging to Christ's nuptial mystery, and their objective participation in the sacramentality of the Church.

In the measure in which the spouses welcome with docility the Holy Spirit poured out during the celebration as their intimate bond of love, they are humanly affirmed in their fidelity and supernaturally consecrated for the service of life and spiritual fruitfulness. Thus they become an active part, as a couple and a family, in the Church's mission. This ecclesial and missionary dimension was not so apparent in the past (and even in the present), because marriage was understood almost exclusively from the point of view of "nature," even if one affirmed that this nature was "elevated" by Christ to the dignity of a sacrament. Hence the tendency to draw attention almost exclusively to the tasks of the procreation and education of children, while the personal and ecclesial aspects remained marginal and extrinsic.

In the light of the Christocentrism of the Council, the properly sacramental and therefore ecclesial dimension of marriage flows from a meeting with Christ, who, by the grace of marriage which specifies the graces of baptism and confirmation, takes up and enriches the couple's being and love for his own purposes. In this Christocentric perspective, the couple is not only blessed and sanctified along the lines of "natural" love, even if care must be taken to integrate this dimension; the two are blessed, consecrated, and placed at the service of Christ's love for the Church. "The Spirit which the Lord pours forth gives a new heart, and renders man and woman capable of loving one another as Christ has loved us. Conjugal love reaches that fullness to which it is interiorly ordained, conjugal charity" (FC 13). Through its offering and welcoming of the sacrament, the Christian couple places itself at the Lord's disposition, to express, in "the language of the body," his own nuptial love for the Church.

9. Cf. Louis Ligier, *Il matrimonio: Questioni teologiche e pastorali* (Rome: Città Nuova, 1998), pp. 133ff.; H. Mühlen, *Una mistica persona* (Rome: Città Nuova, 1968), c.III, §9, pp. 352-438.

The gift of the sacrament is thus given simultaneously to the couple and the Church, because in all his sacramental gifts, Christ loves his Church and makes his children, with her and for her, witnesses to salvation. Through the gift of the sacrament of marriage, Christ makes the spouses not only the recipients of a grace, but full-fledged participants in the Church's missionary witness. Obviously, this supposes faith, the act of faith which founds the sacrament. Hans Urs von Balthasar writes that "Christian marriage . . . must be interpreted a priori from above, in terms of the Christian act that established it as marriage — the act of living Christian faith that always includes love and hope and in which marriage vows are exchanged. This act is oriented directly and immediately to God — as a promise of fidelity to God because, by his promises and revelations, he has first revealed himself as the eternally faithful one in whom man must believe, in whom he must hope, and whom he must love. The promise of fidelity to one's spouse is not to be separated from this promise of fidelity to God."[10]

According to the Swiss theologian, the exchange of consent of Christian spouses has an intrinsically theological dimension, which determines the natural properties of marriage "from above." He continues, "The acts of faith of the two marriage partners meet in God and are accepted, formed and returned to them by God, in whom they find the foundation of their unity, the witness of their union and the pledge of their fidelity. It is God who, in the act of faith, gives the partners to one another in the basic Christian act of self-surrender. Together, they offer themselves to God and receive each other from him in a gift of grace, confidence, and Christian expectation."[11] How can we help couples to live from this faith which commands their love, and to bear witness to the sacrament they receive as charism and mission?

The ecclesial testimony of Christian spouses is rooted in the baptismal faith that lies at the origin of their sacramental bond, and it culminates in the eucharistic offering, the criterion par excellence of the whole ecclesial hermeneutic of sacramentality. God takes the couple's sacramental "one flesh," fashions it, and makes it fruitful from the "eucharistic one flesh" of Christ and the Church. It is here that conjugal love is regenerated at the

---

10. Hans Urs von Balthasar, *The Christian States of Life,* trans. Sr. Mary Frances McCarthy (San Francisco: Ignatius, 1983), pp. 244-45.

11. Balthasar, *The Christian States of Life,* p. 245.

source of Christ's charity and can be lived in truth as coexistence, being-for-the-other and being-together-for-others. Taken up and transfigured by the *agapē* of Christ, *erōs* is purified, made holy, and, through the Church, placed at the service of God and society. This is why the Church keeps watch over the spouses' love, which incarnates both the Gift of God to the world and the response of the Church-Bride to this gift. Hence the greater demand for unity, fidelity and fruitfulness, which proceed from the sacramental gift and from the faith it commands. These demands correspond to the "great mystery" of Christ and the Church; the mystery is truly given, and the couple cannot betray it without also compromising the witness given by the Church. Sacramental logic is a logic of the incarnation, which joins the Eucharist and marriage as two inseparable and complementary expressions of the mystery of the covenant between God and his people.

Modern theology, marked by an extrinsicist understanding of nature and grace, thinks of sacramentality in terms of the elevation of nature; lacking a clear foundation in the act of faith that grounds both sacrament and mission, it allows little room for the ecclesial dimension. Christian spouses appear as beneficiaries of the Church's pastoral action, but not as full-fledged protagonists in the Church's mission. *Familiaris Consortio* clearly goes beyond this perspective, but does not yet achieve a complete integration. The family as "saved" community becomes a "saving" community (FC 49), but its participation "in the life and mission of the Church" (FC 49-65) is still thought out somewhat extrinsically, with emphasis on specific activities of worship and evangelization. But it is the couple's whole being in all its dimensions which is to be seen as an ecclesial being, since Christ takes human love up into his own, divine love, to make it a sacrament of his nuptial relationship to his Church (GS 48). Through sacramental marriage, the spouses are constituted as a "miniature church," receiving as gifts the properties of the one, holy, catholic and apostolic Church. Here we find community of life, priesthood, charity, evangelization, and worship. These constitutive dimensions make the couple into an essentially missionary ecclesial reality, following the example of the great Church of which it is the most basic cell. This is why the canonical form of the sacrament expresses not only the Church's jurisdiction over marriage, but above all the spouses' deeper belonging to the Church by virtue of the sacrament. The basis of jurisdiction is the reality of the sacramental exchange of gifts, in faith.

In the light of the above discussion, the opinion which grants the sacrament of marriage a degree of "secondary ecclesiality" because of the secondary participation of the ordained minister, whereas the sacraments administered by the bishop or priest enjoy a "primary ecclesiality,"[12] does not seem to me to have sufficient foundation. Though this distinction may be useful on the liturgical plane, it seems to me to obscure the internal connection between the sacraments. This connection can best be explained through the nuptial mystery of Christ and the Church, which is the foundation for all the sacraments and grants to marriage a degree of ecclesiality of the first level. Mindful of the shift that took place in Vatican II and in the pontificate of John Paul II, we must insist on the primordial ecclesiality of the sacrament of marriage, even if the development and discovery of this sacramentality have given rise, historically, to strange vicissitudes and much groping in the dark. Too many factors, cultural, theological, and spiritual, demand a recognition of the central place of marriage and the family in the Church's mission, as well as a fresh rethinking of the preparation for and celebration of the sacrament.

The exhortation *Novo Millennio Ineunte* invites us to "begin again from Christ," to take up the task of evangelization at the dawn of the new millennium. More than ever, marriage needs the light of Christ, so that the exchange of gifts that takes place during the celebration and in life might become the source of greater joy for the couple and for the Church. This exchange of gifts is fruitful in the measure in which it remains within the living interaction of Christ the Bridegroom and the Church-Bride. Essentially, this interaction consists in the actualization of Christ's Paschal mystery, which is the intimate substance of the spouses' union, calling them ceaselessly to renew their mutual self-gift "in the Lord" through a very natural recourse to the sacraments of reconciliation and the Eucharist. This is why the sacramental grace of marriage bears fruit that endures in the measure in which it exists in a structural and permanent relationship to the ordained minister, the source and guarantor of the divine initiative of the Lordship of Christ the Bridegroom over his Bride, the Church. This mystery is expressed by the marriage liturgy, whose holy rites transform the anthropological reality of the couple into a sacrament of the union of Christ and the Church.

---

12. Cf. Pierre-Marie Gy, "La célébration du batême, du mariage et des funérailles confiées à des laïcs?", *La Maison-Dieu* 194 (1993/2), pp. 13-25.

The Sacramental Celebration of Marriage,
Symbol of the Spouses' Ecclesial Mission

The sacramental celebration of the marriage of two of the baptized is a highly symbolic event, which introduces a fledgling conjugal love into the mystery of Christ's nuptial love for the Church. This holy rite is not just the starting point along a path; it is a consecration embracing the couple's and the family's whole life, making it an offering to the Lord. This offering is accepted, blessed, and given back to the new spouses as a "mission" received from him, destined to glorify God in the flesh. From the moment of the sacramental exchange of gifts in faith, this mission consists above all in radiating Christ's love for the Church in the spouses' fleshly exchange, in their openness to life, in the education of children, and in various services rendered to society. The success of conjugal and familial love as ecclesial service presupposes a living relationship of personal obedience to the Lord of all gifts, through the grace of the Holy Spirit. The celebration introduces all the divine and human actors in a play of real and definitive exchanges, which have the quality of sacramental symbols bearing an eschatological weight. It explicitly binds the spouses to prolong these sacramental exchanges in their life; at least implicitly, this includes the task of ceaselessly reviving the gift received, through prayer, mutual forgiveness, and a permanent contact with the mystery of the Eucharist, the indispensable source of the spouses' spiritual fruitfulness.

For this reason, it is highly suitable for the sacramental celebration already to include all the parts which will come into play for the marriage's sacramental "success": the spouses' essential consent, the presence of a qualified witness, the epiclesis of consecration, and the eucharistic offering. In the first place, irreplaceably, there is the ministeriality of the spouses. In its document on the sacramentality of Christian marriage, the International Theological Commission analyzes the meaning of the ministers of marriage:

> Since the sacrament of marriage is the free consecration to Christ of a new conjugal love, the spouses are clearly the ministers of the sacrament which eminently concerns them. However, they are not ministers through a sort of "absolute" power, the exercise of which the Church would, strictly speaking, have nothing to do with. They are ministers as living members of the body of Christ, in which they exchange their

oaths; nor does their — irreplaceable — decision make the sacrament purely and solely an emanation of their love. . . . No couple gives themselves the sacrament unless the Church herself consents to it, and they do this under a form different from that which the Church establishes as the most expressive of the mystery to which the sacrament introduces them.[13]

Though essential, the ministeriality of the spouses is neither absolute nor isolated; it is exercised in the company of priestly and lay witnesses, who give the rite a public character by representing the Church. Although theologians are not unanimous in the opinion that the spouses are the ministers of the sacrament, it is considered common opinion, and the *Catechism of the Catholic Church* accepts it: "In the Latin Church, it is ordinarily understood that the spouses, as ministers of Christ's grace, mutually confer upon each other the sacrament of Matrimony by expressing their consent before the Church" (1623). But it seems to me that we might hope for a further development, which would better integrate this singular ministeriality of the spouses into a perspective that is more theological than juridical. To this end, we highlight the importance of the presence of the ordained minister, who symbolizes Christ the Bridegroom, and whose blessing-epiclesis must not be underestimated. The Eastern tradition is full of teachings on this subject and merits a better reception, not in order to bring the Latin tradition into question, but to strengthen and provide a better framework for the ministeriality of the spouses, thanks to the complementary symbolic contribution of the ordained minister. The *Catechism* explicitly refers to this in number 1623: "In the Eastern liturgies the minister of this sacrament (which is called 'Crowning') is the priest or bishop who, after receiving the mutual consent of the spouses, successively crowns the bridegroom and bride as a sign of the marriage covenant."[14]

13. International Theological Commission, *La sacramentalité du mariage chrétien: Seize thèses de christologie sur le sacrament du mariage* (Dec. 6, 1977): EV 6, 472.

14. The text has been slightly modified in the definitive 1997 Latin version, to the disadvantage of the Eastern tradition: "In the Eastern traditions, priests, bishops, or presbyters are the witnesses of the reciprocal consent exchanged between the spouses, but their blessing is also necessary for the validity of the sacrament." Although the *Catechism* speaks in these terms, Bernard de la Soujeole has recently reminded us that the question of the spouses as ministers of the sacrament of marriage is not an official doctrine, but rather a theological opinion which, from an ecumenical perspective, it would be better to revise; cf. "Aspects oecuméniques de la question du ministre du mariage," *Revue Thomiste*, Volume 101 (2001), pp. 565-580.

"In the Eastern tradition, the priest, in addition to assisting, must bless the Marriage. To bless means to act as the true minister of the sacrament, in virtue of his priestly power to sanctify, so that the spouses may be united by God in the image of the flawless nuptial union of Christ with the Church and be consecrated to each other by sacramental grace."[15] In the theological and canonical perspective of the Eastern Churches, the blessing is required for the validity of the sacrament, which is tied to the priestly epiclesis through which the spouses receive the Holy Spirit as the communion of love between Christ and the Church. "It is the action of the Holy Spirit, and not of the spouses, which is primordial: the act constituting marriage is a holy rite."[16] Without a doubt, it is the exchange of consents between the spouses, considered as the indispensable element, which "makes the marriage." But in order for the marriage to become, in the words of St. Paul, "a great mystery, I mean in reference to Christ and the Church" (Eph. 5:32), in order for it to be "in the Lord," it requires the intervention of the Church's ministerial priesthood, to which Christ has entrusted the celebration and the administration of the sacraments, the source of redeeming grace. Such is the more "mystery-centered" perspective of the Eastern tradition which, for both theological and ecumenical reasons, must be taken into consideration for a *rapprochement* of the two perspectives.

In both traditions, the Church remains the sign and guarantor of the gift of the Holy Spirit, which the spouses receive in committing themselves to one another as Christians. "One might say that the role of the priest in Eastern law is that of one who blesses, and in Latin law, one who assists."[17] "In an attempt at a coherent solution between the Latin and Eastern perspectives, one could hold that the spouses and the priest who gives the blessing are the ministers of the sacrament of marriage."[18] Moreover, the presence of an ordained minister (bishop, priest, or deacon) adds a refer-

15. Congregation for the Eastern Churches, *Instruction for Applying the Liturgical Prescriptions of the Code of Canons of the Eastern Churches*, Ch. 10, §82.

16. R. Metz, *Le nouveau droit des églises orientales catholiques* (Paris: Cerf, 1997), p. 213.

17. Metz, *Le nouveau droit*, p. 214; cf. U. Navarrete, "Ius matrimoniale latinum et orientale: Collatio inter Codicem latinum et orientalem," pp. 636-39; also his "De ministro sacramenti matrimonii in Ecclesia latina et in Ecclesiis Orientalibus: Tentamen explicationis concordantis," *Periodica* 84 (1995), pp. 729-33.

18. D. Salachas, "Le sacrement de mariage dans les deux Codes," *L'Année canonique* 40 (1998), pp. 119-49, here 138.

ence to the gratuity of the gift of Christ, whose crucified love always exceeds the dimension of the "elevation" of natural *erōs*. As the *agapē* that takes up, ransoms, and transfigures *erōs*, he is represented by the minister capable of presiding over the Eucharist.

The eucharistic celebration, which usually accompanies the holy rite of matrimony, does not simply furnish the new spouses with particular graces. It signifies, very concretely, their belonging to Christ's Paschal mystery, and their organic link with the source and summit of their conjugal communion:

> In the Eucharist the memorial of the New Covenant is realized, the New Covenant in which Christ has united himself for ever to the Church, his beloved bride for whom he gave himself up. It is therefore fitting that the spouses should seal their consent to give themselves to each other through the offering of their own lives by uniting it to the offering of Christ for his Church made present in the Eucharistic sacrifice, and by receiving the Eucharist so that, communicating in the same Body and the same Blood of Christ, they may form but "one body" in Christ (1 Cor. 10:17).[19]

This very intimate link between marriage and the Eucharist is not only a moral aid for the spouses, or a source of grace for their specific duties; above all, it expresses the couple's sacramental identity, their objective belonging to the witness and the sacramental radiation of the Church. This is why the celebration of the two sacraments together carries a message concerning the spouses' whole life; from the moment of the institution of their family, it traces a path for them of a specific, ecclesial, and missionary spirituality.

Becoming aware of this many-faceted nuptial gift strengthens the spirituality proper to the spouses and propels them into the life of the Holy Spirit, to become protagonists of the Church's mission. If the conditions for this awareness are not present during the sacramental celebration, the couple risks having to make do with a rather limited view of their search for happiness, not really seeing the vocation to the service of God that their fully human love is called to live, under the impetus of the Holy Spirit, as an ecclesial mission. Some may fear that this "ecclesialization" of conjugal and familial love threatens the vocation of the spouses, which is

19. CCC 1621.

rooted in the sanctification of human love. But this fear disappears when we consider that the initial act of faith has, from the beginning, definitively given over into the hands of God whatever spiritual or bodily fruits God deigns to give them in return. "If Christian spouses are able genuinely to make this act of perfect self-giving, their limited community is opened to the universality of the Catholic Church, and their love, which seems to be focused on so narrow a circle, is enabled actively to participate in the realization of the kingdom of God upon earth."[20] The participation of the conjugal communion in ecclesial communion can only affirm the quality of the human love, since it permits this love to draw from the Trinitarian source, opened to us in the nuptial mystery of Christ and the Church. The communion of the spouses grows in the measure in which it opens itself to the archetype of all love, which reveals itself under the species of the Eucharist and in the washing of the feet.

What can we say to those who are not yet initiated into this ideal and who nevertheless request a holy rite for the blessing of their marriage covenant? If it is authentic, their experience of love draws them closer to the Creator and gives them the desire, even the right, to receive, along with the rite, the proclamation of the good news of marriage in Christ. Should this proclamation take the form of a prolonged, pre-matrimonial catechumenate? Without a doubt yes, because this catechesis would have to take up the whole of Christian initiation, including confirmation for those who have not yet received it. For how should the life of faith, hope, and charity be awakened in them without the gift of the Holy Spirit? It does not necessarily follow that candidates who do not want this must be refused the sacrament, unless they are explicitly opposed to what the Church intends to do in the celebration of a marriage of the baptized, and conscious of the reasons for their opposition (FC 68). But an intense pastoral creativity that includes the participation of couples to welcome and prepare those preparing for marriage, should help keep these cases of refusal to the minimum. In this way, the welcome offered to non-catechized engaged couples could have the effect of opening them to Christ, helping them to push their relationship with him a little further, until the day when they can make their conjugal union fruitful through participation in the Eucharist.

---

20. H. U. von Balthasar, *The Christian States of Life*, pp. 248-49. Cf. M. Ouellet, "Mariage chrétien, péché et conversion," *Anthropotes* 16/1 (2000), pp. 19-41. The English translation of this article is published as Chapter 7 of this book.

Then their engagement will not only be legitimate before God according to natural law, but fruitful for the Church and for their own flowering in the Church.

The ecclesial mission of the spouses is love, a love in the image of God, such as that incarnated by Christ in his eucharistic relationship to the Church his Bride. All the dimensions of this mission lead back to love and are unified in the love that descends from the Father of Lights to take up all that is human — man, woman, and child — into the Mystery of his self-revelation and self-gift for the redemption of the world. The spouses' fruitful love always contains a trace and a yearning for that which was solemnly celebrated once, and which afterwards must be nourished at the source of Reconciliation and the Eucharist, so that the Love given to them by God might grow ceaselessly in fruits of unity and service. In this way, their happiness is not merely a private reality, but an ecclesial witness to Christ the Bridegroom, who gives himself and desires to bring the whole world back with him in his return to the Father.

Conclusion

The problem of the ministeriality of Christian spouses has led us from a difficult pastoral situation to a sacramental mystery, where nuptiality is called to play a role that is anything but secondary. At the heart of the exchange of gifts that constitutes the sacrament of marriage, Christ the Bridegroom comes to meet the spouses; he takes up their mutual offering in his own, blesses them with a properly nuptial effusion of the Holy Spirit, and calls them to follow him in the glorification of the Father through a witness of fidelity, unity, and fecundity.

The "exchange of gifts" which takes place in the liturgical mystery reveals to the couple and the Church that God is not only the Author, but the main Actor, of this exchange. The epiclesis and the presence of the ordained minister show more clearly this primacy of the divine Bridegroom and his blessing over a couple that commits itself to placing its happiness at the service of Christ's Love for the Church. The presence of the priest who gives the blessing does not take away the spouses' own, primary ministeriality in the constitution of the conjugal bond; to the contrary, the priest's presence confirms and affirms it by uniting it to the eucharistic offering of Christ, the source and summit of all ministeriality. This complementarity of ministers at the center of the celebration bears a message for the ensuing ministry of the spouses in their everyday life. It invites pastors to place their hopes in the evangelizing potential of marriage and the family, using the necessary means to proclaim Christ to future spouses and to those already married, so that they might become, for the Church and for their children, witnesses to the salvation they participate in through the sacrament.

APPENDIX

Toward a Theology of the "Gifts" of Marriage: Reflections on a Book by Alain Mattheeuws, S.J.

Les 'dons' du mariage: Recherche de théologie morale et sacramentelle
(Brussels: Culture et Vérité, 1996)

This is a book that will mark an important step in contemporary research in the moral and sacramental theology of marriage. Father Alain Mattheeuws presents a firm and bold thesis, "argued through reason," on the integration of the Augustinian "goods" and the Thomistic "ends" in a doctrine of the "gifts" of marriage essentially inspired by the French philosopher Claude Bruaire. It is not easy to give an account of a work of this type, developed through 677 pages of closely argued text, complete with many citations from contemporary authors who have something to say on the theme of gift. My first comment is that the effort of an attentive reading is rewarded by the pleasure of what is discovered and by the sentiment of being witness to a very rich development, subject to still further reflection.

Rather than attempting to summarize the book, which would only betray its richness, I have opted for an overview of its four sections, indicating only a few strong points which, to me, seem more worthy of attention for a theology of the "gifts" of marriage. Let us say from the very beginning that the project is of good quality and well organized: "from being-as-gift[1] to the gift of life, by way of the gift of self" (18). The author offers us an interpretation of the signs of the times, bringing together for the better the expecta-

---

1. *"l'être-de-don."*

tions of the contemporary world, the profound orientations of the Second Vatican Council and the recent pontifical Magisterium, especially that of John Paul II. The result is convincing and refreshing, even if one could wish for a furthering of the thesis in a more "Trinitarian" logic. I will explain this further in the conclusion, after praising the remarkable progress made through Alain Mattheeuws' reflection.

Let us preface this overview with some critical observations about the methodology. The object of the study is "marriage within a theology of gift." The methodology is historical and speculative. The author starts off from the speculative intuition of "being as 'gift'"[2] developed by Claude Bruaire, among others. He then seeks traces of the theme of gift in the evolution of twentieth-century magisterial doctrine, in order to verify whether it is possible to speak of an authentic doctrinal development of marriage in terms of a hermeneutics of the gift. This choice is legitimate and fruitful but, nonetheless, leaves in the dark the elements coming from the patristic and medieval traditions. For example, the Augustinian doctrine of "goods" and the Thomistic doctrine of "ends" are not sufficiently presented in their own right within their historical context. This lacuna affects the overall vision of the "integration of an old and a new treasure: "the 'goods,' before being 'ends' to be reached, are 'gifts' to be received" (16).

Having said all this, let us turn now to the content. "In the beginning was the gift" (23). The first section is ontological and anthropological. It would be better to say "ontodological" because the author adopts Claude Bruaire's metaphysics, which affirms "gift" as being's "name." Man, as a being in spirit, that is to say, "being as gift," is always preceded by and radically "indebted to his being" (47). From this follows a logic of gift in which the subject "given to himself" is "obliged" to give himself, in the image of the absolute Spirit. This Spirit is the infiniteness of Gift. Bruaire describes "the absolute exchange that is the unity of positive infinity" in the following three terms: Original gift, Surrender, Confirmation (71). One easily recognizes the Christian origin of this idea of the Absolute that Bruaire develops "by reason alone," while acknowledging his irreducible and unrepentant debt to faith. Alain Mattheeuws nourishes himself with the same freedom of thought as the Christian philosopher Claude Bruaire, happy to be provoked into thought by his faith. Other studies in Trinitarian ontol-

---

2. "*l'être comme 'don.'*""

ogy are used to confirm this thesis: Ricoeur, Habachi, Hemmerle, Paul Gilbert. Mattheeuws could also have added Ferdinand Ulrich and Hans Urs von Balthasar. The presentation is tightly argued and suggestive. It evokes a sort of "positivity" of contingency, an ontological joy that places the person in a context of gratuity and, consequently, in a climate of being "ethically obliged" as opposed to an "ethical obligation," the latter always being colored by legal exteriority.

The first section closes with a study of the recent tradition in the doctrine of marriage: "from the human being to the person" (127). The texts examined run from Pius XI's encyclical *Casti Connubii,* published on December 31, 1930, to the Instruction *Donum Vitae,* published by the Congregation for the Doctrine of the Faith on March 10, 1987. The author easily identifies the evolution from the question of the human being's obedience to the natural law towards a growing awareness of the human person's dignity founded in Christ, who "fully reveals man to himself and makes his supreme calling clear" (GS 22,1). In this evolution, Vatican II truly marks a "Christocentric" and personalistic turning point that remains the inspiration and the rule of the post-conciliar Magisterium. This is evidenced by Paul VI's vision of conjugal love expressed in the *Equipes Notre Dame* in 1970. The author takes it as a *leitmotif:* "is not the great law of love to give oneself to one another in order to give ourselves together?" (154, 210). The underlying anthropology emerges in light of the doctrine of the image of God *(imago Dei),* interpreted by John Paul II in explicit reference to the Trinity. Here, the theme of the gift becomes predominant, notably in the Pope's catechesis on Genesis, which in turn forms the backdrop for the apostolic exhortation *Familiaris Consortio.* One discovers here the human person's "spousal" structure: "masculinity and femininity are two ways of being a 'human person,' solitude awaiting communion" (211). "Man, the 'image' of God, is 'he who gives himself'" (211).

The second section systematically sets forth the doctrine of marriage from the starting point of Augustine's three "goods of marriage," beginning with *fides.* The author poses first of all the radical question of otherness, in dialogue with Emmanuel Levinas. In order to understand the gift of self it is necessary to define the "position of the other" (218) in relation to the subject as "being-as-gift." For Levinas, the other's face reveals his transcendence, which is essentially an ethical challenge; the other's "face" is the epiphany of God's face and consequently founds an ethics of absolute responsibility. The reciprocity of persons is revealed more clearly with

Bruaire, it would seem, because he bases the human otherness of "being-as-gift" on the fact that man is first of all the "other" for the Creator. The en-counter between man and woman appears, therefore, as "two different 'faces' of the gift" (236). This fundamental element precedes the man-woman dialectic in its manifestation as a struggle, and situates the conjugal relationship in a perspective of welcome and gratuity: "Image of gratuity and superabundance, the man-woman dialectic manifests the true 'history' of gift, wherein all refusal bears death and all welcome bears life" (251).

An overview of "the gift of self in the doctrine of marriage" (257) brings out the inseparability of the conjugal act's unitive and procreative meanings; this doctrine takes up in more depth a view already expressed by the author in another of his works: *Union et Procréation. Développe-ments de la doctrine des fins du mariage (Union and procreation. Develop-ments in the doctrine of the ends of marriage).*[3] "The person is destined to a gift of his whole self. This point is the basis of the discussion on the two meanings of the conjugal act" (287). The anthropological foundation of this ethical norm rests on the Creator's "original gift," which established man in his image and likeness, as man and woman (Gen. 1:27). The author places much importance on this doctrine, which serves to structure the theological presentation of the spouses' mutual gift: body and soul in unity, freedom and indissolubility. John Paul II 's remarkable catechesis on the theology of the body made for the *communio personarum* is well em-ployed in order to confirm the author's thesis. The convergence of ap-proaches is striking. The evil of contraception is made evident, as is the beauty of the gift of self integral to the service of life: " 'Yes' to life, to the gift of life is always a 'yes' to gift of self in truth" (344).

The third section of the book considers the *sacramentum* or God's gift to his people (348). Here we enter fully into the universe of grace. "The gift of Christ, founder of every gift" (361), transforms the created gift of conju-gal love into a sign of the uncreated gift of God to his people. The author approves of the theological opinion which sees in the evolution of the Church's language on conjugal love an authentic doctrinal development. Once again, John Paul II's contribution to this development in the lan-guage of "gift" is substantial. His reflections on marriage as the primordial sacrament bring a new light to the whole sacramental universe: "living a sacrament is not first of all replying to a need, an obligation, a habit or a

3. Paris: Cerf, 1989.

seduction, it is contracting a nuptial bond" (401). In this context an important place is made for the Holy Spirit, a "'formative' milieu in which and by which this gift is given and received" (401). While attentive to pneumatology, the author does not sufficiently exploit the following affirmation made by the Pope: "It is more urgent than ever to *rekindle awareness of conjugal love as gift:* in marriage, this is the gift by which the Holy Spirit, who in the inexpressible Mystery of the Trinity is Person-Gift (cf. *Dominum et Vivificantem,* 10), is diffused into the heart of Christian spouses" (401). The uncreated gift of the Holy Spirit remains, all things considered, placed alongside the gift of Christ, without sufficiently showing the nuptial logic that emanates from his Person and from his role linking Christ and the Church.

The second chapter of this section on the *sacramentum* as such begins by highlighting that "the spousal image underpins the mystery of all sacramentality" (385). The sacramentality of Christ, gift of the Father; the sacramentality of the Church, welcoming of this Gift in the Holy Spirit; and the specific sacramentality of marriage, "as a participation in Divine Love revealed in history and binding Christ Jesus to his bride" (414). The spouses' gift is at the same time "momentary" and "permanent," "consecrated" by Christ's love in view of a mission that is not "simply natural" but is a mission within the Church (415). The liturgy of the "gift" renders publicly and historically visible an exchange of gifts "in Christ's presence, and with him" (424). "God is actively involved"; he does not limit himself to blessing from on high a reality of his creation that is good. Because "authentic conjugal love is caught up into divine love" (GS 48; CCC 1639) (430), "he remains the 'Third' within their mutual giving." His presence inspires and encourages conjugal love in the footsteps of Christ, Bridegroom of the Church, given in the Eucharist. This is the source of the "sacramental affinities" (431) between baptism, marriage and the Eucharist.

"By baptism, man and woman belong to Christ, even in their bodies. They no longer belong to themselves. They belong to Christ. Their bodies no longer belong to them. It is necessary, therefore, that Christ himself gives the spouses to one another and gives up the body of each one to the other, just as he himself gave up his own body" (434). "Through the sacrament of marriage, spouses are invited to enter into this Act of Christ given to the Church for the whole of humanity." They are "the permanent reminder to the Church of what happened on the Cross (FC 13)" (445).

In short, the sacramental gift is a participation of the spouses' love in

Trinitarian love. Perhaps this dimension is not sufficiently underlined. The author does affirm that spousal love is "in the image of the Trinity" (454) but he does not think through to their full conclusion the implications of the existential analogy between God's Gift to spouses and the spouses' gift to God. At the same time he does furnish valuable indications of the involvement of the divine Persons in conjugal love: "spouses love one another with Christ's love itself" (459). Their human love is healed and fortified by "the power of the Spirit, infinite and uncreated Gift" (ibid.). Once "belonging to Christ" in their love has been expressed in principle, everything happens as if the essential remains the inter-human relationship between created persons. Trinitarian communion remains an ideal rather than a reality of participation. In other words, this theology of gift does not really succeed in re-centering spousal love on a radical belonging to the divine Persons and shedding light on the spouses' supreme dignity as a "sacrament" of Trinitarian love. We will examine this later.

The fourth section is a magnificent reflection on the following theme: "the child is a gift, the most excellent of gifts" (459). Here we see an in-depth recasting of the procreational end of marriage in the language of gift. Once more, for the last time, the reflection is developed around magisterial declarations, this time culminating with *Donum Vitae:* "The human being must be respected — as a person — from the very first instant of his existence." (DV I, 1; 480). According to Mattheeuws, no. 2378 of the Catechism gives an excellent summary of the doctrine of the child as gift. He cites: "A child is not something *owed* to one, but is a *gift.* The 'supreme gift of marriage' is a human person. A child may not be considered a piece of property, an idea to which an alleged 'right to a child' would lead. In this area, only the child possesses genuine rights: the right 'to be the fruit of the specific act of the conjugal love of his parents,' and 'the right to be respected as a person from the moment of his conception'" (485). The author demonstrates the logical continuity of the Church's struggle for the child: "having 'fought for' the goodness of marriage as an institution and the goodness of its ends, having emphasized the marriage covenant within the spouses' love (Vatican II), the Church now 'defends' this institution's and this love's 'supreme' gift: the child" (489).

A rather personal interpretation of the instruction *Donum Vitae* allows the author to deepen the reflection on the moral questions linked to artificial insemination, and homologous or heterologous fecundation, in the light of the person of the child seen as a gift. In this context, the principle of the inseparability of the conjugal act's two meanings is adopted and applied once more. "The objective dissociation of the unitive and procreative ends which takes place in homologous artificial fertilization denies both the embryo's dignity and the duty of persons who bodily give themselves to one another. . . . 'Homologous artificial fertilization, in seeking a procreation which is not the fruit of a specific act of conjugal union, objectively effects an analogous separation *(to that of contraception)* between the goods and meanings of marriage'" (DV II,B,4) (527). Because of the child's dignity as a person-gift, one cannot call him into existence other than within an act of conjugal love. The child's right to respect for his "divine" and also truly "human" origin should prevail over any purported right to having a child. "The affirmation of a *right to a child* indicates a refusal of what he is. The *rights of the child* require an unconditional welcome" (497).

The novelty of this argument lies in the person of the child who, from the beginning, as a gift from God, has the right to be loved for his own sake and therefore to be born in conditions in conformity with his "being as gift." The author pushes his interpretation towards its limits in reflecting upon "the human embryo as gift" (529). The embryo is "always" a gift, whatever the circumstances of its conception. It is a gift "in its body," entrusted by God to both spouses in order to be given from "person to person," in conformity with the sacred character of the transmission of life: "from one spouse to the other, from the spouses to the child; from God to the spouses, from God to the child" (544, quoting Jean-Marie Henneaux). In short, every child has the right to be born from an act of love, an act of personal giving that respects his spiritual nature: a "being as gift," personally loved by God, unique Creator of the human soul.

The transmission of life is ultimately inscribed within the Gift to the world of the Eternal Child (554): "God is offered in his Son, who is given up for us from his conception" (555). Each new birth on earth reveals God's Glory manifested in the flesh, even in the obscurity of *kenosis*. "The child is a sacrament of God's vulnerability" (556). This is why the child must be welcomed, protected and recognized in an absolute way, because he testifies to an Infinite Gift in the form of "the gift from person to person in a context of bodily-expressed love" (556).

Alain Matheeuws' *The 'Gifts' of Marriage* certainly represents a major contribution to research in the moral and sacramental theology of marriage. The author's chosen method has the advantage of offering a converging interpretation of the signs of the times such as they appear in contemporary culture and in the Church's Magisterium. This interpretation has the merit of confirming the practical orientations of the Church in the field of conjugal ethics from a new viewpoint, making explicit the rational justification for doctrines professed in faith. Mattheeuws fulfills this task remarkably well. He is marked by a "luminous philosophy" (Habachi) which rediscovers wonder in considering the mystery of being as a gift. His ontodological approach, inspired by Claude Bruaire, resolutely goes beyond the juridical perspective which has dominated the sacrament of marriage's history. The personalistic and Christocentric turning point that took place with Vatican II is taken up and justified in depth, while at the same time continuity with the preceding doctrine of the goods and ends of marriage. Conjugal love emerges with great stature and is explicitly esteemed in its corporal dimension, inseparable from the person as "being-gift."

The question of the ends of marriage, discussed and then discreetly passed over during the Council thanks to an "interlude inspired by the Holy Spirit" is profoundly renewed in dialogue with the expectations and limits of modern culture. The author makes a vibrant plea for the rehabilitation of the child as marriage's supreme gift, precisely from the starting point of authentic human love. The dichotomy between primary and secondary ends is overcome through the spouses' mutual gift which, in order to be true, must remain open to the possible "gift" of a child, given by Him who remains the great partner in their love. Consequently, the authenticity of conjugal love requires that the "third" (both the Divine and the human) be loved for his own sake even before the surprise of the "gift" comes. It is this transcendent gift which founds the child's rights and compels the spouses to pose an act of love at the child's origin, an act which expresses the unity of their persons in the flesh. "Only the conjugal act is worthy of being at the origin of a human person" (Joseph Cardinal Ratzinger). The author's ethical reflection on this point replies to a particularly urgent need in the struggle for respect for human dignity.

In the chapter on the *sacramentum,* the author does well to situate marriage within the nuptial mystery of Christ and the Church, source of all sacramentality. The paschal Gift of Christ and the Gift of the Spirit are affirmed and developed "in parallel," as a source of "being-as-gift" in being obliged to both gratitude and conjugal fecundity. However, the perspective remains strongly ontological and rational, meaning that the Trinitarian logic of this nuptiality is not thought through to its conclusion. Despite all the rhetoric of gift, the author remains conditioned by a philosophical starting point which imposes certain limits on the gift analogy. The image and Archetype remain at a prudent distance from one another. The reciprocal immanence of the uncreated gift and the created gift of persons in the conjugal encounter cannot express itself as radically as it might. It touches upon it in the author's citations but is not sufficiently integrated in the author's own synthesis. For example, little systematic use is made of this inspiring text from H. Denis: "Grace, God's gift in Jesus Christ, is the Spirit himself, Spirit of God, Spirit of Jesus Christ. The Holy Spirit does not give us grace; he himself is grace in us. He is the presence of the loving God in us" (393).

While being affirmed as necessary and sketched in broad outline, the deepening of the grace of marriage from a pneumatological viewpoint remains insufficient. In order to avoid simply placing the action of the Spirit "above" or "alongside" Christ's action, the author could have better highlighted the uncreated dimension of matrimonial grace. Is not the Holy Spirit the "Third" who, as Person-Love, dwells in the spouses' love and sacramentally identifies them with the love of Christ, Bridegroom of the Church? If it is true that by virtue of the sacrament (baptism-marriage) the spouses' love no longer belongs to them but to Christ, why not give more space to the "Trinitarian relationships" within the conjugal and family relationships? As a fruit of intratrinitarian nuptiality poured forth in the sacrament (FC 13), is not the Spirit the nuptial bond that mediates the spouses' mutual gift and allows them to love one another "with the very love of Christ"?

The author's perspective, while firmly anchored in the order of creation, does not completely integrate creation into the covenant. It is true that "being-as-gift" immediately connotes a relationship to the Transcendent Source, but it is the creature-Creator relationship that occupies a grater place and dominates, so to speak, over the covenant relationship. This is why the Spirit appears above all as a presence, a healing and sanctifying force, and not enough as Person-Love, who expresses and gives himself through a fecund human couple. Mattheeuws' predominant perspective is centered on the couple who love "in the image of the Trinity," and much less on Trinitarian Love, which gives itself in a real participation to the couple, and through the couple to the world. In a word, the absence of a more intimate co-penetration of the Archetype and the image confines certain sacramental riches of marriage to the background. The sacramentality of the family is barely mentioned.

In the same sense, the doctrine of the *imago Dei* should be reconsidered in a radically Trinitarian perspective. A theology of gift, over and above ontology, should show how God's gift *ad extra,* every gift from God *ad extra,* is situated within the horizon of the relationships *between* the divine Persons. A superior viewpoint for integrating the reflection on being as gift is to be found here. The gifts of creation, the gift of life, the gift of *fides* and of the sacrament signify, in the final analysis, the gifts of the Father to the Son and of the Son to the Father in the Holy Spirit. Created gifts express and signify the uncreated love between the divine Persons. Thus, human love in its beauty and fragility allows us to see, like a living icon, the Glory within God. The Holy Spirit prolongs in marriage what he does in the relationship of Christ and the Church; he makes of it the nuptial incarnation of the "Nuptial Mystery" *par excellence.* The theology of Adrienne von Speyr and Hans Urs von Balthasar can provide a useful complement to a "theo-logic" of the "gifts" of marriage.

These final remarks in no way diminish the value of Alain Mattheeuws' research. Rather, they confirm his intuitions which give "food for thought" in harmony with the Church and in fascinating dialogue with contemporary sensibilities. The integration of the doctrine of the goods and ends of marriage in a new synthesis of "gifts" deserves to be welcomed as a remarkable achievement, one that will be of great service to the Church's pastoral activity in the long term. If Heidegger's assertion is true that each generation has only one thing to occupy its thought, and if it is also true that the task of our generation is the thinking out of the man-woman difference, Alain Mattheeuws, for his part, will have brought together and produced a substantial and delightful body of thought in order to respond to reply to the challenge and call of Being as Gift.

INDEX

Abortion, 8, 59, 178

Adam, creation of, 26-33; sin of, 131-35

Adultery, 133, 138-39, 142

Agape, 92-93, 94, 96; and eros, 184, 216; and holiness, 108-9; and paschal mystery, 170. *See also* Love

Analogy: of being, 45-47, 158-59; family of Trinity, 21-26; of freedom, 45-47; and primacy of Christ, 45-46; sociality of Trinity, 25; as theological method for Trinity-family relationship, 14, 33-34

Anthropology: and domestic Church, 44-50; presupposition of, 6, 11-18; quest for theology of, 10-11

Anthropomorphism, suspicion of, 18

Aqiba, Rabbi, 82-83

Aquinas, Thomas, 16-17; definition of person, 23; and goods of marriage, 125-26; and Holy Spirit, 189; and *imago Dei,* 180; and mystery of Trinity, 69; and nature-grace relationship, 47; and original sin, 133-34; on sloth, 146; and suspicion of personalism, 18; and Trinity-family relationship, 20-21, 35

Augustine, and analogy of love, 23-24, 98; and Church, 161-62; definition of person, 23; and Eucharist, 156; and goods of marriage, 125, 227-28; and holy family, 118; and human destiny, 71, 72; and *imago Dei,* 180; and incarnation, 158; and Trinity, 6; and Trinity-family relationship, 14, 20-24; and suspicion of personalism, 18

Balthasar, Hans Urs von: and anthropology of the family, 45-50; and conscience, 182-83; and faith, 111, 121-22, 215; and *imago Dei,* 26, 32-33; and complementarity of sexes, 32-33; and impact of Trinitarian theology, 5-6; and incarnation, 157-58; openness of conjugal love, 93-94; and personal identity, 184-85, 186; and sin, 132; and Song of Songs, 83-84; and spiritual fruitfulness of marriage, 65-66; and theological method, 14-17; and Trinity, 16-18, 69, 108-9

Baptism, 51-52; and marriage, 90, 212-13; and original sin, 134; and personal identity, 187

Ecclesiology, of communion, 13

Education, of spouses, 208

Emynian, Maurice, 10

Eros: and agape, 92-93, 184; and Song of Songs, 83-84; and Holy Spirit, 89-90; sanctification of, 171, 216. *See also* Love

Eschatology, and family, 71

Ethics, 177-79, and Christian identity, 179-80; and communion, 190-93; and family, 195-99, 200-204; and grace, 188-90

Eucharist, and domestic Church, 68; and kingdom of God, 173-75; and marriage, 91, 169, 170-72; and mission of the person, 50; neglect of, 142-43; and nuptial mystery of Christ, 150, 156-60, 165-67; and forgiveness of sin, 166-67; and sacrament of marriage, 221

Evangelii Nuntiandi, 41

Evangelium Vitae, 60

Evangelism, 211-12, 217; and culture, 178; and domestic Church, 3-4, 39, 99, 172-73, 200-202; and spiritual fecundity, 103

Evdokimov, Paul, 174; and domestic Church, 42-43; and marriage, 52, 142

Eve, 161-63

Evil. *See* Sin

Evolution, of family, 7-8

Faith, 95-97, 111, 170; and culture, 178; of Mary, 166; and sacrament of marriage, 215-16; and sin, 132-33; and forgiveness, 136

Familiaris Consortio (by JP2): and contraception, 61; and communion of spouses, 128-29, 206; and conjugal covenant, 115; and domestic Church, 42, 43; and development of theology of family, 3-6; and family as image of Trinity, 44; and spiritual fecundity, 122-23; and *imago Dei,* 30-31; and katalogical method of theology, 15-16; and love, 61; and ministeriality of marriage, 213-14; and mission of family, 57, 168, 193-94; and sacramentality of family and marriage, 52-53, 68, 144-45, 150-51, 216; and theological anthropology, 10-11; and Trinity-family relationship, 20-21; virtues of, 200

Family: and communion of persons, 57; as environment for human growth, 35; and ethics, 195-99, 200-202; evolution of, 7; as gift to society, 199-200; holiness of, 110-12; as image of Trinity, 10-11, 20-21, 46, 58; and new creation, 43; rights of, 8; sacramentality of, 13-14, 193-95; and secularization, 7-8; and sin, 125-26; spirituality of, 58-60, 95-100; and Trinity, 5-6, 10-11. *See also* Domestic Church; Family analogy of the Trinity; Family members; Family, mission of; Theology of family; Trinity-Family Relationship

Family analogy of the Trinity: and tradition, 21-26; and Scripture, 26-33; and love, 23-25; and *imago Dei,* 26-33; theological meaning of, 33-36; and anthropological starting point, 34-35; and spirituality, 35

Family members, sacramental consciousness of, 69; theological consciousness of, 60

Family, mission of, 57-58, 71-74; as domestic Church, 42-43; and glory of God, 71-74; nature of, 50; and love, 67-70; and spirituality, 58-70

Fecundity, and *communio personarum,* 34; and ethics, 193-95; and holiness, 110-12; and Holy Spirit, 86-88; openness to, 99-100; and parenthood, 102-3, 110-12, 116-17, 121-23

Forgiveness, 135-38, 166-67

Francis of Assisi, 98

Gaudium et Spes: christocentrism of, 12;
and conjugal love, 91, 114; and issues
confronting families, 7; and marriage, 13-14; personalism of, 9, 191;
and salvation history, 79
Glendron, Lionel, 21-22, 24
God, fatherhood of, 103, 107-10, 111-12,
117-18; fear of, 134-35; freedom of, 17,
45, 46-47, 183; gift of, 97-98; glory of,
17, 71-74; holiness of, 108-9; likeness
to, 31-32, 134; love of, for humans, 71-
73, 108-9; and sealing of marriage,
88-94; and sexuality, 33-34; and spirituality, 97-98. *See also* Trinity
Government, and family policies, 8
Grace, and Christian identity, 188-90;
and nature, 47-48; family as locus of,
59-60; and marriage, 130; in
Mattheeuws, 228-30
Gratitude, 97-98
Greed, 132-33
Gregory of Nazianzen, and family analogy of the Trinity, 22
Gregory of Nyssa, 147

Hemmerle, Klaus, and conjugal love,
63; and human existence, 67; and
spiritual fruitfulness, 65; Trinitarian
approach of, 103
Hinschberger, Régine, 28-29
Holy Family, 30, 117-23, 192-93. *See also*
Jesus Christ; Mary
Holy Spirit: and conjugal covenant, 88-
89; and domestic Church, 43; and
Eucharist, 166; and faith, 95-96; and
fecundity, 86-88; gift of, 86-88, 92,
128-29; love of, 96-98; as living water,
152-54; and marriage, 67-68, 79-80;
and parenthood, 103; and spirituality,
95-100
Hospitality, 99

Humanae Vitae: reaction to, 9-10, and
conjugal love, 62; and contraception,
61, 196, 198
Humans, destiny of, 71-72, 187; dignity
of, 9, 38, 68-69, 178-79, 182, 203-4, 211;
freedom of, 45, 46-47, 183; identity of,
181-83; and meaning of existence, 16-
18; growth of, 35
Human body, and Holy Sprit, 66; and
sin, 138-39

Idolatry, 132-33
Image of God. See *Imago Dei*
Imago Dei: doctrine of, 12-13; exegesis
of, 5, 22, 26-33; and family as Trinity,
10-11; and fatherhood, 107-10; and
likeness of God, 31-32; transmission
of, 134; and Trinity-family relationship, 20-21; and family analogy of
Trinity, 26-33; and sexuality, 32-33;
and "unity of the two," 180-83
Incarnation, 85, 157-59; and personal
identity, 185; and sacramental logic,
216
Industrialization, and the family, 7
Ingratitude, 133
International Congress on the Family,
6-7
International Year of the Family, 20

Jesus Christ: as bridegroom, 85-86, 141,
152-56, 161-65; and Christian identity,
188-90; and covenant, 29-30; death
of, 66-67, 117, 133-34, 159-60, 164-65;
and ethics, 188; and family analogy of
Trinity, 29-30; fecundity of, 102-3;
flesh of, 165-67, 171; on forgiveness of
sin, 135-38; and Holy Family, 120; love
of, 147-48; and marriage, 90-91, 214-
15, 218; mission of, 137-38; as new
Adam, 157-60; pierced side of, 161-65;
resurrection of, 86, 87-88, 159-60, 165.
See also Nuptial mystery of Christ

of, 206-8, 218-23; and conversion, 144-48; ecclesial hermeneutic of, 211-17; and ethics, 191-93, 200-202; and Eucharist, 221; and Holy Spirit, 67-68, 88-94; and love, 89-90, 126-30; in Mattheeuws, 225-34; ministeriality of, 209-11, 212-13, 219; and nuptial mystery of Christ, 150-51; and salvation history, 127-28; and secularization, 8; sign of union between Christ and the Church, 11; and sin, 125-26, 131-44

Sacrament of Reconciliation, 91, 144; neglect of, 142-43

Sacraments, theology of, 209-11, 212-13, 216-17

Sagne, Jean-Claude, 147

Salvation, 154-56; and Church, 171; family as locus of, 59-60; and sacramentality of family, 68

Salvation history, 79-80; marriage as symbol of, 80-88, 106, 127-28

Samaritan woman, 151-56

Scola, Angelo, 31-32

Scripture, interpretation of, 15, 82-83

Second Vatican Council: and contraception, 196-99; and ecclesiology of communion, 50; and family as domestic Church, 38-39, 41-43; hermeneutic of, 11-12; and *imago Dei*, 30-31; and lay ministry, 58-59; and missionary crisis of Church, 99; and nature-grace relationship, 47-48; and marriage, 104-5, 111, 130, 192, 200-201; and spirituality of family, 59-60; and theology of family, 4-6, 12-13, 145; and universality of redemption, 163-64

Secularization, and families, 7-8, 103, 178-79, 207, 209; and life, 38; and spirituality of family, 59

Seraphim of Sarov, 145

Sex, 195-99; and agape, 92-93; as communion, 63; sacramentality of, 197-99

Sexes, relationship between, 21;

complementarity of, 31-32, 110; equality between, 31; and *imago Dei*, 31-32

Sexuality, nature of, 64; in secular society, 7; and *imago Dei*, 32-33, 33-34

Sicari, Antonio, 171

Sin, 125-26; of adultery, 133, 138-39; and conversion, 144-48; and forgiveness, 135-38; as hardness of heart, 135-44; and sacramentality of marriage, 131, 139-44; and original, 131-35; of sloth, 146

Song of Songs, 184; and symbol of marriage, 82-84

Speyr, Adrienne von, and Christian fecundity, 121-22; and confession, 173; and forgiveness, 166-67; and love, 98

Spirituality, of family, 58-60; and family analogy of Trinity, 35; and fecundity, 99-100, 112; and gift of God, 97-98; and growth of persons, 113-17; and Holy Spirit, 95-100

Sterilization. *See* Contraception

Supernatural, problem of, 11-12

Synod on the Family, 5

Temptation, 132

Tertullian, 161-62

Theological method, 14-16, 33-36, 167; in Mattheeuws, 226

Theology of family: and anthropology, 12-13; development of, 3-6; issues in, 6-9; and sacramentality, 13-14; need for new synthesis in, 9-11; and Trinity, 10-11, 20-37

Theology of marriage, 9-11

Thomas Aquinas. *See* Aquinas, Thomas

Time, gift of, 146-47

Trinity, and anthropology, 6, 11-18; and Christian identity, 187-90; and communion of persons, 57, 109; fecundity of, 111; image of, 10-11, 20-37; love of, 168-69; mystery of, 69-70; impact of on spirituality, 5-6; love of, 16-17, 23-